Beach to the Boardroom

Frank O'Hare

Copyright © 2024 Frank O'Hare

The author has asserted his right under the Copyright, Designs and Patents Act 1988 to be identified as the author of this work.

ISBN 9798337683591

All rights reserved. No part of this book may be used or reproduced in any form whatsoever without written permission from the author.

Author's Note

Much of this book is set in the 1980s and 1990s when the world was less politically-correct. The book is an authentic representation of those times. Readers should be aware that some of the content (situations and language) contained in the book has the potential to upset or offend some people.

Preface

My earliest memory of our family holidays consists largely of frayed tempers and playing outside in the rain. Because my uncle had given us a battered old caravan, it became the family rule that we would go camping in Wales or Scotland every year. The routine would always be the same. Firstly, along with our two dogs, we'd be packed into the car at around 3 a.m. to "miss the traffic." The next rule was that my dad would have to make the whole family cry before he'd be ready to set off. During our holidays, his stress level was always off the scale, and the slightest thing would make him explode. Once we'd set off, he'd become the life and soul of the party, and we'd all join in, playing I-spy, singing songs, and telling jokes to break up the journey. Upon arrival at the campsite, it was time for us to cry again as he shouted and stressed over the process of setting up the caravan on its plot. Once settled in, I'd then spend two weeks charging around the campsite with my older brother and sister, where we'd make lots of friends from other parts of the UK. The *cry-sing-cry* routine would be repeated on the return journey, and the friends we'd made would become pen-friends as we'd

Preface

exchange letters with them until we lost interest a couple of months later. Despite the repetitive format, I loved every minute. We might only have travelled 200 miles from home, but to me, I was on my holidays and I was living the dream.

Back then, I would never have dreamt that my future career would revolve around the travel industry, an industry that I didn't even know existed. Yet, I am living proof that a young lad with no discernible talent can go all the way to the top of a highly competitive and fast-paced business such as travel. From the very start, my journey has been a mix of good fortune, good timing, and learning on the job. It's also been a journey littered with horrendous mistakes and bad judgement, which has somehow been overlooked by those people willing to give me a chance - people to whom I shall be forever indebted. However, it's only recently that I've realised how my journey has also been influenced by a number of chance encounters, encounters that seemed random and insignificant, yet on reflection, proved pivotal in shaping my overall destiny. Hopefully, the anecdotes and stories of those encounters will not only keep you entertained, but also provide some form of inspiration. After all, if someone as lacking in prospects as I was can forge a successful career, then there's a chance for us all.

So, after so many years, what was the motivation for me to finally put pen to paper? Well, I was recently invited to give a presentation to a group of hoteliers and travel industry executives at a conference in Istanbul. The theme of the event was "Adapting to Change and Emerging Travel Trends." It wasn't a huge event, but it was well-attended, with around 150 travel professionals filling the auditorium. There was nothing particularly unusual about the event itself; in fact, it was the standard travel industry fare, comprising an earnest and attentive audience looking for assurance and certainty in

Preface

an industry of constant change. The theme of my presentation was "resilience" and how the travel industry always finds a way to EAT (evolve, adapt, and thrive). It was pretty corny, but it was also a neat acronym that I could plan my slides around. So often, the travel industry has to innovate to survive, like a boxer slugging it out in a never-ending final round, rolling with the punches and finding ways to fight back. Whether it's in the guise of terrorism, oil price increases, Brexit, lockdowns, vaccination protocols or plain old weather extremes, each punch has a chance of landing the knockout blow. However, it wasn't so much the topic or the conference that made it such a memorable event; it was the ultimately fortuitous way that I was introduced to the audience. I didn't know whether it had been lost in translation, but as I climbed the steps to the stage, the event compere, Emre Demir, took the microphone and announced,

"Ladies and gentlemen, please give a warm welcome to our next speaker, the great pretender and travel industry veteran, Frank O'Hare."

The great bloody pretender?! I gave him a quizzical look as I took the mic, but he just gave me a reassuring smile and a thumbs up in return. My presentation went largely to plan and garnered a moderately enthusiastic response from the audience, but even before I'd fully stepped down from the stage, Emre was upon me.

"Mr Frank, I am so sorry. I have been told that I introduced you as the great pretender. Of course, I meant to say *great presenter*. I have no idea how I got the words mixed up. Please forgive me."

"Don't worry about it, Emre, I've had much worse," I responded.

Normally I would have left it at that, but the more I thought about it, the more fitting it seemed that at this late

Preface

stage of my career an innocent slip of the tongue, by someone I'd never met before, should so perfectly capture the reason I was in the travel industry at all. In fact, "pretender" summed up my early years in travel and described my entry into the industry to a tee, and, whether or not I liked it, I had somehow now arrived at the veteran stage of my career. So, it was at that moment in the small auditorium in Taksim Square that the idea for this book was born. Emre didn't know it, but his innocent mistake was the catalyst for the warts-and-all story you are about to read. The story of a naive, insecure egotist who somehow managed to carve out a successful career in one of the most bonkers businesses imaginable, the UK travel industry. A career of highs and lows in an industry of highs and lows. A career that was intended to be no more than a couple of summer seasons working as a holiday representative, yet turned into an incredible journey of almost forty years, working with some of the most certifiably crazy characters, in some of the UK's most illustrious travel companies. At each point on the journey, there's a story to tell, light-hearted, whimsical, shocking, and sometimes heartbreakingly sad. Stories all the way from the beaches of the Mediterranean to the boardrooms of the UK. I hope you enjoy the journey as much as I have.

As *Beach to the Boardroom* is based on real events, I've had to exercise some creative licence regarding places, names, and organisations to maintain confidentiality, avoid litigation, and protect the innocent.

Frank O'Hare

Chapter 1

Birth of a Career

We've all said or done something that we are embarrassed about. Sometimes it's because we look at our previous actions through the lens of today's standards and morals, and sometimes we knew full well at the time that what we did was just plain stupid. In one way I'm pretty lucky in that I've been consistently foolish over a long period of time, so what might be devastating to some people is pretty much par for the course for me, however, some memories still send a shiver down my spine. One particular event I made even more unforgettable was during the happiest of times - starting a family. We were pregnant! Samantha and I were living in Manchester and were due to have our first baby on 1 January 2000. A new baby on the first day of the new millennium, super exciting and super stressful. From a business perspective, the months leading up to this point had been equally stressful as we were dealing with the phenomenon christened the Y2K bug, the belief that computer programs and software had been configured in such a way that they wouldn't be able to recognise dates and times beyond the twentieth century. The theory was that when the clock ticked beyond midnight on 31 December 1999 the digital world would grind to a halt, resulting in potential life-threatening events across the world, and in the travel business that potentially meant booking systems failing and planes falling out of the sky. It also meant that some people made a lot of money as the original "project fear" swept through UK businesses. As if from nowhere, an army of tech consultants appeared in boardrooms, charging whatever they wanted to assess IT infrastructures and to do their best to save travel businesses before it was "too late." It was a catch-22 situation which no self-respecting business could ignore, and I take my hat off to whoever coined the phrase "Y2K compliance."

So, from both a business and personal perspective I'd spent most of 1999 in a state of heightened anxiety, but towards the end of the year my focus moved exclusively to the birth of our first child and we gratefully signed up for antenatal classes at St. Mary's Hospital in Manchester. There were around ten couples in the first class, and we really enjoyed it as we bonded with other first-time parents and learned a lot more about the birthing process. At the second class a week later, we heard all about the options for birth pain management and were about to go for a tour of the delivery room when Sam suddenly turned to me with a worried look.

"Frank, I've just realised, I've left my handbag with my purse in it on the back seat of the car!"

"Don't worry, I'll nip out and get it, no problem," I replied.

So, just as they were all collecting the blue elasticated hygiene hats to wear in the delivery room, I turned and dashed out to the car. Thankfully, the handbag was still on the rear seat, so I grabbed it and jogged back. As the group had already gone through to the delivery room, I quickly put on the blue elasticated hat, and with the handbag swinging over my forearm, pushed open the doors to join them. By this stage, the nurse was in full flow, facing the group as she explained how the gas and air device worked. Spying Sam towards the front, I made my way to her side and tapped her arm to let her know I had the bag. However, the withering look she gave me took me by surprise.

"Why do you always have to play the bloody clown?" she whispered.

Bewildered, I responded, "What on earth are you talking about?"

She shook her head with contempt and motioned for me to look around. *Fuck! How could I have got it so wrong?* Not a single person in the group had anything on their heads, but they did have the disposable elasticated blue coverings where they were meant to be, over their bloody shoes! Worse still, some of them had already noticed me and were finding it much funnier than Sam had. I now had several choices:

- Take the "hat" off, go back out to get another and come back with them both correctly on my feet.
- Leave it in place, and front it out.
- Feign illness or an emergency, and retreat to the car.

Bizarrely, I took none of those options, and instead, as the group moved around the room to inspect the leg stirrups, I quickly yanked it off my head and pulled it over my right shoe, and, for some inexplicable reason I began dragging my left leg behind me as though it was a dead weight. For the next fifteen minutes, I followed the group around, blue "hat" over my shoe, handbag over my arm and dragging my left leg behind me. Sam refused to stand anywhere near me. The nurse gave me the occasional pitying look and the rest of the group had both an air of stifled delight and a genuine concern over my mental wellbeing. *Why did I drag my leg around and behave like a total prat?* I've absolutely no idea, but needless to say, we didn't attend the final two classes. Unfortunately, the "birthing incident," as it became known, isn't the only example of my questionable decision-making. On the contrary, I've been a clown on pretty much every continent, and none more so than in my first-ever foray into working overseas in the holiday industry.

The story begins in the early 1980s in North Manchester. Dressed in my best white shirt and navy-blue jacket combo, I was feeling pretty pleased with myself as I stood on the edge of the dancefloor in Bailey's nightclub in Oldham. I was there to celebrate my friend Peter O'Rourke's 18th birthday with a few other members of what we called the 'O' Club. We'd dubbed ourselves the 'O' Club because we all came from Irish families living in our home town of Middleton. On this particular night, we had O'Rourke, Peter - the big, daft birthday boy, O'Sullivan, Michael - coolest, O'Grady, Chris - toughest, in case there was any trouble, O'Reilly, Gary - funniest, and O'Hare, Frank - yours truly, youngest and wimpiest. It was towards the end of the night, I was nursing a pint and tapping my foot to the beat of "I Will Survive" when I felt a slight tug of my jacket sleeve and turned to see a pretty blonde girl in a blue dress, smiling up at me. Immediately, I could feel myself blush as I froze to the spot. This wasn't something I was used to. I'd had nowhere near enough to drink to talk to a girl without almost bursting into tears. Especially as I'd had to limit myself to two pints of bitter shandy, as I'd recently passed my driving test and was driving my dad's old Volvo as the designated driver.

Standing on tiptoes, the girl shouted to make herself heard over Gloria Gaynor.

"Hi, my name's Susan. My mate, Michelle, fancies you. What's your name?"

I was relieved and disappointed in equal measure. Relieved that someone existed who could have fancied me, and disappointed that it wasn't her. I played it as cool as I could.

"I'm Frank. Where is she then?"

"Over there at the bar."

She pointed to the leather-topped chrome stools at the end of the bar. I couldn't believe it. She was pointing at a girl around my age, with wavy dark brown hair, pretty, in possession of all of her limbs…and…she was using one of them…to wave…at me! In a daze, I walked over with Susan.

"Hi Michelle, I'm Frank. What are you both drinking?" I asked, with a false air of confidence.

"I'll have a small white wine please, and you, Sue?" Michelle replied.

"Oh, nothing for me, Frank, I'm driving," replied Susan.

Shit, they're not doing this just for free drinks, I realised, by now almost in a state of euphoria. However, putting my hand in my pocket, the feeling quickly subsided.

"Just hold on a minute, girls, I'll be straight back." With that, I dashed over to O'Rourke, who was standing further down the bar. He turned to face me.

"O'Hare, what's the score?"

"Give me your petrol money now, O'Rourke. I've pulled, and need to buy my bird a drink, but I'm skint."

"No way have you pulled, you pasty-faced fucker. Who with?"

"The brunette over there at the bar. Seriously. She's got a pretty blonde friend with her if you fancy making it a birthday foursome. I can't handle both of them tonight no matter how much they want me to," I chirped, now in full, smug mode. With that, he projectile-vomited all over me. I was pretty much pebble-dashed from the chest down, and stared at him in total shock as he wiped his mouth with the back of his hand and mumbled, "Agh, that's better. I needed that."

"O'Rourke, what the…What the…What the fu…"

"What's the matter with you, O'Hare, you soft arse? Get in the bog and clean it off. Put some smellies on and no one will be any the wiser. Now, where's that bird you were talking about?"

Before I could answer, we were surrounded by three unimpressed bouncers and our night came to a premature end as we were politely advised to leave the premises. O'Rourke took it in his stride.

"C'mon Frank, it's a shit-hole anyway. I'll shout the lads over. Let's get out of here."

Just to rub it in, our official escort walked us past Susan and Michelle, who, after taking in the warm stench that was once my shirt, summed us up succinctly, "Knobheads!"

It was a fairly typical night out to be fair, one that involved alcohol and humiliation in equal measure. To say that I was in a rut was an understatement - by day working as a clerical officer in the Civil Service and by night out with the 'O' Club around the pubs of North Manchester. Weekends were filled with either playing or watching football, followed by some seriously dangerous nights out at Pips nightclub in Manchester, where I'd tread a fine line between being rejected by almost every girl I spoked to, and avoiding eye contact with the various groups of lads milling around looking for trouble. Around that time, I started dating Julie, the daughter of the landlord of our local pub, The High

Sheriff, and, to be honest, it was more platonic than romantic. She was a few years older than me and seemed intent on mothering me, something of a common theme at the time. Julie used to keep the bar open after-hours just for us, and we'd get totally smashed listening to our favourite songs on the jukebox. Her favourite at the time was "99 Red Balloons" by Nena and she'd put it on repeat for what seemed like hours on end. The only problem was that the version they had was the original, which was in German, so we learned to sing every word in German by the time we'd finished. In truth, I only stayed with her because it took the pressure off me having to "cop off" when I was out with the O' Club. Ironically, I probably owe my entire career to Julie. I didn't realise it at the time, but seemingly insignificant events were already coming together to decide my future career path.

Just before leaving work one rainy Friday in January, Chris Maples, my boss, called me into his office out of the blue. Although personable and the first to buy the drinks at social events, Chris was a hard taskmaster, and I feared the worst as I entered his office. With a serious look on his face, he began.

"I want to speak to you, Frank, because I've been watching you work over the last few months and I think you have real potential. You have a positive attitude, your work is accurate, and you're diligent. You're also popular with the rest of the team, which is no mean feat in this place. What I'm trying to say is that I'd like to put you on a fast-track development course normally reserved for graduate employees. It's a two-year course with the aim, should you pass, of graduating from your current role of Clerical Officer to the position of Executive Officer, one grade below my own grade of Higher Executive Officer. So, in three years, if it all works out, you could be 'Frank O'Hare, Executive Officer' and beyond that, you could look at a senior role within the Department of Health and Social Security."

Chris looked as pleased as punch on my behalf and looked for me to mirror his excitement, so I did what I always did, say what he wanted to hear to the point of going a tad over the top.

"You know what, Chris? I don't know what to say. I'm too emotional right now. It's a dream come true. I really can't thank you enough; to think that in another three years, I might be an Executive Officer is mind-blowing," I spluttered, thankful for his compliments but trying to mask any hint of sarcasm. This was the catalyst I needed. I quickly processed the situation. I'd be nearly twenty-four in three years' time, an old man. My life would be over. I had to leave.

Chris continued, "That's just what I wanted to hear, Frank. I knew you'd be thrilled. Look, there's an advertorial here in the Manchester Evening News that shows lots of jobs advertised for this job grade, just to whet your appetite. Take it with you for some light reading over the weekend."

On the bus ride home, I kept the newspaper on my lap with the sole intention of putting it over my head for the rainy walk ahead. But, as I glanced down at the page he'd highlighted, my eyes were drawn to an adjacent advertisement - one that would change my life forever.

Overseas holiday representatives wanted - apply now!

And that was it. The very beginning of what I hoped might be the chance to work a summer overseas, yet turned out to be the start of a whole new life.

Chapter 2

Banana Bob

Within a week of replying to the ad, I received a letter inviting me to an interview with a new holiday company called TAN Holidays based in Leeds, and soon afterwards, I was on my way for the interview at the aptly named "Holiday House" just outside Leeds city centre. O'Rourke gave me a lift there as he owed me a favour following the Oldham nightclub fiasco and I sat in the waiting room among dozens of other hopefuls. As expected, every one of them looked brighter, more confident, and much more employable than me. I only had one card to play, the one marked "bullshit." After around an hour or so of browsing through the various holiday brochures scattered around, my turn arrived.

"Can Frank O'Hare please come through?" came the call.

So, in I went to take my place in front of the interview panel, which comprised three interviewers wearing TAN Holidays name badges: Moira, Head of Overseas Recruitment; Phil, Head of Operations; and Hilary, Director of Overseas Logistics. Following a brief introduction, Moira got down to business.

"Good morning, Frank. We can see from your CV that you've got plenty of overseas travel experience and that you currently work in the Civil Service. Can you tell us more about that?"

"Yes. Because of my father's job, I travelled the world as a child until we settled down in Manchester. I now work in the Civil Service where I deal with international clients because of my language ability," I lied confidently.

"Oh, how exciting. What did your father do for a living?" Moira replied.

Ready and waiting, I continued the tale, "He was a colonel in the army, and because of the sensitive nature of his work in counter-intelligence, we moved around a lot."

"Interesting. So, did you pick up many languages along the way?" asked Phil.

This was like shelling peas and it was all going to plan. I'd spent the last week rehearsing some simple sentences in Spanish and French, as I knew that they were the destinations with the most likely vacancies.

"Well, yes. I can get by in a variety of languages because of my extensive travel as a child, mostly in French and Spanish." I inwardly prepared the sentences I'd rehearsed but was taken completely by surprise.

"How about German?" Phil asked.

German… German… Bloody German?! Before I could stop myself, I went way over the top.

"Well, I was actually born, and spent the early years of my life in Germany. It was idyllic before the…before the…the…the tragedy…the avalanche." The room went deathly silent as I paused for dramatic effect, before continuing in a faltering voice, "Even now, I can hear my nanny singing das old songs to me, 'Hast du etwas Zeit für mich? Dann singe ich ein Lied für dich. Von neun und neunzig luftballons.' I'm so sorry, I'm getting emotional now thinking about how we had to leave under the cover of darkness, and… I never saw nanny again." I then lowered my head, gazed down at my feet, and slowly shook my head. Cue more stunned silence. After a few moments, Hilary responded.

"I'm so sorry, Frank. Please, take whatever time you need to compose yourself."

Phil was the next to speak, now in a soft and respectful tone.

"And where exactly in Germany did you live, Frank?"

Shit, I desperately tried to think of any place I knew in Germany, but my mind was completely blank.

"Oh, it was a small village in the German Alps," I said, praying that there was such a thing as the German Alps.

"Ah, I know the area pretty well, Frank; which village was it?" probed Hilary.

What the hell was the matter with these people? Couldn't they see I was traumatised? I had to think fast.

"Oh, it's tiny, not even on the map actually, and because of my dad's job, even now, I'm not allowed to share that information. It's such a shame we had to leave, as I loved living there, especially the skiing."

Phil's ears pricked up immediately.

"Oh, you skied out there?"

I smiled and slowly nodded.

"Of course. Where we lived, you learned to ski before you learned to walk."

Phil looked across at the other two and I knew that he'd finally seen through the bullshit and it was time to call it a day. But incredibly, he turned back to me and continued.

"Well, to be honest, Frank, although we're interviewing for the summer season, we have an immediate vacancy in the Austrian Alps for a ski representative, and it sounds like you might fit the bill. I think I speak for us all when I say that our only concern is your emotional wellbeing, bearing in mind the traumatic events…the tragedy you shared with us."

I was completely gobsmacked. I was in real danger of blagging my way into a job in a ski resort!

"Oh no. Please rest assured that it's all behind me; it was a momentary lapse because of the pressure of the interview. In fact, if any good came from the tragedy, it motivated me to become an expert in mountain rescue and gain my mountain safety qualifications in Snowdonia."

I'd become carelessly overconfident, and Moira had spotted a chink in my armour.

"My goodness, Frank, why haven't you put any of this in your CV?"

"You're right, Moira, I should have done that, but I didn't feel that it would be relevant for a summer holiday representative's role."

Moira nodded vigorously and continued.

"Okay, Frank, we've heard enough. I feel that you have the maturity, the empathy, and the skill set to become an excellent ski resort representative, and what's more, your honesty has touched me personally. Please leave your contact telephone number and we'll be in touch with the details in the next couple of days."

In a daze, I made my way through the drizzle, back to the car and the waiting O'Rourke. As any good friend would do, he did a great job of bringing me back down to earth.

"Are they fucking stupid? They're giving a retard like you a job in a ski resort?"

He warmed to the task. "Seriously…let's think about this for a minute, O'Hare. The upside is you have lots of confidence, especially for a "ginger." Then again, on the downside, you can't ski, you don't speak the lingo, you're scared of heights, and on top of that, you're as thick as shit!"

With a complete lack of irony, he finished with, "Anyway, my advice is to just believe in yourself and don't let anyone put you down."

As motivational speeches go, it had some room for improvement.

Anyway, within days I discovered that I was to be allocated a ski season in a small ski resort in the Austrian Tyrol, where I would be the TAN ski representative. Even crazier was that it was to be the company's first season operating in the resort, so I would have to set up the ski operation and weekly activity programmes from scratch.

Almost immediately, I was summoned to attend a two-day training course in Leeds, where I realised how far out of my depth I was. Terms like "ski bindings", "red runs", and "airport transfers" were bandied about while I sat there, nonplussed. I desperately tried to get my head around how it all worked and asked as many questions as I could behind the scenes, as I was afraid to ask anything out in the open for fear of being found out. Another three days of training in the Austrian Alps followed, where I tried to soak in every bit of information I could. The focus of the Austrian based training was more on après-ski (arranging the evening entertainment for our guests, such as bowling evenings, sleigh rides, tobogganing, etc.). This was easier, as it largely comprised of drinking and partying. I was dreading the final day of the training though, as that's when we were all to be taken up the mountain to test our ski ability, but not for the first time, Lady Luck smiled upon me, as it coincided with a snowstorm that caused the lift system to be closed. Once again, I'd slipped through the net. From then on, we were on our own, each of us driven by minibus to our allocated resorts.

It was a cold, dark December evening, and I felt physically sick as we arrived at my resort. I was dropped off at the Gasthof Zum Dampfl, an ancient Austrian guest house where I'd been allocated a tiny top-floor bedroom with a shared bathroom for the winter season. As I alighted the minibus, I reached for and touched the English/German dictionary in my jacket pocket for the hundredth time to make sure it was still there. Located in the heart of the village, opposite the ornate church which served as the centrepiece of the village square, it was a storybook scene as the snow came floating down. But I was terrified. I just kept telling myself that although I'd bluffed my way to this point, maybe I was capable of going all the way. I couldn't let the mask of confidence and competence slip now, no matter what lay ahead.

Early the next morning, after a fitful night's sleep, I followed instructions to make my way to the reps' ski office on the main street, dressed proudly in my company uniform with "Ski TAN" emblazoned on the back. The office was shared by all the UK ski companies and the interior was designed like a train station ticket office. Each holiday company had a small section of the counter to work behind to greet their customers when they came in to book excursions, buy ski lift passes, etc. It was already a hive of activity as the other reps were busy putting their company branding on the counter and windows. I could see that all the major brands were represented: Ski Thomson, Ski Enterprise, Crystal Holidays, Neilson and Intasun Skiscene. A short, friendly-looking guy in jeans and a sweatshirt immediately approached me.

"Hi, you must be Frank, the new Ski TAN man, pleased to meet you. My name's Andy, and I'm the Crystal ski rep. I guess that this is your first ski season, right?"

"Wow, I can't believe you know all that information about me. News travels fast," I responded, impressed by his knowledge.

"Not really, you're wearing your full ski uniform and name badge. Only a novice or an idiot would do that with over a week before any punters arrive, and I'm giving you the benefit of the doubt that you're not an idiot."

I'd clearly made a schoolboy error, but as I was quickly finding out, every day was a school day for me.

"Okay, Frank, let me help you here. Your cubicle and workspace are at the end. It's the smallest because yours is the newest company, and as nobody has heard of you, you'll have very few punters, so you'll be out of everyone's way. In any case, we've all worked here for a few seasons, so we have seniority."

It all seemed pretty logical to me, and it made no sense to argue. And, despite his superior tone, he was probably right. I'd certainly need their help a lot more than they'd need mine. Andy introduced me to the other reps, who were busy getting everything ready for the season ahead. The only person not there was the Ski Enterprise representative who coincidentally had the space next to mine and by far the largest work area at their disposal.

"Who's the rep for Ski Enterprise, Andy?" I asked.

"Oh, that's Choco. He'll be along shortly. He's been here for years."

"Really, what nationality is he? Choco is an unusual name," I ventured.

"He's actually English. He's called Mike. It's just that everyone calls him Choco because he's so self-assured that if he was chocolate, he'd eat himself. Hence, we christened him Choco. Don't worry about the nickname, Frank. He loves it; he even has 'Choco' on his name badge instead of 'Mike'.

He's in love with himself, and unfortunately, it's a feeling shared by most of the females in the resort. He used to be a ski instructor, his Austrian mum was a local beauty queen, and his dad used to play rugby for England before making so much money from property investments that they now live as tax exiles in Monaco. He doesn't need to work, but enjoys making money and entertaining the ladies so much that he returns every winter. I've no doubt that he'll tell you all about himself, and how everything is done around here. Anyway, you're in luck. It looks like he's just arrived."

With that, he motioned to the window where a red Porsche Carrera had rumbled to a stop outside. Within seconds, the office door burst open and an impressively handsome and imposing figure strolled in. Well-built and standing at least 6' 4" tall, dressed in a figure-hugging red all-in-one ski suit, topped off with sun-bleached shoulder-length blond hair and mirrored sunglasses, Choco had indeed made a spectacular entrance. There was almost a collective intake of breath as he took a moment to stand stock still, legs apart, and hands on hips as the light from the doorway gave him a hazy halo. It was almost biblical. Having had the desired effect, he made his way to the work area next to mine. Up close, I could see that he had signs of a broken nose which added to his rugged look, and as he turned to face me, I glimpsed my own spotty, pasty face reflected in his mirrored glasses. In a surprisingly cut-glass English accent, he began,

"What the hell do we have here? Why didn't someone tell me it was fancy dress day?"

I was intimidated beyond belief.

"Hi Mike, I'm Frank O'Hare. I'm new here. It's my first winter season and I'm looking forward to working with you." I had no idea what I was saying, and he knew it.

"Look, Frank, old-boy, point one, feel free to call me

Choco, and point two, you really don't need to tell me it's your first season; everything about you reeks amateur-hour. You're dressed like a clown and clearly have all the charisma of a bag of dirty washing."

To be fair, he'd nailed my strengths, and I now waited for him to start on my weaknesses. Instead, he slowly took off his sunglasses and his steely blue eyes bored into mine.

"Look, Frank, rightly or wrongly, I care about the reputation of this ski resort, so I'll ask you three questions:

1. Do you speak German?
2. Have you skied before?
3. Have you any experience working in a ski resort?

"You don't even have to give me an answer, because I already know that the answer is 'no' to all three. So, as we've just over a week before the season starts, I'm going to make it my business to make sure that you don't embarrass yourself and everyone else when it does. Listen to me closely and you'll learn how things are done around here."

He then motioned to the small storeroom at the back of the office.

"Okay, Frankie boy, clean that out, put two chairs and a table in there, and I'll give you an hour of my time each day until the season starts. Never be late, and be sure that I'll want some kind of payback at some point."

True to his word, over the next week or so, he taught me more than I could ever have expected. From our very first session, it was a total eye-opener. I was all ears as he imparted his wisdom.

"Okay, let's get started, Frank. How many arrivals do you have this month?"

"Well, only eight people in the first week, but I'll

probably average around twenty-five arrivals per week across the whole season," I responded eagerly.

"Poor sod, only twenty-five arrivals? I've got eighty-five of the buggers arriving next week and average well over 100 per week for the rest of the season," he gloated.

"But I don't understand. Surely, the fewer guests you have, the easier it is to manage. There's less chance of getting complaints, and it also gives you more time to go skiing?"

"Good lord, Frank, have you no concept of basic economics? Okay, let me give you a crash course. All your guests need to go up the mountain if they want to ski, right?"

"Well…yes," I muttered.

"Well, you sell them a lift pass and get a 3% commission from the lift company. They mostly need to hire skis and boots, right?" he continued.

"Yes."

"Well, that's another 10% commission for you from the ski and boot shop. They'll also need to exchange their traveller's cheques and English cash for local currency, right?"

I was starting to get the gist as he continued.

"Well, you exchange their cash and sterling traveller's cheques at a better rate than they can get directly from the bank, but the bank will give you preferential "rep rates." It equates to around £4 for you for every £100 you've exchanged, and you'll be changing £1,000's every week. Look, besides your pittance of a salary and the "legitimate" commission you get from your company for selling excursions such as tobogganing and sleigh rides, there are a million other ways to make money in a ski resort, and you don't have to do anything other than be here to collect it. It's not like the summer; the beauty of the winter season is that you have a captive audience. Every guest is coming to ski, which means that they need a lift pass to get up the mountain, they might need ski lessons, and they need to rent skis and boots. They can't book any of this stuff in advance, so they book it all with us when they get here, and we earn a commission on every sale made, typically from 5% to 15%, and Bob's your uncle!" he exclaimed, as the early winter sun streamed through the office windows.

"So, Frank, my dear boy, the more customers you have, the more money you make. A ski season is a bloody gold mine. Even a numbskull like you could earn around £700 per week from an arrival of fifty guests, and that's without your salary and all the other free stuff you'll get from around the village, such as free food and drink from restaurants for recommending them to your guests. If I don't walk away with over £30k at the end of a four-month ski season of hard partying and skiing, I'm doing something wrong. And don't think I'm stupid enough to drive my Porsche around when the punters arrive. No, you'll see me driving an old Volkswagen Kombi van. I'm a poor old ski rep without a penny to my name, just like you, Frank. The Porsche gets put away in the garage next to the Merc and the motorbikes. In some ways, I wished I looked as poor and wretched as you do so I could get even more sympathy from the punters," he continued, without pausing for breath. He summarised my first tutorial with one final practical piece of advice.

"Now, if you only remember one thing about being a ski rep, it's the same as being a boy scout; always be prepared and always do your homework. If you mainly have beginners arriving, then think in advance what questions they will want answers to - *Where does the ski school meet? How do you put skis and boots on?* etc. If they are more advanced, then they need to know where the best mountain restaurants are, which are the least crowded slopes etc. Just make sure you do your homework, Frank. Now, let's take you down to the ski shop to get you some proper kit."

So, off we went, to "Herr Herbert Ski," the main ski shop at the bottom of the ski lifts. It was Herr Herbert himself who greeted us, and after a brief conversation in German, Choco turned to me.

"Okay, Frank, it's all sorted. He's going to give you a generous discount on everything. Let's start with the ski boots - what size shoes do you take?"

"Size eleven," I replied.

"Okay, it's important to get a pair at least a half-size smaller than that, so they aren't loose on your feet. Here's a pair of size tens which will be a cosy fit," he said, as he handed me the first pair on the rack.

They were, without doubt, the most hideously crippling footwear I'd ever clamped to my feet. Not only did they feel like concrete, they were bright bloody yellow!

"Okay, listen closely, Frank. The best skiers always have the longest skis, as they need to be good skiers to handle long skis. The totty all know this, so if you have longer skis, they'll be more attracted to you. So, even though you can't ski, we're going to give you skis of two metres. You'll be fine. Better still, they're bright yellow, to match your boots."

Of course, most of this was complete hogwash. Ski boots should be worn for support and comfort just like any other item of footwear, and no way should you give a raw beginner skis of that length. It was Choco's way of having some fun at my expense, but it was only much later, after weeks of hobbling around like Tim Cratchit and falling arse over tit on the baby slopes, that I realised that.

"Okay, Frank, next up, let's get you out of your polyester fire hazard of a coat. Unless you're a decent skier, you don't want to be seen out on the slopes with your uniform on, so let's get you a proper ski jacket."

On cue, Herr Herbert came through holding a bright yellow puffa jacket. I had to admit; it was super warm and much better quality than my uniform ski jacket.

"It's a bit bright, Choco," I commented.

"Nonsense. You're in a ski resort, not a bloody morgue," he chortled.

"Fair enough. How much is it?"

"1600 Austrian schillings, around £80."

"£80! I can't afford that. My other anorak cost £19.99 from C&A."

"Look, Frank, it's the only one he has in your size and he's reduced it from £150 just for you. He'll also throw in a matching yellow ski hat and let you pay in instalments. What more do you want from the poor guy?"

With that, he threw me a yellow bobble hat with the word "Herbert" emblazoned across it in black lettering.

"Choco, it says Herbert on it!" I whined.

"Of course it does. He's only giving you the discount because you'll be advertising his ski shop when you wear it, you plonker."

Before I knew it, I'd walked out of there with yellow skis and boots, a bright yellow ski jacket, and a yellow bobble hat with the word "Herbert" written on it, and I still felt I'd got a bargain. Choco was simply helping Herr Herbert get rid of the crap from the previous season that he couldn't sell, but I was so much in awe of everything, I couldn't have cared less.

The next few weeks flew by as Choco and the others introduced me to key local contacts, helped translate for me, and got me up to speed with how things worked.

My first few arrival days came and went without too much trouble. I was relieved that I'd only had a handful of guests in the resort at any one time, and as most of them were beginners, they believed much of the well-prepared advice I gave them. I also discovered that I had a knack for selling tickets to our après-ski events, such as tobogganing and sleigh rides, so I was slowly building my confidence. The most pleasing aspect was that my guests seemed to like me, and they all scored me highly on the customer service questionnaires at the end of their holiday. When it came to assessing our performance, the questionnaire scores were the deciding factor, especially when deciding on future employment. My high scores weren't too surprising, as I'd been working like a dog to be liked by my guests, carrying skis for their children, helping families get fitted with skis and boots, and giving them discounts on everything I could. You name it and I'd do it if it meant they'd be complimentary about me on the questionnaires.

It was now almost six weeks into the season and I'd successfully created an alter ego for myself, which was plausible enough to give me some credibility with my guests. It went like this - I'd been skiing since an early age and I'd been in the Alps working as a ski bum in various resorts for a few years, mainly partying, working in ski shops, and giving ski lessons in my spare time. I had now decided to work as a ski rep as I loved helping people.

I liked my alter ego much more than the real me and was pleased with how the story rolled naturally off my tongue. Deep down, I knew that it was all a delicately balanced house of cards, but I was totally unprepared for the agony and humiliation that was about to come my way.

My most recent influx of guests was my largest to date and included a group of twelve skiers from Bristol with the lead name of Harrison. I knew I'd have to be on top form with them as they'd brought their own skis and boots, and hadn't booked any lessons. The likelihood was that they were experienced skiers.

After my welcome meeting, they came to see me to ask where the best ski runs were for a mixed-ability group. Of course, I had this all prepared and happily gave them various routes and plans for them to spend the next couple of days on the mountain. By now, I'd picked up lots of ski lingo from listening to the other reps and could happily "talk" ski even if I couldn't actually "ski" ski. It transpired that the Harrison group were part of a ski club who skied every week at their local dry slope. They were all competent skiers, so when they invited me to ski with them, I used my usual excuse of carrying a hip injury from some heli-skiing I'd done on the nearby Kaprun glacier before the season started. Their group leader was Bruce, a friendly, bespectacled, balding guy in his early thirties who had the strongest Bristolian accent I'd heard. From the moment he greeted me with, *ol roight me ole mucker?* I barely understood a word he said. Luckily for me, they were a lovely bunch and booked lots of excursions and après-ski events, so I could rest easy. However, no matter how much I tried to convince myself that everything was fine, the fact remained that I still hadn't gotten to grips with the most important basics; the ability to ski and, beyond some essential words, the ability to speak the local language. Clearly, this had to change if I was to be taken seriously, so I again turned to Choco for help.

"No problem, Frank, it's about time you did something about the lingo. It's been painful listening to you speak English with a loud Austrian accent, and still expecting to be understood. Luckily for you, I know just the lady to help. She's a semi-retired English teacher called Frau Berger. Here's her telephone number. Give her a call and book yourself in for some lessons."

In terms of the skiing, Choco again wanted me to know that he was about to do me a huge favour.

"Frank, my dear boy, you are about to get an offer to die for. I am personally prepared to take you up the mountain and give you your first proper ski lesson. If you listen to what I tell you and I don't get bored senseless by your inane northern drivel, I may even give you a follow-up lesson. Now, bear in mind that I've taught kings and princes to ski in the past, so I will expect some form of payback at some stage. What that looks like, I've yet to decide," he said with a grin.

Keen to get down to business, I called Frau Berger that evening. She was friendly and happy to help, and although she lived too far away for me to get there on foot, she agreed to collect me from the church square and take me to her house for German lessons. She was booked up for a couple of weeks, so pencilled me in for her first available slot in a few weeks' time. Better still, she gave me a discounted rate for committing to an eight-week course. *Wunderbar!*

With the German lessons sorted, I could now focus on my skiing, and later that week I went to meet Choco outside Herr Herbert's, at the bottom of the chairlift, as arranged. Wincing in agony from my tiny ski boots, yet resplendent in my new canary yellow puffa ski jacket and matching "Herbert" bobble hat, the kindest thing you could say was that I was warm - in pain, but warm. As many skiers will testify, even without wearing kids' ski boots, being in pain is a rite of passage for the newbie skier, as is suffering a modicum of embarrassment as you try to make sense of how hurtling down a mountain with two planks attached to your feet can be in any way deemed "fun." None of this registered with me though, as I was living the dream. Frank O'Hare, the lanky, spotty, oft-mocked "strawberry blonde" office clerk from Middleton, was now gazing out across the snow-clad mountains of the

Austrian Alps and rubbing shoulders with alpine royalty such as Choco. It sounds ridiculous now, but I was almost bursting with pride.

Before long, I heard the deep rumble of Choco's van. Heads turned as he pulled up to his reserved parking spot outside the ski shop. True to form, and looking like he'd stepped straight out of a Wham video; tall, tanned and strutting, Choco had arrived. One chairlift-ride up the mountain later, we got started with my first ski lesson. To be fair to Choco, he showed great patience, and a couple of hours later, he'd coached me to the point where I could slowly cruise along, turning in wide "snow plough" arcs across the snow. We stopped for lunch in a cosy mountain hut and I felt like I was one of the ski crowd at last. Having said that, I soon realised that I'd made the novice mistake of taking off my ski boots during lunch and almost cried as I tried to clamp them back onto my feet at the end of our break. If not for the three mulled wines consumed over lunch, I might well have given up there and then. Being the celebrity he was, Choco had been joined by three pretty female skiers, and as they chatted away in German by the door, they blew kisses to me as Choco motioned in my direction. *If only the O' Club could see me now!* Stepping back outside into the freezing, yet sunny afternoon, Choco left the girls and came across to where I was fumbling with my gloves and goggles.

"Hey, Frank, old bean, you've done so well that I'm going to let you ski down a run on your own, while I ski with the girls on the adjacent slope. This one here is the best for you. It's officially an intermediate run, but it's very easy. We'll be on the steeper slope just over there, so I'll be able to look across and see you. If you get into any trouble, I'll be there. Take your time and don't worry. We'll meet up again at the restaurant in half an hour. I think one of them fancies you, so make sure you don't make an arse of yourself."

With that, the four of them skied further along the path and took off down the steeper slope. Immediately, the confidence I had in the morning drained away, and despite the hot mulled wine, every part of my body felt frozen. My boots were so tight that my toes had melded into a single digit, and my skis felt like a huge pair of wooden clown shoes with a mind of their own. I looked down the slope, and it looked like the North Face of the Eiger. Worse still, it snaked down in full view of those on the chairlift directly above. I tried my best to gee- myself up. *Come on Frank, there are families with kids skiing down it. Pull yourself together man!*

So, ignoring all of Choco's advice on how to ski, I bent low into a crouch, lent back from my ankles, waited until the coast was clear, and slowly wound my way down. It all started well, but by the third turn, I had picked up too much speed and had forgotten how to slow down. With my arms flailing, and dangerously close to other skiers, my left ski slid over my right and impaled itself into the mountain. For a split second, I came to a sudden halt before my boot released from the ski, and off I went, sprawling down the mountain, head over heels. Within a few metres, my other ski released, and I careered on my merry way, bouncing and pirouetting over the bumps, crashing down the hill in a blur of bright yellow. It was a weird feeling, as I felt totally detached from my body as I bounced along and eventually came to a stop on an icy ridge halfway down the run.

Heavily winded, goggles smashed, and wiping the snow from my eyes, I heard cheers and whooping from the direction of the chairlift. *Cheeky sods!* I gave a theatrical bow in their direction, but knew that my problems were only just beginning.

Too far and too icy to stumble to the bottom of the run, I had no option but to try and walk back up the slope to recover my skis. In the meantime, I hoped that a competent skier might collect them on their way down and bring them to me.

To the great amusement of those on the chairlift, I spent the next twenty minutes trying to scramble a few metres up the slope before sliding back down and repeating the process. As each minute passed, I became more exhausted and helpless. I was close to reaching full panic mode when I noticed a sleek red figure skiing on the adjacent slope.

I must have sounded like a wailing banshee as I howled across the slope.

"HELP. HELP. MIIIKE…MIIIIIIKKKE…BLOODY HELL, MMMIIIIIIKKKE!"

Goodness only knows why I reverted to his real name, but Choco and the three girls continued to ski down without so much as a sideways glance. I heard the echo of my own voice, *MIIIIKE, MIIIKKKKE, HELP!* reverberating around me. Except it wasn't an echo; it was coming from the chairlift, where the delighted skiers joined together to chant my cry for help.

"HELLLPPP, MIIIIIKE!"

I couldn't believe the cruelty of it, but they were having the time of their lives. All nationalities had joined in now, holidaymakers, locals, old, young, healthy, infirm; the world joined together in harmony to mock the pitiful, bedraggled figure of Frank O'Hare. It was like I'd never left home!

After what seemed a lifetime, I finally recovered the skis, and with the help of a kindly lift operator, came back down the mountain on the chairlift with a vow never to put another pair of skis on as long as I lived. My fragile ego couldn't take the risk of further humiliation, so despite the cold, I packed the telltale canary yellow coat and hat in my backpack and cut a dejected figure as I limped back, ever colder into town.

Later that afternoon, showered and back in my uniform, I made my way to the rep's office for my evening duties. Choco was already there with a long queue of holidaymakers waiting to cash in their traveller's cheques and book excursions with him.

"Hey, Frank, what happened to you today? Leaving me with three hot German chicks to service was well out of order. And because you abandoned us, I had to give special attention to the one who fancied you, and now she's invited me to her flat for dinner tonight. The things I do for you!"

As he was saying this, a group of boisterous girls from Birmingham reached the front of his queue.

"Hey handsome, can you change some traveller's cheques for me please?" said the girl at the front of the group.

Choco gazed out at them dispassionately, and with a weary tone explained, "Look ladies, as there's a few of you, and you're only here for a week, can we set some ground rules?"

The girls nodded as one, and the maestro continued.

"By all means flirt with me, but if you do, please bear in mind that I shall be making love to you by the end of the week. So, if you aren't ready for that, then please don't flirt with me in the first place, as it won't be fair on those who do want a piece of me."

If I'd had a sharp knife, I'd still have struggled to cut through the layers of testosterone this guy was producing. Unbelievably, they all nodded and looked at each other as if to say, *well, you can't say fairer than that.* Even more bizarrely, the girl at the front turned to one of the others and shouted,

"Oi Tina, did you hear that? Don't go spoiling it for the

rest of us. No prick-teasing - either let him shag you or keep well away."

Tina retorted with a thoughtful, "Fair enough, Linz."

With that, Linz turned back to Choco.

"Okay, Choco, no problem. While we're here, can I book eight of us in for the toboggan evening on Thursday night, please?"

What can I say? When in full Choco-mode, he was one of those rare creatures whose aura and self-confidence transcended rational behaviour.

Shortly afterwards, a happy-looking Harrison clan came bounding into the office with Bruce leading the way.

"Hi Frank, moi luverly. Can we exchange some traveller's cheques, and book in twelve people for the fondue evening for our final night this Friday?"

"Sure thing, guys. You all look happy; how was your day today?" I replied.

"The. Best. Day. Evvverrrr!" they sang in unison.

Bruce elaborated, "You won't believe this, Frank, but we saw the best wipeout ever. This clown in a bright yellow coat and hat fell head-first down the mountain right underneath the chairlift. Spectacular. Lost both his skis and then spent hours crawling up to get them and kept sliding down again every time he almost got there. It wasn't even a steep run. He just had no coordination and kept trying to climb over the icy bits when the easy, soft snow was right next to him. We went up and down that run three times while he was still sliding around on his arse. He shouldn't have even been on the mountain; he was a complete tosspot, the type of idiot who gives skiers a bad name."

Seething inside, I tried to keep calm.

"That's strange. Normally, you'd expect someone - maybe a better skier - to collect his stranded skis on their way down, and take them to him to stop him going through all that pain. It sounds like pretty poor etiquette, and it's extremely unusual," I said.

This only made matters worse.

"But you don't understand, Frank. You needed to have been there. The guy was a complete fuckwit. We think he was pissed. He was in some kind of yellow-themed fancy dress and just kept shouting, 'Help, MIIIKE, MIIKE, HELLLPP.'"

With that, the whole Harrison group fell about laughing.

"Seriously. He was a complete buffoon, Frank. In fact, we christened him 'Banana Bob, the fucking knob.'"

My seething anger and sudden hatred of all things West Country was only matched by the relief I felt that they hadn't realised the true identity of the "fuckwit." With a thin smile and a lame, "Well, I'm glad you all had fun out there," I changed the subject and admitted defeat. If only I'd known then that things were about to get worse - much worse.

Before long, the time for my first German lesson had arrived, and I was super motivated to conquer the language. At least then, I'd have something to show for my increasingly embarrassing winter in the Alps. Armed with a pen, notepad and my English/German dictionary, I set off to meet Frau Berger outside the church at 8 p.m. where we'd planned for her to collect me in her white Mercedes. It was a perishing cold night, and I felt glad to be wearing my yellow puffa jacket and matching hat again, safe in the knowledge that the Harrisons were away partying on their final evening, so "Banana Bob's" cover couldn't be blown.

With snow falling, it was great to see that the Austrian reputation for punctuality remained intact as Frau Berger's white Mercedes pulled up directly outside the church a couple of minutes early. With striking grey/blue eyes and auburn hair set high in a bob, Frau Berger looked younger than I expected. She returned my wave with a warm smile. As I approached her car, I could see that the front passenger seat was full of textbooks so I opened the rear passenger door, sank into the warmth of the leather seat and found myself next to a cherubic toddler strapped into a baby seat, happily gurgling away. I instinctively reached across to touch the toddler's hand while bellowing out a hearty, "Guten abend, Frau Berger."

The next few seconds remain a blur. I remember looking up at the rear-view mirror and seeing a look of fear on the face of Frau Berger. I also remember an ear-shattering scream, and her shouting something along the lines of, *AAAGGGGHHHHH. AAAAGGGHHHH. HELFT. HELFT. SCHNELL DIE POLIZEI ZU HOLEN!* I'm less clear about how quickly I was dragged from the car by the police, and what their response was to my wild-eyed plea of, "There must be some mistake, officer. Mrs Berger is my German teacher," while waving my £1.99 Collins English/German dictionary at them. It didn't help that they didn't understand a word I said – that, and the fact that "Mrs Berger" was now slumped against the outside of her car, clinging onto her baby, wailing hysterically and pointing in my direction. I vaguely remember another white Mercedes pulling up with an elderly lady driver looking at her watch and shaking her head.

However, I do clearly recall being sat in a police cell later that evening, and being asked for the name of a German speaker who could represent me, as I had been accused of the attempted abduction of a minor. I was living a nightmare. I couldn't make sense of anything and was shaking with fear. A couple of days earlier, I'd been on the phone to home telling them how happy I was, my mum bursting with pride that her youngest, "Little Frankie," the laughingstock of the family, had hit the big time. Now, here I was, my career over before it had started, and on the verge of spending the rest of my life behind bars. I didn't have the heart, or the bottle, to tell the police to contact my manager at TAN Ski, but I couldn't think of anyone else who could help me, until I blurted out, "Mike!"

The police officers looked at each other, bemused. "Mike?"

"Ja, Mike. No, Choco. Choco, the English ski representative. Reiseleiter, bitte. You must know him?"

"Ah, Die Choco. Der Englische reiseleiter?"

"Ja. Ja. Ja. Choco, bitte. Danke schön."

I'd packed almost every German word I knew into a couple of sentences, and it seemed to work as they nodded and left the cell. After what seemed like an age, the cell door opened again and in walked Choco. Despite his serious expression, I felt like a puppy dog when its owner returns home from work.

"What the fuck have you been up to this time, Frankie boy?"

"I've no bloody idea. I went to meet Frau Berger for my German lesson as we arranged, and next thing I know, I'm bloody Nelson Mandela!"

"You really are a thick bugger, Frank. You got in the wrong car, and to make matters worse, you apparently tried to grope the woman's baby!"

"Choco, please believe me. I did nothing of the sort. I just held the baby's hand. I mean, I just leaned across and touched him. I mean… Oh fuck!"

I then babbled incoherently.

"Have you spoken to them? What are they going to do to me? Did you tell them I'm innocent? Please don't let them hurt me."

"Look Frank, I told them the truth, that you are a thick

northern bastard from England who shouldn't really be in the job, but I have been helping you learn to ski and arranged for you to take German lessons to help you blend into a civilised society."

Despite one insult after another, I nodded along with him in complete agreement.

"The problem is that you got into the car of the daughter of the deputy chief of police, and although I've made them see it was just an unfortunate misunderstanding, they say you must be kept in the cell overnight to think about your actions and teach you a lesson."

I couldn't believe what I was hearing. I was a free man. But as soon as the euphoria died down, reality kicked in again.

"Shit, Choco, it's airport transfer day tomorrow morning and I'm meant to be on the coach at six-thirty, taking all the departures up to Munich Airport for their flights back to the UK."

"Don't worry, I've thought about that. They'll let you leave here at 7 a.m. so I'll tell the coach driver to make the first pick-ups on his own and stop off at the police station to collect you on the way to Kitzbühel. They should get here around seven-thirty, so you'll have plenty of time. You'll have to give some story to the punters as to why you are getting picked up at the police station. Anyway, it's well past your bedtime now, so get your head down and let me get back to the very eager young lady I had to leave to come and sort your mess out."

"Look Choco, I don't know how I'll ever be able to repay you," I mumbled.

"Oh, I do, Frank. From now to the end of the season, I want 50% of all the commission you earn from money exchange, après-ski events, lift passes, the lot. We'll settle up every Monday morning when you'll hand over the cash."

With that, he blew me a kiss, gave a thumbs up sign, turned around, and off he went. Honestly, I couldn't have cared less about the deal; he was welcome to the money and I would happily pay him every week until the end of the season.

On a hard, cold bed, I got little sleep. I couldn't help thinking about the situation. I wrestled with the notion of whether Choco was actually a friend or foe. Yes, he delighted in belittling and making fun of me at every opportunity, but he was there when I needed him. And, despite any payback he demanded, I'd learned more from him in these few weeks than I could have from a lifetime of training courses.

Aching all over, I was awoken early the next morning by the keys opening the cell door and, just as Choco had said, the coach pulled up outside the police station with a collection of sleepy holidaymakers already on board. With renewed vigour, I jumped onto the microphone.

"Good morning, ladies and gentlemen. Apologies for joining you a little later than planned, but some of my guests lost some valuables this morning and I had to come to the police station to help translate for them."

I could see a few nods of approval from the Harrison group at the back of the coach, but it was clear that nobody cared. Despite my tiredness, I was now absolutely buzzing.

A couple of hours later, as we approached the airport, I handed out the holiday questionnaires, and once completed, handed them in at the Ski TAN airport desk and changed into one of the spare uniform jackets we kept at the airport. I was now ready to welcome the new arrivals. A few minutes later, I could see Bruce from the Harrison party running towards me.

"Hey, Bruce, I thought you would have gone through passport control by now?" I chirped brightly.

"The others have, but I realised that we hadn't returned the holiday questionnaire, so here you go. Thanks for everything, Frank."

With that, he handed me the completed form and rushed off towards security and passport control. Alone at the desk, it was the perfect opportunity to have a quick read to see what they'd said about me, just in case I had to find the nearest bin. My eyes immediately fixed on the three key questions.

Score
Knowledge and helpfulness of your resort representative 5/5
Availability and punctuality of your resort representative 5/5
Professionalism of your resort representative 5/5

I quickly scanned to the bottom of the form to read the comments.

Frank (aka BANANA BOB) is the best ski rep we've ever had - he is a credit to your company and you need to look after him. BTW please buy him a new ski jacket!

They'd all signed the message individually - all twelve of them. I don't mind admitting that I welled up with emotion. Whether it was the effects of the past few days or the fact that people still liked me for just being me without all my bullshit stories, I couldn't say. I don't know whether they knew all along that I was Banana Bob or they'd realised when they saw me wearing the yellow ski jacket on the coach that morning, but it didn't really matter, all was forgiven, and without knowing it, they'd now made Bristol my favourite place in the whole of the UK.

That incident proved to be a turning point for me. From then on, I dropped the facade of fake achievements and just told the truth. It turned out that people didn't think any less of me for being an inexperienced and eager-to-please lad trying his best to help make their holiday the best he could. Customer feedback like theirs certainly didn't do any harm to my reputation within the company, and through a mixture of good fortune and lots of sucking up, I got enough high customer feedback scores to see me successfully complete my first-ever winter as a holiday rep. Surprisingly, that was to be Choco's final ski season as I later learned that he'd fallen in love with the daughter of one of Turkey's most prominent hotel chain owners and relocated to the south-west coast of the country to help them develop their hotel portfolio. I had absolutely no doubt that he'd take the switch to the Turkish hospitality industry in his stride. His extrovert, self-indulgent style might not be to everyone's liking, but when you have as much confidence and charisma as Choco, then success is pretty much guaranteed, whatever the task at hand.

Looking back, I wondered whether he knew it was to be his final season. Maybe that's why he was so generous with the knowledge he shared with me. Whatever the reason, and whatever his shortcomings, working with Choco had hardened me and given me a confidence I hadn't felt before. I was now more determined than ever to prove that I could make it for more than one season in the travel industry.

Chapter 3
Costa Bravado

There is no doubt in my mind that if social media had existed in the 1980s, then my career would have been over before it had even begun. Not so much because of anything I would have posted, but more because of the existence of the mobile phone and the way every misdemeanour is recorded and shared in the blink of an eye. In my view, social media is the modern-day Colosseum; the gladiators being those combatants brave enough to post their stories and views, risking the thumbs up or thumbs down from the fervid audience. On the likes of X (aka Twitter), it can be tempting to get drawn in and comment on the conversations that pique your interest without thinking too much about the consequences. I once joined a thread to point out a factual flaw in an argument. The speed at which I was told to "crawl back into my hole" stopped me from entering the fray again. More recently, I happened across TikTok and for a short spell became obsessed with swiping up to watch the short videos, sometimes for hours every day. Luckily, I had enough self-awareness to delete the app before I became addicted. However, it was on TikTok that I saw something that captured the essence of social media to a tee. The video in question featured a middle-aged lady called Norma, and it was set to a faint, melancholic musical background. Norma talked earnestly into the camera to share her story.

A year ago today, the terrible curse that is Covid took my loving husband of twenty-five years away. Six months later, my sweet younger brother tragically died in a motorbike accident, and I didn't think I could ever cope with so much grief. But my friends and family rallied around and helped me through my darkest hours, and I owe them so much.

After being diagnosed with cancer last week, I know that those same friends and family will come through for me again. Yet, as I watched the sunrise this morning, I felt lucky; lucky to have lived the life I have, lucky to have such loving friends and family around me, and lucky to be alive.

Life is precious, but it is short; shorter than we can ever imagine. Please savour every moment as though it is your last. Don't waste a single second. Smell the roses. And be thankful you are living your best life.

I became a little emotional as I read Norma's story and decided to leave her a message to wish her all the best, but, as I clicked on the comments section, I had to do a double-take as I read the very first response to her video. In three brief words, the whole crazy randomness that is social media was captured, because the very first response to Norma's heartrending video was, '*Shut it, Bitch'*. Of course, the messages below this were all supportive, but I couldn't help staring at the three words at the top of the page, and, as I did, I glanced at the username of the person who'd written it. I'd expected it to be from a keyboard warrior with a pseudonym such as *@wolfman* or *@hellsangel666*, but the reality was much less exotic. The author of the vitriol wasn't hiding at all. It was brazenly attributed to *@basingstoke.paul.* Now, I don't know what it was about Norma's video that enraged Paul so much, but I do know that if he'd witnessed some of my antics in my first-ever summer season as a holiday representative, he would have been far from amused.

Shortly after my eventful debut ski season, my newfound confidence was further boosted when I was offered my first summer season. This is what I'd set my heart on. Although I'd learnt so much, my winter season had been a struggle as I was so far out of my comfort zone. On the other hand, summer was right up my street. After all, how much was there to learn about drinking in bars and lying on a beach? No new jargon to take on board, no awkward equipment to master, and no slopes to embarrass myself on. Bliss! The only slight problem was that we could be allocated anywhere across the summer portfolio, with France, Spain and Yugoslavia (as it was then) being the main options. I desperately wanted to work in Spain, and was prepared to do almost anything to achieve that aim.

Before learning our allocated summer destinations, we had to complete another training course, this time located on the Spanish Costa Brava. We were to meet at the head office in Leeds, where a double-decker coach would collect us to take us down to Dover, through France, and into Spain. At this point, lots of my decisions were still based on advice given by Choco, and one tip he gave me was to dress for the position I wanted, rather than the job I had right now. So, as I was desperate to work in Spain, it made sense to me that I rocked up at the meeting point dressed in the most Spanish-looking clothes I could find: White jeans, brown sandals, no socks, a light blue shirt with most of the buttons undone, and a white pullover casually tied around my neck and shoulders. Among the parkas and duffle coats worn by everyone else on a cold and wet Yorkshire morning, I stood out like a sore thumb. Back then I think that my biggest strengths were stupidity and naivety. At the meeting point, I was pleased to see that Phil, from my first interview, was leading the training course, and Hilary was one of his assistants, so my confidence was high. Once everyone was on board the coach, Phil took to the mic and laid down the law.

"Okay, before we set off, I'd like to welcome you all to the three-day training course which will take place in Lloret De Mar, on the Spanish Costa Brava. We have a mixture of new recruits and a handful of staff who have already completed a winter season on board today – forty-two of you in total. Irrespective of that, the only thing that matters is your performance on this training course. We hope you will all be successful, but it's very rare for everyone on the course to pass, so please apply yourselves properly and take nothing for granted."

To be honest, my winter season under Choco's tutelage had given me a bit of an ego, and I was slightly miffed that I was being treated the same as the brand-new recruits, so I took Phil's warning with a pinch of salt. I sat next to a skinny, dark-haired lad called Terry from Liverpool. Despite not having worked abroad before, he exuded confidence. He'd been guiding river tours on the River Mersey for a couple of years, and was used to dealing with passengers and giving commentary. We hit it off immediately. He welcomed me with,

"Hi, I'm Terry. What time are you due on?"

"Sorry?" I replied.

"What time are you due on?" he repeated.

"What?"

"I presume that, dressed like that, you're the cabaret act. What have you got in your bag, a Julio Iglesias wig?"

"Nice one. That must be the famous non-existent scouse wit I've heard so much about. I'm Frank. Pleased to meet you," I fired back.

We exchanged a few football-related insults and became firm friends in a matter of minutes.

As we made our way down the motorway, Phil took to the mic again. There might have been a ruthless streak in him somewhere, but his appearance was that of a genial geography teacher, complete with thick corduroy trousers and a chunky woollen pullover. With his unkempt curly hair, and probably in his mid-forties, he reminded me of Jasper Carrott, but without the jokes.

"OK everybody, to be successful as an overseas holiday representative, you need to be able to communicate clearly and concisely, and be comfortable using a microphone. With that in mind, we have a stack of travel brochures at the rear of the coach downstairs. Please take one of these and choose a destination or a landmark and rehearse its main selling points. During the journey, we'll call you up to the front of the coach at random to spend five minutes on the microphone selling your destination of choice to the rest of us. Your aim is to make us fall in love with it."

This was great news. I'd spent lots of time on the microphone during the winter so I could do this in my sleep. I nonchalantly took a magazine, which focused on Paris and its biggest tourist attraction, the Eiffel Tower. I immediately flicked through the pages, looking for the best bits, and as I did, Terry sparked into life.

"I thought you wanted to work in Spain for the summer?" he questioned.

"I do, why?"

"So, why are you talking about somewhere in France? If you do a really good job, they might think you love France, and will give you a job in one of the French resorts. Be careful, Julio. Anyway, the Eiffel Tower is just a bloody big pylon; everyone knows that."

Crazily, I let Terry's comments play on my mind, and instead of properly focusing on the job at hand, I planned to do just well enough to get by without impressing too much or giving the impression that I actually liked Paris or France. It was bloody madness. I glanced across at Terry, who was calmly looking out of the window.

"Anyway, where's your magazine?" I asked.

"I don't need a magazine. I'm going to talk about the greatest city on earth, Liverpool."

I said nothing, but fully expected him to fall flat on his face.

In another hour or so, Hilary came on the mic and called up the first couple of girls to the front to have a go. They looked around my age and were clearly nervous. One of them rambled on about Athens for the full five minutes and made it sound like the most uninteresting place on earth. The other dried up after around three minutes, attempting to sell the delights of Cornwall. They obviously needed lots more practice, but I thought that overall, it was a decent first effort from them both. I was itching for my turn to show them how it was done, but supposed that they'd go through all the newcomers first. However, my chance came sooner than expected.

"Okay, we've heard from two of our new staff; now let's hear from someone who has already had a winter season under his belt. Please, can Frank O'Hare make his way to the front of the coach?"

As I reached down to take my notes, Terry again piped up.

"I thought you'd done this before, mate. Why do you need notes?" he asked.

I smiled back at him and left them on my seat. He was right. I could do this blindfolded. So, I sauntered nonchalantly to the front and turned to face the sea of expectant faces, all with notebooks at the ready…and I froze. My mind went blank, and I even felt myself blush. A few vacant moments later, after looking down for my non-existent notes, I randomly started to yell into the microphone.

"Some people say that the Eiffel Tower is just a big pylon, but for me, it's much more than that." I squawked.

Then, from absolutely nowhere, I blurted out, "Most people think that it's named after its creator, Gustave Eiffel, but actually it's called the Eiffel Tower because of the pigeons on the top. Every time you look up, you get an eye-full."

This generated some nervous laughter, so I latched onto it like a drowning man.

"The man who really designed the Eiffel Tower was a French guy who only ever wore beach sandals, Felipe Felopp."

Fewer people were laughing now. I knew I was making a complete fool of myself, but I just couldn't stop myself from going under.

"By the way, when we reach France, make sure that you never have more than one egg for breakfast, because one egg is 'un oeuf.'"

For some inexplicable reason, I then let out a huge, "Wayhaaay!"

I mumbled on, largely incoherently, for another couple of minutes and finished the shit show with,

"No, seriously, you gotta visit the Big Paris Pylon; IT'S GREEEAAATTT."

And that was it; the most unprofessional, slap-dash, car-crash of a performance you could imagine. All that was missing was, *My name's Frank O'Hare. You've been a great audience. Thank you and good night!* The spectacle was greeted by utter silence from the dumbfounded audience as I made my way back to my seat. Terry greeted me with genuine concern in his voice.

"Jeez, mate, I thought you'd done this shit before. Were you taking the piss? It has to be a set-up, right?"

I was in shock and felt like crying. I couldn't look him in the eye, but tried to front it out.

"C'mon, Terry, I can't tell you now, but you'll see why I did it like that in due course."

Hilary immediately jumped back on the microphone.

"OK everyone, we'll take a break now and continue a little later. In the meantime, can Frank please come back to the front of the coach?"

I could see that Hilary had vacated the seat next to Phil, so he was obviously the one who was going to give me the warning. Or worse. As I took the seat next to him, he was almost whispering to keep his temper under control.

"OK Frank, what on earth was that? It was an embarrassment to yourself and, more importantly from my perspective, to the company. For an experienced member of staff to act in such an immature and unprofessional way reflects poorly on our recruitment process. We'll try to recover the situation later, and you will get the chance to redeem yourself, but make no mistake, Frank, we'll be watching you closely from now on, so you need to get your act together. You'll be going back on the mic again before we get to Spain, and each time you do, you'd better be well-prepared and word-perfect every time, otherwise you'll be going straight back to the UK. Okay, go back to your seat."

He looked so disappointed that I actually felt sorry for him, but not as much as I did for myself. I was like the kid with the inflatable family, and I'd let them all down. To make matters worse, I could hear Choco's voice in my head, *Don't forget, Frank, always be prepared, and do your homework. You aren't bright enough not to.*

As I reached my seat, Phil returned to the mic.

"Hello everyone, we hope that you've had time to reflect on the last presentation from Frank. We feel bad for him, as we'd asked him to put together an overly humorous and ill-prepared presentation as an example, and although he went a bit overboard, we think he got the message across well enough. The message is this; whilst there is always room for humour in any presentation, it must be within reason and be there to support the main message you are trying to convey, not the other way round. The purpose of your presentation is to inform and educate in an interesting manner. We are not looking for stand-up comedians. I'm only going to say this once. We are a professional organisation and we expect professionalism from our staff. Please prepare properly and don't waste your chance."

Phil had saved my embarrassment, and, for the time being, my job. But in a way, it made me feel even worse because I was back to doing what I'd always done, putting on a facade and pretending to be something I wasn't. I knew I'd failed, and that I was back in the last chance saloon. The only good thing was that my over-inflated ego had been well and truly popped.

Terry was also back to his old cheery self. "You sly old

son of a gun. You kept that one quiet, Frankie boy. You've gone up a couple of levels in my estimation. You're now on minus two!"

"Ah, nice one, Terence. Yeah, I wasn't allowed to share it with anyone beforehand. I must admit, I felt a bit of a prat having to talk shite like that, but you have to do what the boss wants, I guess."

Over the next few minutes, I had a queue of lads and girls slapping me on the back and shaking my hand with comments such as - *You had us fooled there, mate - I knew that nobody could genuinely be that bad* - and the memorable - *I told my friend, Sue, that it was a set-up as soon as I saw the comedy Spanish waiter outfit you were wearing.* On the positive side, the humiliation had stung me into action, and while Terry and others around me slept, I devoured every single magazine and every word I could about France, Paris, and the Eiffel Tower. No way was I going to be humiliated again.

Throughout our journey through France, more and more people were being invited onto the microphone to present, including Terry. Up he went, with next to no preparation and no notes to fall back on. I feared the worst and was mentally prepared to distance myself from him if he was anywhere near as bad as I was. But blow me down with a feather; delivered in a strong scouse accent, he was the consummate professional. Almost word-perfect, he gave a potted history of Liverpool, highlighting its many attractions, their historical significance, and the reasons they were worth visiting. No nerves and no unnecessary pauses, it was informative, entertaining and endearing. *The Bastard!*

It was now one presentation after another, each one a step closer to what I hoped would be my redemption. When my name was finally called, I could feel the tension rise as I took my place at the front of the coach once more. Phil glared at me as he handed over the microphone, and I mentally went through my checklist:

1. *Deep breath*
2. *Hold the microphone against the chin*
3. *Scan the audience at forehead level*
4. *Talk with a smile*
5. *Don't rush*

I was super nervous, but I had one thing in my favour. I hadn't been afforded many natural assets in life, but in the absence of any physically redeeming features, I had been blessed with an excellent short-term memory. I'd realised at school that I could read a few pages of text, take it in, and remember it virtually word for word for a couple of days afterwards. It never worked if someone told me something, but if it was written down, then I was in business. Strangely, if I had to read the same thing again the following week, then I wouldn't recognise a word of it. But it's a skill I've milked within an inch of its life my whole career.

The problem with my first effort was that I'd been far too busy trying to show Terry that I didn't need to prepare, and consequently, wasn't able to wing it when push came to shove. Instead, I went blank and fell back on a juvenile comedy routine. There was to be no mistake this time, as I'd now done my homework. After a slightly rushed start, I hit my stride and eulogised Paris like never before. The Arc de Triomphe, The Louvre, The Grand and Petit Palais, Notre Dame, Montmartre, and, of course, the Eiffel Tower. I was allowed to talk for around ten minutes until I came to a natural close. The relief coursed through my veins. I was back in the game. Phil remained deadpan, but I knew that he would have been equally relieved that I hadn't embarrassed him again.

We had a couple of more chances to speak on the microphone as we practised airport welcome speeches and safety checks, but both Terry and I were on a roll and were near word-perfect each time. We couldn't stop telling each other how much better we were than the others for the remainder of the journey. To say that we were pleased with ourselves was an understatement. This wasn't a good sign.

As the coach finally pulled into Lloret de Mar, despite it being early spring, the weather was lovely and sunny, and there was the faint scent of salt in the air blowing in from the seafront. I was beyond excited. This was what I'd dreamed of. Not everything was open yet, but the resort had the feel of something that was coming to life and I already loved it. Once off the coach, we formed a queue to check into our hotel, where I would be sharing a twin room with Terry.

"Let's have a look at your passport pic then, Frank," he piped up.

"It's not worth looking at, Terry. It's only a year or so old."

"C'mon, let's see it, you ugly bugger."

So, I passed it across without thinking much about it.

"Spencer? Spencer? Fucking Spencer?" he cried.

"Yeah, so what? That's my middle name. Big deal," I responded.

"Big Deal? Your name is FRANK fucking SPENCER!"

Now, for those of you not aware, Frank Spencer was the name of the lead character in the hit comedy series, Some Mothers Do Have 'Em. He was basically a clown of a man whose stupidity got him into lots of scrapes. It was probably the biggest comedy show of the 1970s, and Frank Spencer was the byword for a blithering idiot.

"You are right, Terry. My parents should have known that years after my birth, there'd be a TV programme starring an idiot called Frank Spencer."

"I don't care, Spennie. I think it's hilarious," he said, as he fell about laughing.

What I didn't know at the time was that handing Terry my passport and letting him see my full name would prove to be a stroke of genius, and would ultimately keep me in a job. Predictably, I demanded to see his passport, but it didn't give me any ammunition other than seeing that his middle name was Albert. So, from that moment on, to each other, we became Spennie and Bertie.

The plan for that afternoon was for us all to go out in smaller groups to find as much information about the resort as we could - things like where the post office was, where the nearest bars were, and how far it was to the beach. This would involve lots of walking, speaking to locals, asking directions, and exploring what Lloret had to offer. The information we gathered would be used the following day as we presented mock welcome meetings in front of the group.

We teamed up with four girls: the two who first presented on the coach, Natassa and Joy, from Yorkshire; Kim from Australia; and Sally from Cardiff. I was in my element for two reasons: first, it gave me the chance to use my schoolboy Spanish to ask questions of the bemused locals, and second, I could swan around in my white jeans looking like a local. Although, what the locals made of a deathly pale, skinny, freckle-faced ginger-haired lad asking them questions in broken "Dondy esty el post officy" Spanish, goodness only knows. I didn't care, in my book, I was one of them.

Around an hour into the exercise, we came across the Beach Boys Bar, which seemed to be just opening up, so Terry suggested we go in and ask a few questions about what entertainment and food they offered. It was almost empty inside, and the barman greeted us straight away in English.

"Hi folks. Don't tell me…you're new reps doing some resort fact-finding?"

With his long black hair, moustache and dark brooding looks, he appeared Spanish, but his accent was unmistakably cockney.

"How'd you guess?" squealed Kim.

"Well, I think that the pens, clipboards and serious expressions gave it away most," he laughed. "Anyway, I'm Ricky. Welcome to the Beach Boys Bar. Seeing as you're the first reps to come through the door this season, let me give you all a drink on the house."

Kim was the first to reply. "Wow, that's great, mate. I'll have an orange juice, please."

"Same here," shouted the other girls.

"Look ladies, when I offered you a drink, I meant a proper drink. It's well past midday, and it's the local custom."

To be fair to the girls, they stayed firm.

"Sorry, we can't risk it. None of us are sure of passing the course, so we can't risk alcohol."

Of course, as Terry and I thought of ourselves as big shots, and also had zero willpower, we immediately accepted the offer.

"Go on then, just the 'uno', thanks," I said.

With that, Ricky poured four glasses of orange juice and passed them to the girls, and then poured what looked like half a bottle of vodka into two glasses, before adding a splash of orange juice.

"There you go, lads. In case your boss comes in, you've all got orange juices."

To me and Terry, this was heaven, and it was getting better by the minute.

"Look, if any of you work the summer in Lloret, you'll always get free drinks in the Beach Boys Bar as long as you recommend us to your punters and bring some of them in here with you now and again."

I had found my natural habitat at last. I wanted to work in this resort so much, it almost hurt. By the time we finished the drinks, the girls had got all the information we needed, not only about the Beach Boys Bar, but about the rest of the resort too, as Ricky told us everything we needed to know. It turned out that his mum was Spanish and his dad was from London. He'd been born in London, but his parents had split up when he was twelve, and he came over to live in Spain with his mum after that. He and his business partner bought the Beach Boys Bar three years ago, and it was one of the most popular bars in the resort, especially with the British. As we left, he shouted across.

"Come back later tonight, guys. It'll be much busier, and we'll have some live music on."

"That's a shame. We have more work to prepare tonight. In any case, our boss has warned us that anyone caught drinking and staying out late will be for the chop," Kim responded.

I was already light-headed, and the last thing I wanted was to risk anything by going out on the town, so there was no argument from me.

Later on, in the hotel dining room, there was excited chatter from each of the groups as we exchanged stories from our day exploring Lloret. The six of us agreed not to mention our visit to the Beach Boys Bar, and after dinner, we went down to one of the allocated meeting rooms to prepare our presentations for the following day. The girls wanted to do the lion's share of the presentation as they felt that they still needed to impress, and we were happy for them to take the limelight. After a couple of hours of fine-tuning the presentations, we returned to our rooms to get some well-earned rest.

"Hey, Spennie, you tired?" Terry asked.

"Bloody exhausted, mate. Two more days of this is going to be pretty full-on."

"Exactly. That's why we need some downtime," he continued.

"What do you mean?"

"Well, you heard what that bar guy said - free drinks and live music down at the Beach Boys tonight."

"Bloody hell, Bertie, are you mad? You know what'll happen if we stay out too late and get pissed."

"What are you talking about, Spen?" he continued. "I'm talking about an hour or so, innocently relaxing in a bar and then back in bed well before midnight. In any case, Phil and the others are on one of the top floors, and we're on the first, so we'll be in and out without anyone seeing us. Anyway, we've got two keys, so you can come back early if it's not your scene."

Half an hour later, we breezed into a much busier Beach Boys Bar and were greeted like homecoming kings.

"What'll it be, boys? Same again?" shouted Ricky above the general hubbub.

"Yes please, Ricky, mate," we chimed.

After serving us the drinks, Ricky immediately turned to two girls standing near us at the bar.

"Hey girls, these guys are the ones you should ask, not me. They're local holiday reps and know the resort inside out," he shouted to them, while winking at me and Terry.

The girls turned to face us, and I could see that they were probably five years or so older. One was blonde, the other brunette, both quite pretty, and clearly up for some fun.

"Hi boys, we're Sheila and Jackie from Glasgow. Who would ye be then?" smiled the brunette.

Before I could speak, Terry was straight in.

"I'm Bertie from Liverpool, and this is my mate, Spencer, from London. We're both holiday reps just winding down after a tough day at the airport."

"Och, get you. In that case, where can ye recommend for a good time?"

"Well, other than back to my place, here is as good as anywhere. Especially now that you've met us!" Terry flirted.

Her friend, Jackie, then turned to me.

"Och, I'm not sure Spencer here is capable of giving us a good time!"

Playing the part of Spencer, from London, seemed to galvanise me.

"Sorry Jackie, I didn't quite catch what you said. Did you say you wanted someone to show you how it's done? If so, you've met the right guy," I said confidently, in my new southern accent.

She laughed. "Och, you're a cocky wee lad. Just what I might need later on!"

Ricky came over again to join the conversation.

"Everyone ready for another drink? It's all on the house if you're with these two fellas."

With that, he poured two large vodkas for me and Terry, and two cocktails for the ladies. The next two hours passed in a blur of flirting, sexual innuendo, and more drinks, until Jackie turned to me and said,

"OK Spence, isn't it about time you two gave us what ye promised? How about coming back to our apartment to prove you're not all talk?"

"Your wish is our command, ladies," Terry laughed.

By now, I'd lost all sense of time, and feeling worse for wear, hoped that adrenaline would see me through.

"I'll just nip to the loo before we go." I said, as I went to freshen up.

As soon as I reached the toilet cubicle, the whole room started to spin, and I vomited everywhere before collapsing in a heap. The next thing I heard was Terry's voice through the door.

"What the hell are you playing at, Frank? You've been gone twenty minutes. We are waiting at the bar. Hurry up, man, they want you."

"OK Terry, don't worry. I'm on my way," I slurred.

I only have a vague recollection of what happened after that, but I do remember two doormen picking me off the toilet floor and dragging me past the bar, towards the exit. It was like being out with the 'O' Club all over again, as they dragged my limp body past Terry and the two girls, who were waiting for me to give them the "good time" I'd promised.

Once outside, dizzy and disorientated, I looked for somewhere to collapse. Feeling like shit, I made my way to a shop doorway, slowly curled up in the foetal position, and fell asleep. I vaguely remember Terry's voice telling me he was leaving to go back with the girls, and that this was my last chance. I waved him off with a slurred, "Alright, give 'em one for me." Even by my standards, this was a low point.

Sometime later, I felt someone grab hold of me. Once again, it was Terry.

"C'mon you daft bugger. It's three o'clock in the bloody morning, and in your state, it'll take us at least half an hour to walk back to the hotel."

"Did you go back with the girls?" I grunted, half asleep.

"Yes, but nothing happened because I thought you'd bloody choke on your own vomit. I made my excuses and came back for you. Anyway, I was too drunk to do anything, but at least I can still walk and bloody talk."

I still felt like shit, and could hardly stand without Terry holding me up, so that's the way we staggered off towards the hotel. I don't know whether my drink had been spiked or whether it was a combination of the lack of sleep, stress, heat, and alcohol. Whatever it was, I must have felt like a dead weight to Terry, but he battled on manfully. It was dark. Every street looked the same. And we soon realised that we didn't have a clue where we were going. Before long, we came to a patch of grass and a bench where Terry sat me down.

"OK Frank, you stay here. You're too bloody heavy, so I'm going to go on ahead. It won't take me long to find the hotel, I'll bring you back a pair of trousers, a fresh shirt, and some water. You stink and look bloody hanging, mate. We can't risk you being seen in this state."

I laid down on the bench and waited for his return, and in what seemed like no time at all, I was being woken again, but this time, it wasn't by Terry; it was by the sunlight. It was bloody morning! I glanced down at my watch and saw that it was almost 6 a.m. The morning sessions started at 8 a.m. And breakfast started at 7 a.m. Terry must have fallen asleep back in the room.

Despite feeling parched, I felt much better now, and slowly gathered my senses. Terry was right. I was filthy and stank of vomit. I tried to get my bearings and luckily, in the light, everything was a lot easier. I recognised a couple of landmarks and realised that I was around fifteen minutes from the hotel, if I got a move on. I stumbled along as quickly as I could, and when I got to the hotel, I thanked my lucky stars that our room was on the first floor, so I could easily take the emergency staircase rather than the lifts or the main staircase leading from the reception area.

Once on the first floor, I checked the coast was clear, and dashed to the room with no one seeing me. I'd made it! I quickly dumped my clothes and went straight to the shower. Every muscle ached, and I felt like death, but we had arranged to meet the girls at breakfast to do some final prep for the day ahead. Terry was nowhere to be seen, but knowing him, he'd probably be having a sneaky fag outside with some of the hotel workers.

Showered, shaved, freshly clothed, and with double helpings of aftershave and mouthwash, I entered the rapidly filling breakfast room. The girls were already there, and I made my way over to their table. Natassa was the first to react.

"Morning Frank, you look bloody knackered!"

"Yeah, I didn't get much sleep last night. Just couldn't get comfortable," I lied.

"I'm not surprised after what Terry did."

"What?"

"Haven't you heard?"

"Heard what?"

"The management team took it in turns to wait in reception, overnight, until around six this morning to catch anyone who had broken the rules and gone out on the town. Apparently, they caught three people coming back pissed in the early hours, and Terry was one of them. He came over to the table earlier to apologise and say goodbye to us. Terry and the other two lads are being sent back to the UK on a flight later this morning. We thought you knew. He told us how you'd tried to persuade him not to go out, and threatened to report him to Phil to stop him, but that he wouldn't listen. He asked us to thank you for trying, and to wish you all the best for the rest of the training course."

I couldn't take it in. My head was banging like a drum,

just trying to piece the story together. I had nothing adequate to say, but to my everlasting shame, I mumbled, "If only he'd have listened to me. I tried my best," and shook my head.

As we made our way to the main meeting room after breakfast, Hilary made her way over to me and took me to one side.

"We can only apologise for the upset Terry must have caused you last night, Frank. We caught him trying to sneak back into the hotel at around four this morning, and I'm sorry to say that he had been drinking heavily. We had to let him back to your room to collect some of his clothes before letting him sleep it off in a spare room. I hope he didn't disturb you too much. He wasn't the only one, but we were the most disappointed in Terry, as he showed so much promise. He told us how you'd tried to stop him, and he wanted us to pass his apologies on to you."

"Thanks for that, Hilary. He didn't wake me when he came into the room, so it was really no problem from that point of view. I think it's out of character. Can't he be given another chance?" I pleaded.

"I'm afraid not, Frank. We can't give second chances for deliberately flouting our rules. It's always the ones you'd least expect, but it's better to part ways now than give them a job and find out later. We've arranged for them to fly back to the UK today, so it should be a stark warning to everyone else on the course."

The rest of the day, and indeed the rest of the training course, passed by in a haze of guilt. But, from then on, I did exactly what I was asked and was pretty much the model pupil.

On the final day, we were told whether we had passed the training. It transpired that another four trainees hadn't made the grade, and again, they were flown home while those of us who had been successful were issued with our summer uniforms ahead of the return coach journey back to the UK.

On our final evening, the management team gave the go-ahead for us to join them for a few drinks "within reason" after dinner, and as fate would have it, the first bar we went in was the Beach Boys Bar. There were around forty of us in all, and we made for a largely happy and celebratory bunch as we made our way into Beach Boys. I walked beside Phil as we entered, and soon caught Ricky's eye behind the bar. I don't know whether it was a sixth sense, but he treated me as a complete stranger when he came over to serve us.

"Hi there guys, what can I get you?" he asked politely.

Phil ordered a small beer and, I ordered an orange juice because I couldn't be bothered with anything stronger. Seconds later, a smirking Ricky handed Phil his beer and served me a large glass of orange juice, which, upon tasting, was at least 50% vodka. We went to sit in one of the booths away from the bar area, and Phil wanted to get something off his chest.

"You know, Frank, at the start of this training course, we had doubts about you, especially after your disastrous presentation on the coach. You didn't seem to take it seriously. But since then, we've been impressed by the way you knuckled down and distanced yourself from those who were just here for the ride."

I knew he was referring to Terry, so this was my chance to defend him.

"Well, to be fair, Phil, from the little I knew of Terry, I found him to be honest and maybe a bit misunderstood. I think he was unlucky not to have made it."

It was pretty feeble, but it made me feel a little better.

"Ah Frank, I admire you for seeing the good in everyone.

It's part of what makes you ideal for this kind of role. Trust me, the job can soon wear you out if you haven't got that."

Feeling like a fraud despite the praise, my blood suddenly ran cold. Coming in through the door, and heading straight for us, were the dynamic duo, Sheila and Jackie! A bit worse for wear, dressed in high heels, scanty skirts, and bikini tops, they were turning heads and stomachs in equal measure. Phil was still talking as they approached, but all I could hear was the sound of impending doom.

"Well, what have we here? The wee sicky boy, Spenny. Have ye recovered from ye first pint, wee laddie? How about making up fer the other night and giving us that good time to ye promised," screeched Sheila.

It was clear that this wasn't the first bar they'd been to, as they staggered and held onto each other for balance.

"Anyway, where's yer mate, Big Bertie? At least he tried to get it up. Better than sleeping in a fuckin' shop doorway! Anyway, who's this wee fossil yer with t'night Spence?" pointing at a bemused and unamused Phil.

As they fell about laughing, Phil looked at me coldly, and I knew I had to act fast.

"I'm sorry, ladies, but I think you've mistaken me for someone else. My name is Frank, and I'm just out for a quiet drink with a friend."

I was speaking in the broadest northern accent I could muster, hopefully, to put some doubt in their minds.

"Fuck off, ye English bastad. Yew and yer mate were happy enough to buy us drinks on Monday night on a promise to shag us, but ye couldn't take yer drink, could ye, Spencer, wee laddie? Ye got pished out of yer wee heed. What happened to all the 'I'm a holiday rep and can get free drinks anywhere' shite you were telling us? Where's the free drinks now?"

I was bloody mortified. With Phil now scowling, and me being on the brink of losing my dream job, I had to throw the dice again.

"Look, I've told you both. My name is Frank, not Spencer. I've no idea what you are talking about. Come to the bar with me and I'll prove it."

Before Phil and the two girls could move, I dashed to the bar and called over to Ricky. Out of sight of the others, I flashed a 5,000 peseta note at him.

I theatrically shouted across, "Excuse me, barman, can you please answer a question from these girls?"

"Yeah, sure," Ricky responded impassively.

"Okay," I said to the girls, "ask him if I was here on Monday night."

"Hey sexy. Wasn't this skinny prick in here on Monday night with his scouse mate, giving it large and getting pished? You were serving us shots all night, remember?" asked Sheila.

I desperately hoped that Phil hadn't heard the words "scouse mate," and that Ricky would save my bacon. He looked me up and down slowly, before eventually turning back to the girls.

"I've never seen this guy before in my life, never mind on Monday. Believe me, I'd remember if two stunning girls like you were with an ugly mug like him. I do remember you both from the other night, but you weren't with this guy."

With that, he turned away and went back to serving other customers.

Thanking my lucky stars, I turned back to the girls.

"Now, if you don't mind, can you please leave us alone?" I said with renewed vigour.

Sheila turned to Jackie. "Och, it's probably not him after all, Jackie. These two look like a pair of puffs anyway, and wee Spencer was a cockney…and much better looking than this twat."

With that, they staggered off to harass a group of German guys further down the bar. I knew I wasn't out of the woods yet, and could hardly bring myself to look at Phil, but he was the first to speak.

"What the hell was that all about? Looks like you've got a doppelgänger walking around the resort giving you a bad name, Frank."

I threw my head back and laughed much too loudly, then swigged back the rest of my vodka.

"I'm going back to the hotel, Phil, before things become any more bizarre. I've had enough excitement for one night, and don't want to be late in the morning."

"Good thinking, Frank. See, you're leading by example, yet again."

I couldn't get out of there fast enough, and started on my way back to the hotel. As I did, rather than feeling pleased, elated, or even relieved, I don't think I'd ever felt worse about myself. The reason I'd knuckled down, and got my act together, had nothing to do with being professional or leading by example; it was because I was scared. Scared of losing the job, scared of friends back home finger-pointing and saying that they knew I'd fail, and scared of being found out as a waster, and a charlatan. I was giving the impression of doing the right things, and sometimes actually doing the right things, but for all the wrong reasons. It was as though I wanted to just play at being professional and responsible when it suited me, or when I was forced into it. I was tired of playing games with myself, and had no real idea who I was trying to impress. I'd only been successful to this point because people either mistakenly believed in me, sacrificed themselves for me, or had their own ulterior motives. Yet, whether it was Phil, Terry, or Ricky, one thing was for sure, left to my own devices, I would have been out on my ear long ago. I had been lucky, but it couldn't last, and I knew it.

There are a few times in life where you can point and say, "That's the moment the penny dropped," and that walk back to the hotel was one of them. Enough with the facade and trying to be the smartest idiot in town. From now on, I was going to do things properly, and have a real go at doing whatever was required to be the best I could be at the job. Forget just wanting to be a holiday rep for the image. I wanted to be proud of myself for the right reasons. I can't say that it was an overnight change, but from then on, there was a change in my attitude, nonetheless. I realised that the ones who I made fun of, those I called "try-hards," were the ones who were given the best positions and the most responsibility. They had the trust and the respect of the management, whereas I had scraped through by pure chance and serendipity. From here on in, I was going to be one of the try-hards, and if anyone wanted to make fun of me, let them. At the end of the Costa Brava training course, we were informed which resort we had been allocated for the summer, and I was over the moon to be told that I had been given the Costa Brava, and, more specifically, the resort of Lloret de Mar. In that sense, it was mission accomplished - tarnished, and with some harsh lessons learnt, but mission accomplished, nevertheless.

Once back in the UK, I had a two-week turnaround before reporting back to Leeds to board the Costa Brava bound coach once more. The main differences were that this time, I wasn't dressed like a Spanish waiter, and I was no longer pretending to be something that I wasn't.

By now, Lloret de Mar had a completely different look. The weather had warmed up, and there was a buzz around the town. Shops and cafes were now fully open, and there was a palpable excitement as the resort geared up for the coming summer season. I was thrilled to be allocated the largest hotel in the resort, the Hotel Don Juan. It was a huge building of over 2,000 bedrooms set in a central location, and well-known in the UK holidays market. The hotel was separated into different blocks - red, blue, green, etc. to make sense of its sprawling layout. As it was so busy, there were two of us working at the hotel for Tan Holidays; myself, and a more experienced rep from Essex called Helen. Helen was there to show me the ropes and explain everything I needed to know, and this time I listened intently. With half-board prices starting at £79 by coach, we had hundreds of weekly arrivals, and group bookings of twenty or more weren't uncommon. With no airs and graces, it suited me down to the ground. I also had a couple of other, smaller hotels to look after, but my performance at the Don Juan would ultimately make or break me.

As most of the reps from the other companies were more experienced than me, I copied a lot of their ways of doing things, and none more so than Robert from Thomson Holidays. Robert must have been around thirty years old, which seemed ancient to me, but he was super organised, and exuded calmness and professionalism. Although he was unfailingly polite towards me, he kept his distance and went about his business with minimal fuss. In the past, Robert would have been someone for me to make fun of, but the new me viewed him as someone to learn from and look up to. Once the season started, the flights arrived, the coaches rolled into town, and I learned my trade. I got better at identifying problems before they arose, became a dab hand at defusing difficult situations, and quickly learned that it paid dividends to stay on the good side of all hotel staff, especially the hotel receptionists, as they often had the ultimate power of allocating the rooms. My organisational skills also improved, and despite the high number of arrivals, I was proving popular with guests of all ages. The scores on my customer questionnaires were amongst the best in the region.

As we built up to high season my life was a maelstrom of airport transfers, guest welcome meetings, hotel visits, health and safety checks, excursion guiding, and problem-solving. Add in finding rooms for overbooked customers, and there was hardly a moment to spare. We officially had one day off per week, but that was often compromised by an unforeseen incident, such as a customer being arrested or taken ill, but I was loving every minute of it. It's hard to describe how happy and proud of myself I was back then; proud of my job, proud of the uniform, and even proud of the cramped apartment I shared with three other reps. I was working as a summer holiday representative for an actual holiday company, so I had already exceeded my wildest dreams. Each time I arrived at the Don Juan to stand behind the rep's desk, I must have radiated genuine happiness. I'd check that my information books were all neat and tidy, the company notice board was up-to-date, and I'd shout out "Hola" to anyone within earshot. Looking back, I think most people thought I was a bit simple and felt sorry for me. I was thin as a rake, red-raw from walking around in the blistering heat with no sun protection, and consequently had a face that was a mix of peeling skin and congealed freckles. I could easily have been mistaken for the victim of a cruel medical experiment.

On one particular evening, I popped into the hotel to double-check that everything was ready in advance of my next batch of arrivals so that the check-in would go smoothly. It only took a few minutes, and I was on my way out again when I looked across to the Thomson Holidays desk and instantly fell in love. Sitting there was the most gorgeous holiday representative you could ever imagine. To say she was a better-looking version of the blonde singer from ABBA would be to underplay it; she was an absolute stunner. She looked a few years older than me, with a dazzling smile and amazing ocean-blue eyes, and it was clear that I wasn't the only one who was drawn to her. She had a queue of holidaymakers snaking out in front of her desk booking excursions like there was no tomorrow. It was like watching the Pied Piper in action as the mostly male queue had quickly formed, and she was taking money for excursion bookings like it was going out of fashion. Back in the UK, I would have blushed, lowered my head, and scurried out without making eye contact. But, bolstered by self-confidence and an incredible lack of self-awareness, I waited around until she was free to talk. Twenty minutes later, I had my chance.

"Hi there. I'm Frank, the TAN Holidays rep. I've not seen you here before. Doesn't Robert normally cover the Don Juan?"

"He does, but I'm helping him out during high season. By the way, I'm Anna."

Her voice sounded southern and quite posh, and I decided, there and then, that I wanted to marry her.

"Oh, I wondered why you were here. It's two hours later than the usual visiting times. You'll need to change your noticeboard so you don't confuse people."

Why the hell was I talking about bloody noticeboards?

She smiled sympathetically and started to pack her things away. I became desperate.

"It looks like you've taken a lot of cash there, Anna. Do you want me to walk you back to your hotel or your car?"

"That's very sweet of you, Frank, but I have my moped

outside, and I need to make a couple of other hotel visits before I finish."

"Ah, me too," I lied. "Which hotel are you finishing at?"

"The Hotel Miramar, at around nine," she beamed.

"Unbelievable. I'm due there in an hour to drop off some rooming lists. I'll see you there. We can pop out for a quick drink after that, before you go home?"

"Sounds like you've got a deal!"

She laughed and smiled so enthusiastically that I couldn't believe my luck. Of course, I had no reason to be anywhere near the Hotel Miramar, but I wasn't going to miss the chance to get to know Anna a little better.

I raced back to my apartment. Showered, shaved, and smelling almost 100% of Paco Rabanne aftershave, I rocked up at the Miramar with ten minutes to spare. I asked the receptionist if Anna was there, and was delighted to hear that I'd arrived first. All I had to do now was to pretend to be doing something official, shuffle a few papers and wait...and wait...and wait...and...wait.

It was almost 11 p.m. by the time I realised she wasn't coming. I didn't think for a moment that she might have fabricated the Hotel Miramar visit to fob me off. I preferred to think that she'd been kidnapped, or maybe had a minor accident on her moped. I would casually remind her of our missed rendezvous the next time we met and ask her out again. I wasn't going to give up on the lovely Anna that easily.

Over the next few days, I pined for Anna to return to the Don Juan, but every time I looked across at the Thomson desk, it was good old dependable Robert on duty. Then, later in the week, I could see that Robert was getting a hard time from some of his guests, and voices were being raised to the point where even the normally unflappable Robert seemed ruffled. It got weirder when I saw him handing over wads of cash to each of his guests. Once the hullabaloo had died down and he was alone, I went across to him.

"Is everything okay, Robert?" I asked.

"Not really. It's been a hell of a week," he responded, looking exhausted.

"How come? Overbookings?"

"No. We've been infiltrated by a phantom rep."

"What?"

"You won't believe it, Frank, but some girl has been travelling up and down the coast wearing a Thomson uniform, pretending to be a rep. And, she's been selling excursions to my guests."

"What?" I was stunned.

"Exactly, Frank. God only knows where she got the uniform from. She even has a book of genuine Thomson excursion tickets. It's been mayhem. Our guests have been turned away from excursions and venues everywhere. The cheeky bugger's even been offering discounts. No wonder she sold so many. We reckon in the space of just over a week, she's walked away with around three grand, and we're still counting!"

"Have they caught her?" I asked.

"No. All we know is what our guests are telling us. Apparently, she's a real looker, and has a few aliases… Julie…Jane…"

"Anna?" I added helpfully.

"Yes. How did you know?"

"I met her…here in the hotel. She was definitely a looker, and very plausible. I even arranged to meet her for a drink, but she stood me up." We stood in silence and shook our heads before I continued. "You know what, Robert? This sounds bad, but if ever a girl has balls, it's her. It's genius -

simple, but bloody genius. It's all cash in hand, and she knows she's got at least a week before anyone will ask any questions. There are so many excursions, and mistakes with bookings, as it is. She's probably got a uniform for every holiday company out here."

"To be fair, I'd probably feel the same if she hadn't caused me so much hassle, Frank. Apparently, she's so believable that we reckon she might have been a rep for real at some point, and figured out that it's easier and much more profitable to just pretend to be one whenever she feels like it."

I longed to cross paths with "Anna" again at some stage during the season, but although I kept an eye out wherever I went, she was far too clever to stay around the scene of her crimes for too long.

The rest of that first summer season flashed by in a blur of late nights at the airport, happy and unhappy holidaymakers, hotel visits, and excursion guiding. Being permanently tired became the norm, as I packed in as much sun, sea, and partying to make that season a standout memory some thirty years later. Alas, like everything else in life, my first summer season as a holiday rep had to come to an end, and, as I'd spent so much of the summer hopping on and off coaches, it seemed fitting that this would be the mode of transport to take us back to Leeds, as the close of the season was upon us.

It was a weary and largely hungover group of reps who were collected that morning from the Lloret de Mar office. The previous evening had been a heavy night in a summer of heavy nights, and I nodded in and out of consciousness as the coach made its way up the coast to pick up more staff for the long journey back to Leeds.

A couple of hours later, we arrived at the final pick-up point, the coastal resort of Roses, in the far north of the Costa Brava. As the final few staff members climbed on board, a group of us discussed which resorts we wanted to be allocated for the upcoming winter season. Although I would have preferred a "Winter Sun" destination, I still had some unfinished business with skiing, so I was about to say that I was hoping to get back out to an Austrian ski resort, but, before I had a chance to speak, I was suddenly dumbstruck.

"C'mon Frank, it can't be that difficult! Where do you fancy this winter?"

"What are you looking at, man? Haven't you seen boats in a harbour before?"

"Bloody Hell, Frank, have you had a bloody stroke? Just answer the question, man."

But I couldn't answer the question. I couldn't even think of what the question was, because as I looked over my friend, Alan's shoulder, and out across the harbour, there on the jetty in front of the plethora of sightseeing tourist boats, was a girl selling cruise tickets to a queue of smiling late-season holidaymakers. Nothing unusual about that. Nothing unusual in the fact that it was a pretty girl dressed in the uniform of the local tourist association. More unusual was the fact that the girl had the most amazing figure and ocean-blue eyes, and despite now being brunette, it was the same girl I had met three months earlier back in the Don Juan Hotel. The same girl that I had fallen in love with. The same girl who stood me up. The same girl who was making a fortune selling imaginary excursions and boat trips. And the same girl who almost certainly wasn't called Anna. I smiled to myself and slowly nodded off to sleep without sharing her story with the others. As I drifted away, I invented a whole persona and lifestyle for Anna. In my mind, she was now one half of a super-attractive Bonnie and Clyde style couple who travelled the world operating their scams, gambling their spoils and mixing with the social elite. As my sleep became deeper, their exploits became so sophisticated and lucrative, that they'd reached Bond-villain status.

To this day, I still occasionally wonder what new scam she's involved in, and whether the digital age has made her life easier or harder. More than likely, she'd have embraced the anonymity that technology affords and be all over social media, fleecing anyone gullible enough to be lured into her web. If she is, then let's hope that *@basingstoke.paul* never comes across her - he'd be bloody livid!

Chapter 4
Art of the Interview

The set-piece drama of the job interview has always fascinated me. During my career, I've only had a handful of formal job interviews as a prospective employee, but I've interviewed many eager job applicants over the years, and witnessed brilliance and incompetence in equal measure. One of the best-intentioned, but worst, pieces of advice given to a potential interviewee is to "just be yourself." If I was just going to be myself at the TAN Holidays interview in the early 1980s, I might as well have stayed at home. It's hard to think of a worse piece of advice. If you care anything about the cat-and-mouse, and high drama of the occasion, why on earth would you spoil it by simply being yourself? As an interviewer, I've learned that simplicity is key, and I follow four basic rules:

1. Create a relaxed and friendly environment.
2. Be enthusiastic, yet honest, about the role and organisation.
3. Listen carefully, and ask relevant, precise questions.

4. Ensure each interviewee walks away knowing they have been treated fairly and respectfully.

Unfortunately, some interviewers use the interview as a power trip, which makes the fourth rule virtually impossible to achieve, and others prefer a "one size fits all" approach, religiously asking the same set of questions irrespective of the role or what the interviewee tells them, which negates the third rule.

I remember sitting in on one interview where the interviewer, Stewart, asked, "Can you describe yourself in three words?"

The interviewee replied, "Lazy," and then stayed silent.

Although risky, I thought it was a response that showed a sense of fun and was worthy of further discussion. However, Stewart ploughed on, keen to get through his pre-prepared questions.

"Don't worry if you can only think of one; it's a pressure situation. Now, where do you see yourself in five years' time?" he continued, head down, reading from his list.

I sat there thinking that the answer to that question was, *if the standard of this interview is anything to go by, then anywhere except for here!*

No matter how well prepared you are, and how many times you have been through the process, there is always room for a surprise, and the following incidents will live long in my memory.

In 2015, I was leading the travel department of a major media organisation and we posted a job vacancy for the newly created position, Head of Digital Performance. It attracted lots of interest, so much so, that after the initial CV screening, we had around a dozen first-round interviews lined up. And because it was a Bank Holiday week, we had most of the interviews backed up over a two-day period. I'd asked Dan Broadbent to join me in the interviews. Dan was our Finance Business Partner, in his mid-fifties, and he'd been in the business forever. He had a good grasp of what was needed in the role, and I trusted his judgement. He was also good company, but in an understated and unique "Dan" way. He had a knack of getting inadvertently caught in embarrassing situations and then he'd recount each hapless tale in such a factual, unemotional manner that he would have you in stitches. Consequently, his nickname within the business was "Deadpan Dan."

He'd just had his latest skirmish. It was the start of the week, and Dan was on his usual Monday commute on the packed train from Woking to London. During the journey, he needed to go to the toilet, so pressed the "open" button on the automatic toilet door, only for it to open and expose a lady sitting on the loo. Taken by surprise, she screamed and Dan panicked. The train suddenly juddered, and he fell into the cubicle in front of her. The door started to close with them both inside, so he stuck out his foot behind him to stop it fully closing. Amid the woman's shouts of, *"get out, you pervert!"* some other passengers pressed the "open" button again and pulled at his leg from the outside. As the door opened, out hopped a devastated Dan, apologising to all and sundry as the teary woman told him in no uncertain terms that he should be ashamed of himself. Fast-forward to the office, and a flushed-looking Dan related the story in the most deadpan way imaginable, reciting the facts as though he were reading a kidnapper's ransom note. If it was me, I'd have embellished it to high heaven, but he saved what little emotion he felt for the end.

"To be honest, Frank, I'd love to get my hands on

whoever designed that locking mechanism," he said, before trotting off to the office restroom.

Anyway, the interviews on the first day were coming thick and fast, and by late afternoon, we had reached interview number six. As we waited for the interviewee to arrive, I turned to Dan.

"I'm glad you're taking so many notes, Dan. I'll need help remembering all the details,"

"No worries, Frank, I'm old school; the devil is in the detail" he replied.

"The next one in is Robert Jones. Works at Expedia. The CV looks promising," I observed.

"I was thinking the same, Frank. He's also got some media experience as he worked briefly at News Incorporated," Dan agreed.

"Fingers crossed!" we said in unison.

Five minutes later, Robert joined us, smartly dressed in a sharp navy-blue suit and white open-necked shirt, a confident handshake, and a disarming smile. We introduced ourselves and Dan scribbled away as I began the session.

"Thanks for coming in today, Robert," I opened.

"No problem, Frank, feel free to call me Rob," came the reply.

"Okay Rob, we've read through your CV and would like you to talk us through your biggest achievements in your most recent roles."

"Okay, in my current role, it's pretty easy to pinpoint my greatest achievement, as last year my team achieved a year-on-year increase in online booking conversion of +22%."

"That's impressive, Rob. Can you talk us through the steps you took to achieve that, and in particular, your own input into the success story?" I challenged.

Rob came straight back with, "Well, by using Google

Analytics, I'd noticed that the keywords being clicked on most were…Excuse me Dan, what's that you've written on the top of your notepad?"

As he spoke, Rob had shifted his focus to my right, and glared at Dan's notepad, in particular the word he'd written in brackets, and in capital letters next to Robert's name, "Robert Jones (BLACK)." Rob now raised his eyes to stare directly at Dan.

"Can you please explain what you mean by that word?"

Dan looked bemused, but replied calmly, "It's just my notes on the interview. I hope you don't mind me taking notes while you're talking."

"It's not the notes I'm talking about, Dan. It's the word next to my name. Why have you written the word 'Black'?"

Dan's look quickly changed from bemused, to extremely flustered.

"It's nothing…It's just that we've had a lot of interviews today and it helps me remember."

"WHAT! You've written it so that you can remember that I'm black? I'm the black one of today, am I?"

Now clearly shaken, Dan dug himself deeper.

"No, it's not like that. I've done it with all the interviews. Here, look."

With that, Dan shuffled his papers and showed Rob his notes from a previous interviewee, where he'd written the words "Red-Hair" next to the name, Lucy Grant.

"I can't believe that you even think that writing 'BLACK' is the same!" shouted Rob, becoming more upset.

Almost shaking with anger, Rob stood up and announced that he couldn't continue the interview and would be taking this further. I walked Rob back to the office reception to hand his pass back and tried to smooth it over enroute.

"I'm sure he didn't mean anything by it, Rob. He's really not that kind of bloke."

Rob remained silent, although he did shake my hand before disappearing down the escalators and out through the external doors. I scooted back to the interview room as quickly as I could, and when I got there, Dan made an unconvincing stab at levity.

"Did you tell him he's got the job?" he said.

"I'm not sure that this is something to laugh about, Dan. You'll need to let HR know what happened straight away."

"C'mon Frank, you know it was totally innocent. I don't see what the issue is. Everyone knows I'm not like that. I'm sure he'll soon realise that he's got hold of the wrong end of the stick."

Within two days, Dan was suspended pending a full investigation and an internal message was circulated to say that he was taking some time out for personal reasons. Four weeks later, a goodwill gesture of £20,000 was accepted by Rob, and Dan came back into the business following his month-long suspension.

Except that he didn't.

On his first day back, he was called into the office to be told that his contract was to be terminated with immediate effect on the grounds of gross misconduct. Of course, the way Rob reacted was understandable and warranted, and diversity, equity, and inclusion training quickly became an integral part of the business.

Following an unsuccessful appeal, 55-year-old Dan was unemployed. His fifteen years of service counted for nothing, his reputation was in tatters, and with no severance package, only a murky undercurrent of whispers and gossip remained. So it was with some trepidation that I met him for lunch a few weeks later. I won't ever forget it, and the life lesson it taught me.

It was a drizzly, dreary day as we took our seats at the restaurant, and I was prepared for an equally bleak hour of listening, being sympathetic, and discussing how unfair life was. However, nothing could have prepared me for this version of Dan. He looked relaxed and happy, and he bore no malice whatsoever.

"No excuses Frank, it was a stupid thing to do and I feel so sorry for the stress I must have put Rob through. The fact that I didn't mean any harm is irrelevant. In life, it's not what people say or do that has the most effect on you; it's the way they make you feel, and it was wrong for me to make Rob feel that way. I regret it deeply and have reached out to him. I'm meeting him for breakfast next week as I want to apologise in person."

I asked him how he felt he was treated by the company, especially after so many years of loyal service.

"Look Frank, I always play above the line, so I have no excuses. I was out of order and deserved to pay a price. That price wasn't mine to decide so I can't control it, but I can control my reaction to it, and I refuse to be bitter and hold any grudges. Blame lies below the line, and it's a nasty, dangerous place to be. It's even worse than Liverpool. No, seriously Frank, blame and regret suck your lifeblood. It's not for me."

I was flabbergasted and uplifted. We spent almost two hours in the restaurant, and his positivity was infectious. When it was time to go, he turned to me and smiled.

"Don't worry about me, Frank. When you're a hammer, you view everything as a nail, and I'd been a hammer for far too long."

There had been no hint of face-saving. Every word he'd said was heartfelt and genuine. I felt in awe of his strength, self-awareness, and lack of bitterness. I felt humbled, and it made me question myself, and my own values, knowing deep down that if the positions were reversed, I would have been a seething mass of self-pity, blaming the company and the system in equal measure. I kept in touch with Dan, and a year later, he started his own business, ironically, an executive recruitment company employing a small team of five people.

I'd love to say that this is the most dramatic incident I've witnessed in an interview situation, but it pales into insignificance compared to the late 1980s and 1990s when some interview techniques could best be described as no holds barred.

Following my first years working for TAN Holidays, a much bigger organisation bought the company, the International Leisure Group (ILG), and I slowly rose through the ranks. Then, in late 1990, I was asked to join the ILG recruitment team, to recruit and train overseas staff for the all-new Summer 1991 TAN Holidays programme. The recruitment started in November, and there was plenty of excitement as we formed a new "Specialist Products" division, which combined TAN Holidays with our "18-30 Crew" programme. The brochures had been printed, and we were ready to roll. The new division was considered to have a bright future, as the "18-30 Crew" brand was already a big success. We broke new ground by taking recruitment on the road, and the "ILG Recruitment Roadshow" toured the UK's major cities to find the best talent.

The roadshow was way ahead of its time and was uncannily similar to today's X Factor format. Around twenty of us would travel across the country on board a double-decker coach, and as we'd advertised in the local press for overseas holiday representatives, there were hundreds of candidates waiting for us in each city, with queues of hopefuls snaking around the recruitment venues. We'd tell them little in advance, only that they had to be aged between nineteen and thirty years old, have a reasonable height-to-weight ratio (really), be prepared to answer whatever questions we'd ask, and that we didn't have to give a reason if they were rejected. Brutal.

For the first round of interviews, we'd sit on panels of five and invite candidates through, six at a time, and fire questions at them for ten minutes, at which point, a big hooter would sound and we'd mark on the list whether they had made it through to round two. We'd then invite the successful candidates back individually, and ask more questions, this time based on their CVs. Finally, we'd ask them to perform for us - sing a song, sell us an item of our choice, or tell some jokes, to show that they had the confidence to interact with an audience.

One of the "18-30 Crew" interviewers on my panel was a Scottish guy called Jamie. I disliked and was intimidated by him in equal measure. He was one of those chubby yet solidly built types, with slicked-back hair, in his late twenties, and sporting the type of red-purple tan that was more sun-bed than sun-kissed. He was full of his own importance, permanently pleased with himself, and was on the back of a season in Ibiza. Where, according to him, he'd *shagged for Scotland*, and made a *fucking fortune* in sales commission. Brash and bullying, he loved to see the candidates squirm, and I felt ill at ease whenever I was near him. At our final roadshow in Edinburgh, maybe because he was on home soil, Jamie had his arsehole setting turned to maximum during the first group interview sessions.

"Would ye have sex with a punta if it meant they'd buy more excursions?" he asked one girl.

She was no more than twenty years old, dressed in an

immaculate black trouser suit, hair tied back, and clearly nervous. She sat stunned and struggled for a response.

"C'mon, answer the question, wee lassie," Jamie barked.

Blushing and close to tears, she blurted out, "I'm not sure. Is that what I'd have to do?"

Jamie stared straight at her, his beady bullet-blue eyes showing no emotion.

Slowing his speech right down, he uttered, "Well, if it's something you'd consider, then you'll not be coming back for the second round, wee lassie, because I don't employ slags."

Tears flowing, the girl got to her feet and walked out of the room. I'd heard enough.

"Why did you speak to her like that? How would you like it if someone spoke to a member of your family that way?" I said, seething.

"If she can't take a bit of banta without crying, she wouldn't last five minutes out in resort. You stick to your poncey TAN questions and mind your own fucking business, you lanky wet fucking lettuce."

Unbelievably, a couple of the others laughed at his insult and I'm ashamed to say that I sat there and took it without firing back.

The second stage of the interviews began later that day, and the CVs were duly shared with the panel. Jamie threw his copies of the CVs back into the pile with a dismissive, "I dnae need a CV to tell me whether someone can do the job. It takes more than a fucking CV to impress me."

As soon as I saw the first candidate walk through the door, I sensed trouble for the poor lad. Slim, medium height and build, with John Lennon glasses and Marti Pellow ponytail, he'd been put through from the first round by Richard Brown, a member of the head office HR team for whom Jamie had no respect as he'd never experienced the "firing line" of working overseas. There were four of us on the panel: Me, Jamie, Richard Brown and Pauline Woods, who, as Director of Operations was the most senior person on the panel. The afternoon session began, and the unsuspecting victim introduced himself as Christos, a 24-year-old from Kirkcaldy in Fife, a town situated around thirty minutes north of Edinburgh.

Jamie opened with the standard, "Why do you want to work overseas?"

"Ye have clearly never visited Kirkcaldy!" replied Christos confidently.

Except for Jamie, we all laughed.

And, so it continued, with Christos demonstrating a flair for self-depreciation that belied a steely determination and ambition to be successful in life. We learned that his Scottish father met his Greek mother on holiday on the Greek island of Skiathos in the 1960s, and a whirlwind romance followed. Christos spoke Greek and had worked at his parents' Greek restaurant, so had plenty of experience dealing with the public. Everything was going well as this bright and confident candidate engaged us with his relaxed style, and made us chuckle with his easy wit. He had "overseas holiday rep" running through him like a stick of rock. Unfortunately, our resident silverback felt his role as the dominant male was under attack by the slender, yet charismatic Christos. Jamie went onto the front foot and upped the ante.

"What would you do if I gave you a pair of scissors and told you to cut off your ponytail?"

Christos calmly responded, "I'd probably say no to that, as Richard told me earlier that as long as my hair is clean and tied back, then it doesn't break company rules."

"I don't care about company rules. If you are working for

me in Spain, then the girly ponytail comes off," hollered Jamie.

"In that case, if I'm successful, I'll have to hope that I get posted somewhere else," came Christos's measured response.

The tension was now increasing.

"Are ye trying to be a smart arse, laddie?" Jamie responded with menace.

"No. I'm just trying to do my best to get an overseas job with your company, and then hopefully work every minute of every day to make you and the company proud."

It was textbook stuff from Christos, and Jamie was seething that he hadn't been able to rattle him.

We then moved on to the final part of the process - the candidate's chance to perform - and it was my turn to introduce it.

"OK Christos, if you were to be successful today, a large part of the job would be welcoming, selling to, or entertaining your holidaymakers. With that in mind, we'd like you to stand up and…"

"Stop right there!" barked Jamie. "Instead of asking ye to sing a song or anything naff like that, we're going to do a role-play, laddie. You're going to play the part of a coach transfer rep, and I'm a punta who you have just dropped off at the hotel, and I'm not happy with my room. OK?"

Jamie got off his chair and marched menacingly towards Christos. He stopped directly in front of him, forcing him to take a half-step back. Christos looked up into Jamie's eyes, a few inches above his own. I was now becoming scared on Christos's behalf, but felt helpless as I exchanged anxious sideways glances with Richard and Pauline.

"Are you taking the piss with that room, pal?" Jamie began, bizarrely affecting an English Lancashire accent for the role-play.

"I'm sorry. What seems to be the problem, sir?" Christos responded.

"You're the fucking problem, pal, putting me in a shit-hole of a hotel room," shouted Jamie.

"I'm sorry you feel like that, sir. I have three more coach drop-offs to complete and then I'll come back, look at the room with you, and if it is sub-standard, I'll see if the hotel can move you to a different room."

"Are you calling me a liar? I'm telling you the room is shite and I want to move NOW." bellowed Jamie.

At this stage, Jamie's nose was almost touching Christos's forehead, and the tension in the room was such that I could hardly breathe.

"Please sir, let me buy you a coffee and I'll be back as soon as I've dropped the remaining passengers at their hotels. It will only take twenty minutes at most," Christos continued calmly.

"Are you deaf, wee laddie? (back to Scottish). You move me to another room now or I'll deck ye, ye…ye LONG HAIRED POOFTA!"

There was a stunned silence in the room and Christos was now visibly shaken. Licking his dry lips in vain, he bowed his head wearily and muttered to himself, "Och mon, I cannae be doing with this," and turned to walk away.

As he did so, Jamie sensed victory.

Smugly, he shouted after him, "You'll never have the backbone to be a holiday rep, wee laddie…"

However, he didn't get to finish the sentence, because as Christos turned, in a single movement, he crouched low, and putting all his weight onto his left foot, he raised his right leg high and swivelled backwards in an effortless arc, crashing the heel of his right foot hard against Jamie's right cheekbone. For a split second, Jamie stayed upright, red-faced and eyes bulging, before falling heavily backwards and crashing through the tables, sending the CVs high into the air, leaving them scattered across his prone body. He'd been knocked clean out. Silently, and without a backward glance, Christos exited the room.

We crouched over Jamie as he came around.

With his glazed eyes flickering, he muttered, "What the fuck was his problem?"

As he was helped to his feet, I glanced at my copy of Christos's CV and smiled to myself as I read the sentence I'd highlighted under the "Hobbies and Interests" section, the one I'd not had a chance to question him on, the one that said - *Personal Achievements: Captain of the East Coast kick-boxing team.*

It seems strange now, but no action was taken against Christos over the incident. I sometimes wonder if he ever realised his ambition to work in the holiday industry, or whether Jamie ever started to read CVs and subsequently discover some humility. Unfortunately, I very much doubt the latter.

A few weeks later, and with recruitment complete, everything was set for an exciting summer season ahead, but unfortunately, as far as ILG was concerned, there wouldn't be any more summer seasons. In March 1991, it was announced that the International Leisure Group was officially bankrupt, and as such, closed for business. This was like a bolt from the blue, and I had no idea what to do next. All I knew was that my fledgling career in the travel industry had come to an abrupt halt.

However, the demise of ILG was to strengthen the hand of their competitors, and none more so than the fast-growing Lancashire giant, Flytours Holidays, and, with the summer season almost upon us, they were advertising for overseas-based staff. So, off I went for an interview with their head of recruitment, Joan Tyler.

Joan was refreshingly down to earth, and her easy, motherly, Lancastrian manner made me warm to her immediately. Asking me lots of questions about working for ILG in Spain, she asked me to say a few words in Spanish, and I told her in Spanish that I'd left home that morning at 8 a.m., travelled for an hour to reach the interview, and met a lovely lady called Joan Tyler who offered me a job on the spot.

Joan answered in Spanish, "Eres muy descarado, Frank!" (You are very cheeky!).

I complimented her on her excellent Spanish accent, and I sensed that I'd impressed enough to earn a job offer of some kind. Joan shared that Flytours was expanding quickly and needed experienced staff, so my hopes were high. Sure enough, within a week, I received a call from her.

"Hi Frank, Joan Tyler here, from Flytours Holidays. I'm delighted to say that following your successful interview, we are pleased to offer you a position as an overseas area manager for this summer season."

I was thrilled to be offered an area manager's position straight away, and conscious of the fact that the summer season had already started, I was equally eager to know which part of Spain I would be working in.

"That's great news, Joan. Thank you so much. Where will I be based?"

"We'd like you to fly out to Crete next week," came the response.

"Crete...in Greece?" I replied, somewhat taken aback.

"Yes, it's one of our biggest overseas operations. The season has already started and unfortunately the existing area manager has had an accident and cannot continue in the role. I'm sure that you will love the challenge, Frank."

Having a challenge was pretty low on my priority list at this point, and the fact that my CV said that I was someone who loved a challenge was nothing more than a lazy copy from virtually every other CV I'd seen - not something to be taken seriously.

"That's great news, Joan. I thought I might be in the running for a job in Spain, based on my experience and language ability, but of course, you are right, I love a challenge, and Crete sounds perfect," I lied.

"I knew it, Frank. You're a great fit for the role. If you can come into the office for a briefing early next week, we'll get you on a flight out to Greece the following Saturday."

Chapter 5

The Cradle

The island of Crete was a journey into the unknown for me, as was Greece in general. It had never been on my radar, yet it was about to become home. It was a hot and sunny Saturday afternoon in May 1991 when my flight touched down at Heraklion International Airport. I was met by the head representative, Nora Patarakidis, who was to take me to meet our handling agents, Adamis Tours. The role of a resort handling agent, or "ground handler," is a much-underrated piece of the holiday jigsaw. Their purpose is to ensure that the local operation runs as smoothly as possible, everything from arranging the coach transfers and excursion programmes, to making sure the hotels are paid. From an area manager's point of view, if you have a well-respected and efficient ground handler, it makes your life so much easier, and Adamis Tours was known to be one of the best. During the journey from the airport to Heraklion, Nora proudly told me she'd been living on Crete for over fifteen years. Originally from Edinburgh, she'd fallen in love whilst on holiday, both with a Greek boy and the island of Crete itself. She'd learnt the language, got married, and had a baby, all within three years of setting foot on the island. She was also a PR machine.

"It's the largest and most southerly of all the Greek islands, Frank. It witnessed the birth of the Minoan civilisation over 2,000 years ago, then came the Roman and Byzantine eras, followed by the Venetian and Ottoman occupations, before being liberated in 1898. It has some of the most valuable historical structures in the world, and is home to the world-famous Samariá Gorge, part of our own national park."

She spoke so passionately that it was hard not to be impressed. She continued to tell me about how the Cretans offered the fiercest resistance during World War Two, and then finished with a flourish.

"…and from a tourism point of view, we have some of the most beautiful beaches, and most historically important architectural sites in the world. We are truly the cradle of civilisation!"

Nora's passion and animated storytelling made the thirty-minute journey fly by, and she had me sold on the island long before we arrived at the office, where I was warmly welcomed by the agency owners, brothers Odysseus and Dimitris Adamis. Beneath halos of cigarette smoke, they brought me up to date with the local operation. It was in that first meeting that I learned the fate of my predecessor, who had left the island three weeks earlier. Until now, I'd been told precious little about the man I'd replaced, a chap called Steve Archer, who by all accounts, had been a popular and effective leader. He'd also done a good job of setting up the office and training the staff in advance of the summer season. The season had started well with many positive customer feedback scores from holidaymakers.

So why did he leave?

Steve lived in a staff apartment in Agios Nikolaos, the main resort on the east of the island, and he had a number of passions - his burgeoning career, partying, and flirting with women, being the main ones. However, on one crazy night, the last two of those passions snuffed out the first. Steve was one of the "work hard, play hard" types who put the hours in at the office, and combined it with an equal amount of time in the bars and nightclubs. And, as a tall, dark, Greek-speaking, ex-public schoolboy, he had a lot of admirers.

It was three weeks into the summer season, and after a long day in the office, Steve went out for a few drinks to the bars around the port with Giorgos, one of his hotelier friends. The night flew by, and in the early hours of the morning, they found themselves in a nightclub where they were chatting with two English girls, Jill and Katy, who were on a girls' holiday. As is the way with these things, Giorgos put on the Greek charm and left with Katy to go back to her hotel, while Steve stayed, chatting away with Jill. He was enjoying the chat as much as the chase, as not only was Jill a super-attractive lady in her early thirties, but she was also a smart and ambitious corporate lawyer, a subject he'd studied at university. Relishing the conversation, but feeling a little worse for wear, Steve arranged to take Jill out for dinner the following evening and volunteered to walk her back to her hotel. Walking side by side along the narrow streets leading to the port, Steve was firing questions at Jill as they got to know each other better.

"What three skills would you say you have that make you stand out against other lawyers?" he ventured.

"Hmm, well, from a business perspective, I'd say I have the best attention to detail, and I also have an incredibly analytical mind," she responded confidently.

"And the third?" Steve pressed.

Without pause, Jill continued, "Well, it's not really business-related, but I reckon I give the best blow jobs in England, and probably in Greece, too."

They both burst out laughing before Steve continued with a flirty, "Here's a little-known fact for you, Jill. Did you know that statistically 100% of women who don't give me a blow job go on to pay for their own drinks?"

"Well, I certainly don't want that to happen to me, Stevie-Boy, so I reckon I'd better get to work," she snorted.

Steve laughed nervously, unsure of how serious she was, but before he could say anything, Jill had dropped to her knees on the narrow pavement, loosened his belt, and opened his zip. Seconds later he leaned against a shop doorway, closed his eyes, tossed his head back, and was thinking to himself, both how lucky he was and how right she was.

"OH MY GOD!" shrieked a voice, suddenly interrupting his moment.

In his hazy condition, Steve was vaguely aware of some movement nearby, but the fact that Jill hadn't missed a beat, coupled with his heightened state of ecstasy, meant that he didn't take too much notice.

"OH, MY GOODNESS! Cover your eyes, children!"

Startled into action, Steve turned to his left to see a group of holidaymakers approaching, complete with sunhats and beach towels. At the front, leading the group, was Karen, a horrified Flytours Holidays rep; one of Steve's own team. Gobsmacked, he glanced at his watch.

"Fuck, it's quarter to eight in the fucking morning!" he whispered to himself.

He'd lost all track of time and suddenly realised that he was on the main pathway to the port where Karen was taking her guests to catch the boat for their half-day excursion to Spinalonga Island, an ancient, disbanded leprosy colony.

Wild-eyed, Steve frantically pulled at Jill's head, but she was having none of it. Like a dog with its jaws clenched around a meaty bone, there was no way she was stopping. Her fingers were clenched lock-tight to his buttocks, and she was determined to finish what she'd started. Then, with perfect timing, Jill altered the angle of her mouth and, with a final lunge of the neck, proved her earlier boast. Steve threw his head back in an *I don't give a fuck* moment of pure ecstasy, and with his head arched backwards, eyes flickering like the spinning reels on a one-armed bandit, he reached his climax.

"OH FUCK - YES!" he bellowed, just at the point Karen was leading her guests past him, with the parents' hands shielding their children's eyes.

"Morning Steve," she hissed.

"Uggghhh…morning…Karen."

They were the last ever words Karen heard Steve utter, as later that day he handed in his notice due to "personal reasons," and took a flight back to the UK two days later. As the brothers finished telling me this crazy story, it did cross my mind that now I'd arrived on the island, the least I could do was find Jill!

The Flytours office, where I would work, was directly across the street from the Adamis office, and was much less plush. Situated on the fourth floor of a converted apartment block, it comprised a tiny open-plan space with three desks and fax, copy and telex machines. In the hallway was an old and creaky toilet and another small and stuffy office, which was to be mine. The three desks in the main area were occupied by our admin staff: Linda, Melanie and Kevin. Linda was the senior person, married to Giorgos, a local coach driver. Melanie was the more junior office assistant from Newcastle and was straight out of university. And Kevin was the "admin/airport representative" meaning that on the days when we had flight arrivals, he would go to the airport and manage the operation, ensuring that our arrivals were transferred to their hotels without delay. The role sounds easy enough, but it's one of the most difficult and crucial jobs in a resort. When you have multiple flights arriving on the same day, a fixed number of coaches to fill, and flights delayed, making sure people are transferred to their accommodation in the quickest time possible is a real skill. Linda was a ghostly-pale, dark-haired Glaswegian; round-shouldered, thin as a rake, and at around six-feet tall, had the limp appearance of a discarded Halloween decoration. Melanie was equally pale, fair, and much shorter. Kevin, on the other hand, was a chubby, ruddy-faced chap of around thirty-five years of age, and with his garish red-framed glasses, had the look of a jaded children's TV presenter. However, it wasn't his appearance that would set Kevin apart, it was the fact that he was incapable of answering a simple question with a straight answer. The type who, instead of telling you the time, tells you how the watch works. Our first meeting was a fine example.

"Hi Kevin. I'm Frank, the new area manager. Where do you come from back home?" I asked.

"I came over from Gran Canaria where I was working last winter," he replied.

"No. I mean, where do you come from back in the UK? Is that a Geordie accent you have there?" I said, thinking he'd misheard me.

"I went to university in Durham. That's probably why you think that," he responded without elaborating further.

"So, you aren't from that neck of the woods, then?" I continued, no longer in the least bit interested.

"I studied languages for three years," he replied, wide-eyed and unblinking.

Being our first meeting, I wasn't sure if I'd made a mistake and not asked what I thought I had. Or maybe he was hard of hearing.

At that point, Linda kindly explained, "He's from Stoke. You'll get used to him. He's a bit of a twat."

Kevin also had another strange habit in that he always introduced himself using his full name, Kevin Hand, rather than plain old Kevin. And he'd usually follow it up with a lame, "So, whether it's my hand or my face, you're still talking to the Hand!"

That aside, I couldn't help wondering how he organised everything at the airport, dealing with customers, reps, and coach drivers alike. Surely, he must annoy and confuse the hell out of everyone. In time, I would discover the answer to this in spectacular fashion.

Despite being a huge island, it didn't take me long to get used to the operation, and to keep things ticking along. Steve had set it up well. One of my first jobs was to assess each of the welcome meetings, where the reps would inform our new arrivals about the local area, attractions, and excursions. Coincidentally, my first port of call was to see Karen in action. Hopefully, she had fully recovered after witnessing Steve's "indiscretion."

She held the meeting on the huge terrace of the Elounda Krini Hotel, and had around forty guests in attendance, all eager to hear about the delights of Crete, on this sunny Sunday morning. I could see that the guests liked her. She was informative, relatable, and she sold excursions like hotcakes. She was the best excursion seller on the island, and you could see why.

It's incredible how an accent is interpreted. Karen had a strong Lancashire accent, and with phrases like, *I won't harp on and mither you no more coz it's crackin' flags out there,* I got the feeling that the crowd could have listened to her all day. After I had congratulated her on a job well done, and got in the car to make my way back to the office, I glanced in my rear-view mirror to see Karen riding away on her company moped. I noticed she wasn't wearing her crash helmet, so I made a mental note to speak to her when she called the office later that evening. When she made the call, the exchange was brief.

"I just wanted to say well done again, Karen, for an excellent welcome meeting, and by the way, I noticed you were riding your moped without wearing a helmet. Please make sure that you wear it from now on."

"It's okay, Frank. It's not the law to wear it in Greece," she replied cheerily.

"Maybe, but you know that if you ride a company moped, it's compulsory that you wear a helmet, Karen. Please do it; it's for your own safety."

"Okay Frank. Will do."

A week later, it was the day that the representatives came into the office to hand in the money they'd taken for excursion sales, known as "liquidation day." Who should be the first to arrive? None other than Karen, pulling up to the office after her 30km ride to Heraklion...again without her helmet on. I met her at the door, and as nobody else was within earshot, gave her a sterner talk this time.

"Karen, I reminded you last week to wear your helmet when riding your moped, and you've driven all the way from Malia without wearing it."

"Aw, I'm sorry Frank. I've just had me 'air done and didn't want t' spoil it."

"Come on, Karen, this is about safety, not vanity. You might not care, but I do, and I'm not prepared to have it on my conscience, so this is your final warning," I snapped, probably too harshly.

"Aw, I'm really sorry for upsetting yer. It won't happen again, Frank. Promise."

"Okay, let's leave it at that, Karen. By the way, we should be talking about your great sales performance again this week, not a helmet."

I was now six weeks into the role and things were going pretty well. With high season round the corner, Crete was top of the mini-league versus the other Greek islands, and in terms of customer feedback and excursion sales, we were well ahead of plan. So, I was in high spirits as I shared an evening of fine food, wine, and Greek dancing with the Adamis brothers, their wives, and some of the senior agency staff in one of Heraklion's finest restaurants.

At around midnight, on my drive back to my apartment in Kokkini Hani, a small village twenty minutes to the east of Heraklion, I slowed down as the cars coming in the opposite direction had come to a standstill because of an accident between a car and a motorcycle. My heart missed a beat as I immediately thought of Karen, but as I got closer, I relaxed as I could see that the bike was much bigger and that the motorcycle rider and car driver were both okay and talking to each other at the front of the stationary cars. Speeding up once again, I saw a red moped overtaking the queue and speeding towards me. A Greek-looking chap in his mid-twenties was driving, with a blonde girl of a similar age riding pillion. Nothing odd about that, other than the fact that the girl riding the pillion was Karen, the bike was Karen's company moped, and neither of them were wearing helmets. They didn't see me as they sped past, but I knew that I now had a serious problem on my hands, and once back in my apartment, I spent the night in fitful sleep as I toiled with what to do for the best.

The next morning, following a couple of calls to the office back in the UK, I was ready. At 11 a.m., Karen pulled up on her bike, a red helmet securely fastened to her head, and the picture of relaxed happiness. As soon as she came in, I called her through to my office.

"Hi Frank. What a luvvly day today. Aren't we so lucky to be livin' here?" she beamed.

"Look Karen, there's something we need to talk about," I responded.

"Aww, what's the matter, Frank?"

I took a deep breath.

"I was driving back late last night from Heraklion and saw you riding the other way with your boyfriend."

"Aww, that's nice. You should have waved to us," she said, unconcerned.

"No. The reason I'm telling you is that you didn't have your helmet on again."

Karen looked at me with a quizzical expression.

"But I wasn't driving last night. Manolis was."

"C'mon Karen. It doesn't matter who was driving. In any case, neither of you had a helmet on. This isn't a game, Karen. You've already had two warnings."

"Okay, Frank. I'll make sure I remember from now on. Is there anything else?" she said with a disarming smile.

"I'm sorry, Karen, but you've already had a final warning, and it's too serious a subject to treat as a joke. The head office has been informed, and you are booked on a flight back to the UK on Tuesday."

Karen just stared, open-mouthed.

"But that's in four days' time! You can't be serious, I luv it 'ere. I'm going to get engaged to Manolis. I'm the best seller on the island. You can't do this. Who do you think you are? You have no right."

"I have every right, Karen. Staff safety is my responsibility. Look, I don't want to do this, but you've given me no option. I'm sorry for you, and you'll be missed, but the decision has been made."

"Please Frank, just give me one more chance. I won't do it again. I promise!"

Her tears were now flowing and I could feel myself cracking. I wanted to give her another chance with every fibre of my being, but knew that it would undermine my authority, and ultimately be the wrong decision.

I shook my head and said, "Sorry Karen, you've had your chances. I can't trust you, and I won't take the risk."

I felt terrible and could hardly hold eye contact with her.

Rightly or wrongly, this was an episode, and a decision that I've always looked back on with some regret. *Could I have been more compassionate and less of a heartless bastard? Was I trying too hard to be tough, as I was new to the role?* It certainly didn't help me in the popularity stakes. Within a day, the whole community of reps knew what had happened, and several of Karen's friends held it against me, frosty and uncooperative for the rest of the season. Additionally, we started to get overbookings at Manolis's family hotel, so it seemed that grudges were being held by them, too. Ultimately, I reconciled my decision through the lens of Karen's parents. Had I given Karen another chance, and she'd ignored me to the point of having a serious accident, how would they have felt about my leniency? If nothing else, though, it proved the strength of Karen's relationship with Manolis. In 2015, they celebrated twenty years of marriage, have three children, and run a thriving car rental business on Crete. If you're reading this now, Karen,

I'm not surprised that business is booming; you always were a great salesperson.

I was grateful that the Flytours HR team, back in the UK, had been fully supportive of my decision. They even sent her replacement, Julie, out on the same day Karen returned home.

Julie had impressed everyone with her enthusiasm at the interview stage and had been put on the standby list for her first job overseas. We'd lost our best performing and most popular member of the team, and now we had a new member of staff to train up before the height of the summer season. There was no time to lose. I asked that Julie be brought straight to the office upon her arrival for an initial briefing. As she entered the room, I was struck by her confident poise, although I feared for her in the Greek heat as she was freckle-faced with light ginger hair. I also noticed that she was dragging her right leg behind her and asked if she had hurt her foot.

"No, it's a degenerative disease which affects my lower leg and foot. Unfortunately, it won't get any better," she replied.

This presented a new challenge as the hotels were spread across the island in such a way that it meant reps often needed a moped to cover the distances. This was impossible for Julie. We moved staff around so that we could place her in the smaller resort of Sissi, and agreed that she could travel to her hotels by taxi if she needed to, rather than walk. I called head office that night to ask if they knew about Julie's leg condition. They did and had assumed we'd be able to work around it. In any case, Julie was our only option at such short notice. However, within weeks, we began to receive complaints from our customers, berating us for the cruelty of making Julie walk to each hotel in the increasing heat. By now, her foot was red and swollen, and dragged hideously behind her. Soon enough, the customer feedback scores from Sissi reached an all-time low, with threats of legal action over the way we were treating Julie, yet, no matter how much we insisted, she refused point blank to take taxis as she didn't want to be treated differently to the other reps.

With the heat and stress of August just around the corner, we asked Julie to take an admin job in the office and to swap with Melanie, but again, she refused. The only role she would consider would be as airport controller, effectively swapping with Kevin Hand. Julie was unimpressed with Kevin's organisational skills and felt that with some basic training, she could do a much better job as she was well-organised and had plenty of admin experience. It seemed a sound enough decision as Kevin wasn't the most organised and had a habit of causing confusion and chaos when the pressure was on. Kevin begrudgingly accepted the compromise and agreed to give it a go. For the next two weeks, Julie would shadow Kevin at the airport and we'd make the swap permanent after that. Unbeknown to me, this seemingly simple decision proved to be the catalyst for one of the greatest cock-ups of my career.

Competition amongst UK tour operators was at its height in the 1990s, and being the largest and most southerly of the Greek islands, Crete was often in the middle of the price war. The secret weapon for Flytours at this time was the "Sundeal Holiday." The "Sundeals" would be advertised at incredibly cheap prices, especially for last-minute bookings, and were typically found on posters in travel agency windows, screaming something like:

SUNDEAL - 7 NIGHTS B+B - 3* HOLIDAY IN CRETE - £69!!!

The price was unbeatable, and people would book in their droves. The catch was that the accommodation was to be allocated upon arrival at the destination, so the customers didn't find out which resort or hotel they'd be staying in until they arrived on the island. This concept allowed us to fill empty hotel rooms that we'd already pre-paid for at the start of the season. Paying for the rooms in advance meant that we could negotiate rock-bottom rates as the hotel received the money whether we filled them or not. It was a huge success.

However, it was the "Sundeal" concept that almost sealed my fate.

The airport scene was set - it was now deep into July, the flights had been delayed all day, and tempers were frayed. Kevin was being his usual awkward self and confusing the hell out of customers, coach drivers, and staff alike. For good measure, Julie was also doing her best to undermine and criticise Kevin at every turn.

Welcome to airport transfers day.

The arrival of a group of Geordie lads from the late evening Newcastle flight was a great example of Kevin Hand in his prime. One of the new arrivals began the discourse as he approached the clipboard-holding Kevin.

"Hi there. We've just landed on the Newcastle flight," he said.

"Excellent. Welcome to Crete on behalf of Flytours Holidays. What is the lead name of your group, please?" replied Kevin, without looking up from his clipboard.

"Well, I'm Steve, but me mate, Lee, booked it, so it's probably under the name of Hunt, but we make it double-barrelled and call him Lee Waddock-Hunt."

Cue lots of laughter from the group.

"And can you tell me the number of travellers in your

group, and the name of the resort you have booked?" a deadpan, Kevin continued, still not making eye contact.

"There's eight of us, all going to Malia. Is it any good, like?"

Ignoring the question, Kevin ploughed on, "Sorry, but we don't have anybody by the name of Waddock-Hunt. Are you sure you've booked with Flytours Holidays?"

"Apologies. It was a joke, mate. 'Waddock-Hunt.' Get it? The surname is Hunt; forget the 'Waddock' bit," a bemused Steve responded.

"Sorry. We have no Waddock-Hunt on the list," Kevin insisted.

"No. Like I said, it's just Hunt, times eight, man!"

"In that case, please make your way into the coach park and look for the blue bus with a Flytours sign in the front window," Kevin droned.

"There are hundreds of blue buses out there, man, and lots of them have Flytours signs in the window. Does ours have a number or anything?"

Kevin was now in his element.

"Just ask the driver when you reach the coach park," he continued, ignoring the queue forming behind the Geordie lads.

"Which driver?"

"The driver of the coach."

"But we don't know which coach, man!" exclaimed another exasperated member of the party.

Kevin now had them just where he wanted them, and was nearing peak fuckwit mode.

"Just look for a Flytours sign in the window, sir."

"BUT THEY'VE ALL GOT…"

Just before it got out of hand, a new voice intervened.

"Hi there, lads. Maybe I can help? The Malia coach is

coach number four, third from the left, as you go through that door. Have a great time in Crete. You'll love Malia; it's party-central," rescued Julie, before turning to Kevin with a stage-whispered, "You are such a twat. What the fuck is wrong with you?"

Eventually, it was time for the final flight of the night from Glasgow, and three Flytours coaches were left in the car park. It was 1.30 a.m. and the end was in sight. Two queues formed in front of Julie and Kevin as they checked off the final arrivals, Kevin having written the accommodation names on the flight list for Julie to check off. As it was the final flight, Julie would take one of the coaches to the east of the island, Kevin would go on the second coach destined for the south, and the third coach would go without a rep, but with an English-speaking driver, to the western resorts of Rethymnon and Chania. Kevin's coach, and the Rethymnon coach, were the first to fill and made their way out of the airport as Julie welcomed the final two arrivals, an elderly couple, holding hands, and smiling warmly at her.

"On behalf of Flytours Holidays, welcome to Crete. You are our final arrivals of the evening, so you must be Mr and Mrs McEwan," Julie beamed.

"Och, thank you. That's right. It's our first time in Greece. Our family has paid for the holiday to celebrate our sixtieth wedding anniversary," Mr McEwan beamed back.

"Oh, what a lovely family you have. I'm sure you'll have a great time, and, as you are a Sundeal booking, we've placed you into the Pension Nostalgia, a lovely little bed and breakfast hotel in the charming resort of Amoudara on the east coast of the island. Unfortunately, we have a few stops to make enroute, so it might take a couple of hours or so to get there, but we'll go as quickly as we can."

"Nae bother. Better to be late in this world than early in the next," Mr McEwan replied.

"That's lovely. Please let me help you with your cases and I'll take you to your coach," Julie offered, before limping off with them into the coach park.

So, Kevin and Julie's first joint airport day came to an end, seemingly with no major issues. All was well, and it was a job well done. *Or was it?*

Kevin was looking after the Pension Nostalgia, but saw little of the Mr and Mrs McEwan during their week-long stay, as every time he visited, they were out exploring the local area. Dimitris, the hotel manager, said they were having a great time and not to worry. The week flew by, and on the day before their return flight, Kevin left the transfer details with the receptionist to let Mr and Mrs McEwan know what time the airport coach would collect them the following day. However, in the office later that afternoon, Linda received a call from an agitated and anxious Mr McEwan. Linda listened as he explained that their holiday had been booked for two weeks, not one week, and they shouldn't be going home yet as they still had a week of their holiday remaining. Linda said that she would check it out, and called the Flytours duty office, who in turn called the Glasgow travel agency where the booking had been made. Confirmation duly came that their booking was only for one week and not two. Despite more protests from Mr McEwan, he eventually conceded that they would be ready to depart at six-thirty the following morning.

The next morning, the Pension Nostalgia was the first pick-up stop and Julie was the transfer representative. Upon arrival, there was no sign of the McEwans, and the door to the hotel was locked. Julie rattled it and shouted, "Is anybody there?" as loudly as she could. Stepping back, she then heard a faint, "Hellooo," from the side of the building. As she walked around to see where the voice was coming from, she spied Mr McEwan leaning over a second-floor balcony, waving to her.

"We cannae get oot of the room, wee lassie. We're locked in!"

"Just come down the stairs to reception and open the door from the inside, Mr McEwan," Julie responded.

"Ye dnae understand. We can't get oot of our room. We're locked in!"

A bemused Julie then heard the main hotel door being opened, and she was greeted by a tired-looking receptionist who sheepishly apologised for oversleeping. The receptionist handed Julie a key and asked her to go up to the McEwan's room while he opened the other rooms downstairs. Nonplussed, Julie slowly climbed the stairs, as her foot had already started to swell. Once she reached the McEwan's room, she was stunned to see the room door locked by a padlock. The key in her hand was a padlock key! She quickly unlocked it and opened the door to a smiling Mr and Mrs McEwan, who apologised for keeping her waiting. As they descended the stairs, the McEwans explained that there hadn't been a lock on the door when they arrived, so the owner kindly bought them a brand-new padlock and made sure they were safely locked in the room every night. He then let them out again whenever they called down to reception.

"Dimitris himself came to let us out on Wednesday morning, and he's the owner," Mrs McEwan announced proudly.

Julie couldn't believe what she was hearing. Two customers had been effectively imprisoned for a week, breaking every possible health-and-safety regulation, and yet they seemed as pleased as punch. Julie kept hold of the padlock as proof for when this was inevitably taken further. Armed with the knowledge that this was no ordinary couple, when they again complained that they'd booked for fourteen nights and not seven, she reassured them.

"We've checked with your travel agent back in the UK, and they've confirmed that your booking was only for one week, Mr McEwan."

Around two hours later, upon arrival at Heraklion airport, Mr McEwan made one last attempt and tapped Julie on the shoulder again.

"We dnae want to cause a problem here, but we want to speak to your manager as we have definitely booked for two weeks, not one."

"I'm sorry, Mr McEwan, but I'm afraid that you will have to leave on the Glasgow flight today, in accordance with your reservation," Julie replied firmly.

Then, as if from nowhere, another voice sounded.

"Excuse me. Can I help?"

"Maybe. Are you in charge here?" asked Mr McEwan.

"Yes. My name is Kevin Hand and I am the airport controller for Flytours Holidays here in Crete."

"Thank goodness. Someone in authority, at last. Hopefully, you can help us. We're Mr and Mrs McEwan. We don't have our booking reference with us, but we have booked for two weeks and you're sending us home a week early!"

A half-hearted shuffle of papers later, Kevin announced, "I'm sorry, but according to my departure lists, you are definitely booked on today's Glasgow flight. Luckily for you, it has been delayed for two hours which will give you another two hours on our lovely island."

The elderly couple exchanged confused glances before Mrs McEwan shook her head and muttered, "Och, Bill, leave it. Let's just go home." And off they went towards the check-in desk.

Around the same time, the phone rang in the resort office and Linda answered. As she spoke, she hurriedly sifted through the departure lists on her desk and covered the phone with her hand as she shouted over to me.

"We have a problem, Frank!"

"Why? What's wrong?" I answered.

"This is the Hotel Filoxenia in Rethymnon. They have a couple waiting in reception for their flight pick-up and the coach left the resort without them."

"Oh shit! Never mind though, we can get them a taxi to the airport if the worst comes to the worst. Which flight is it?"

"It's the Glasgow flight," she confirmed.

"We should be okay, as it's delayed. How come we missed them?"

"This is where it gets worse, Frank. Their name is McEwan…and there's two of them!"

I instantly had that feeling you get when you know something is seriously wrong, but you're not sure why.

Linda continued "I've checked the flight lists and the room manifests. There's only one set of McEwans booked on the Glasgow flight today and it's the McEwans we've left behind in Rethymnon. The McEwans we've put on the plane *are* booked for another week, like they told us."

"That's impossible, Linda. We checked with the duty office and the travel agent, and they confirmed they had only booked for seven nights," I replied.

"I know, but I think I know what's happened. There were two separate Sundeal bookings with the lead name McEwan on the Glasgow flight last week, a young couple staying for one week, and the elderly couple staying for two weeks. It looks like Kevin didn't check the booking references properly at the airport, so he mistakenly sent the young McEwans who had booked for seven nights to the hotel in Rethymnon which was intended for the elderly couple who had booked for fourteen nights. He then sent the elderly McEwans to the Pension Nostalgia on the other side of the island, which was meant for the young couple who booked for seven nights. In short, we've cocked-up, Frank!"

Just to make a day of it, Melanie joined in the fun too.

"But I don't get it. Why did the travel agent confirm that the elderly McEwans had only booked for seven nights?"

Linda took it in her stride. "Because the booking reference we gave the duty office was from the rooming list, which didn't take into account that we'd swapped their hotels. So, we called the travel agent of the young McEwans, who, of course, confirmed it as a one-week booking. We called the wrong fucking travel agent!"

My mind was working overtime to take it all in, and I tried to take control.

"Okay Linda, call Julie at the airport, now, and see if the McEwans are on the plane yet. There's a delay, so we might be able to rescue the situation."

Julie confirmed that the flight had just boarded, but would be held on the ground for at least an hour because of the delay. She could request permission to go airside, onto the plane, to explain the situation and try to off-board the elderly McEwans. At best, this was a hugely embarrassing strategy, but in the absence of any other options, we agreed to let her go ahead.

Of course, we hadn't factored in the simmering tension between Julie and Kevin at the airport. He demanded that he take control as the airport staff knew him and would be more likely to give him access to board the flight, so Julie reminded him she had a much better relationship with the McEwans. In the end, they compromised, and the airport granted permission for them both to board the aircraft, on the proviso that Julie go in a wheelchair as her foot was heavily swollen by now, and she was struggling to walk. So, like two negotiators in a hostage situation, they set off across the baking tarmac towards the Boeing 737, their mission clear - to keep us all in a job.

Having been notified in advance, the cabin crew waited at the top of the aircraft steps as a puffing and panting Kevin heaved the wheelchair backwards up the front steps with Julie sitting red-faced, with the padlock glinting on her lap. Once safely onboard, Kevin took to the microphone, and with Julie manoeuvred into the aisle in front of him, facing 189 bewildered faces, he started his address in typical Kevin Hand fashion.

"Dear Flytours Holidays passengers, my name is Kevin Hand, and I am the airport controller here on the lovely island of Crete."

At this point, Julie, twisted in her chair, and attempted to grapple the mic from Kevin's hand, spitting, "No, you're not. I'm the airport controller now. Let me speak, Kev!"

For a surreal fifteen seconds, there was a flurry of hands and fingers as they wrestled for control of the microphone. A sweating Kevin emerged as the winner, amid anxious glances between the stunned cabin crew.

Bizarrely, he continued as though he was starring in an episode of The Bill.

"We have reason to believe that there are two passengers named McEwan on board who have booked a two-week holiday yet are trying to leave after a week. Can you please make yourselves known and we will escort you back to your accommodation, free of charge."

Amid the stunned audience, you could just about hear a faint sob to the rear of the plane, followed by a muffled, "Please just leave us alone," in a weary Scottish lilt.

Julie now took over. "Give that bloody mic here, Kev. I can see where they are. Wheel me forward."

With that, Kevin pushed Julie slowly and squeakily down the aisle while she spoke menacingly into the microphone.

"Dear Mr and Mrs McEwan. It was a simple misunderstanding. We've spoken to Dimitris, and he's happy to lock you back in your room."

She raised the padlock above her head and waved it around as the wheelchair squeaked its way towards their seats. Once they reached the McEwan's row, Julie made eye contact with them and continued the onslaught.

"Please come back to us, Mr and Mrs McEwan. The real McEwans need these seats!"

The adjacent passengers had heard enough and formed a protective circle around the elderly couple, and in a scene reminiscent of Braveheart, the verbal retorts from those nearby became louder.

"Stop using a wee lass in a wheelchair to protect you, ye fat bastard!" one yelled in Kevin's direction.

"Let them go home, ye heartless bitch," another aimed at Julie.

"Once they've got the McEwans, och, they'll come back for more," added another.

"This is how the Nazis started. Dnae let them take any of us!"

And on it went as they warmed to the theme.

The cabin crew had seen enough and stepped in to save Kevin from potential physical harm, and, with help from the ground staff, helped him reverse Julie back to the front of the aircraft. By now, Julie had taken full leave of her senses and was waving the padlock in the face of any encroachers like a crucifix to a vampire. If there was ever a plot, it had been utterly lost.

In one final Exorcist-like head-twist, as Julie's wheelchair bounced down the aircraft steps, she turned and bellowed, "YOU'RE THE WRONG BLOODY McEWANS!"

In a collective state of stunned silence, the faces of all on board were glued to the aircraft windows as they stared wide-eyed at Kevin and Julie being escorted back across the tarmac and into the terminal building. Once the terminal door was shut behind them, the aircraft erupted as the passengers burst into spontaneous applause in a show of support for the elderly Scottish couple. Sadly, the euphoria was punctured a few seconds later by the captain's announcement.

"Owing to our unfortunate and unforeseen onboard incident, I'm sorry to inform you that we have lost our revised departure slot and will have an additional delay of approximately one hour. On behalf of Flytours Holidays, I would like to apologise for any inconvenience caused."

Later that evening, we managed to get the "right" Mr and Mrs McEwan on a flight to Manchester and arranged a taxi to take them the rest of their journey back home to Lanarkshire. Considering the inconvenience, they took it well, although they made it known that we hadn't heard the last of it.

The following morning, a bedraggled quintet of myself, Kevin, Julie, Melanie and Linda, met in the office to survey the damage. As we reviewed the debacle, it didn't reflect well on any of us. An elderly couple had been forced to end their holiday a week early. A second couple had been stranded for almost a day without a flight home. We'd added a further delay to an already delayed flight. And besides the inevitable claims for compensation, we'd caused reputational damage to both Flytours Holidays and yours truly. Ahead of the meeting,

I'd decided to shoulder the blame, as I was ultimately in charge of the operation and I'd had enough of blaming others for my own shortcomings in the past. Despite that, the meeting still descended into some world-class finger-pointing.

Kevin kicked it off by blaming most of the problems on Julie (and some of them on Linda, too).

"If the office administration had been better, then none of this would have happened," he hissed.

"You mean that if you weren't such a stupid twat, then none of this would have happened," Linda immediately fired back.

Julie placed most of the blame on Kevin, but also partly on her medication, which made everyone back off. Then Kevin brought the meeting to a close with a flourish.

"But of course, none of this would have happened if I'd been left in sole charge of the airport operation. You have to question that decision. As they say in Greece, 'The fish rots from the head.'"

With that, four pairs of eyes turned and set themselves firmly in my direction. Ultimately, the customer care and smooth running of the operation were my responsibility, so I knew I had nowhere to hide. As I was new to the company, I also knew that I was in a vulnerable position, so it was with a heavy heart that I dialled into the weekly head office call later that day.

"Hi Frank. Anything major to report from last week?" asked Neil, my area manager.

"Not really… Oh yes, we had to put two people on a later flight back to the UK, as their own flight was full."

"Oh. How did that happen?" Neil questioned.

"Well, we put two other people on the flight in their place."

"Ah, I see. Was it a medical emergency?" he continued.

"Not as such. It was basically because they had the same surname, but it's a long story and you're not going to like it. I've almost finished the report and will have it with you by the end of the day, but before that, I want you to know that I take full responsibility for what happened."

Without going into all the details, Neil flew out to Crete to carry out an on-site investigation, where, thankfully, the Adamis brothers gave me a glowing reference and Neil showed fairness and understanding as he pored over the facts. Under normal circumstances, I doubt he would have gone to such lengths, but the Scottish press had gotten hold of the story, and the Daily Record headline of, *Holiday Hell for Scottish Pensioners,* only added fuel to the fire. The article explained how the couple had been imprisoned in their room for most of their holiday, had been forced to go home a week early, and then, once they'd boarded the return flight, two members of Flytours staff had tried to drag them off the plane whilst waving a padlock at them and calling them "the wrong McEwan's." The saddest part was that there was no sensationalism or fake news in the report; we really had made it hell for them. One particular part hurt the most. Towards the end of the article, it said,

Despite repeated pleas to speak to someone in authority, the couple were told that the area manager was "too busy" to speak to the elderly couple.

It went on to say that this "uncaring and faceless" attitude was symptomatic of the unprofessional shambles the couple had to endure. I was instantly christened Faceless Frank, in some quarters, for a time after that. Had I known that the McEwan's wanted to speak to me, I'm not sure whether I would have had the conversation with them; it seemed a pretty mundane issue at the time. However, it taught me another valuable lesson. Since then, I've never shied away from speaking to customers, or indeed anyone, who wants to air a grievance face to face.

So, my summer of 1991 in Crete, the cradle of civilisation, was almost my last for Flytours Holidays because of a cock-up that was to be written into all of the training courses as an example of how not to manage airport operations (you're welcome). It cost the company in terms of both negative PR and monetary compensation, and I was relieved to have been given the benefit of the doubt. The flip side was that "Faceless Frank" was synonymous with shambolic resort practice for some time after. Maybe that was fair. And maybe it wasn't.

In truth, I didn't really think that I should shoulder the whole blame. I didn't think that Linda, Melanie, or even Julie could be held accountable either. No. I knew that on this occasion, it was Kevin Hand who Rocked the Cradle.

Chapter 6

Skipper

I couldn't have wished for a better life than being in my twenties and working overseas as a holiday representative. Despite the low salary, my accommodation and travel expenses were taken care of and the rest was mostly a blur of partying, sunshine and happy faces. However, there were some drawbacks, and one of those was deciding what to do in between each holiday season. As there was a gap of around six weeks between a summer and winter season, you'd face the dilemma of what to do and where to stay for those weeks every year. Even if you took a two-week holiday, you still had to find somewhere to live for a month. Quite often I'd rely on the hospitality of family and friends. So, at the end of the 1988 summer season, I was delighted to receive a call from my cousin, Andrea, with the news that she was going away with her long-time boyfriend, Mark, for two weeks, and would I be interested in dog-sitting, Skipper, while they were away?

Andrea and Mark first met in Llandudno where Andrea was taking her first step on the nursing ladder, working as an assistant nurse at Llandudno General Hospital. Mark had travelled to Wales from Surrey as part of a lads' rugby weekend, and Andrea was enjoying a night out with the girls at a local disco bar in the town centre. Just as the girls were getting ready to leave the bar, in bounced the fifteen boisterous rugby players from down south, all wearing fancy dress costumes befitting the night's theme of "London underground train stations." The first guy through the door was also the largest, standing at around 6' 5" and weighing in at a hefty seventeen stone. He almost knocked Andrea over as he scrummaged his way into the bar. He apologised, and Andrea stared at this hulk of a man who held an inflatable plastic chicken in one hand and a six-pack of Australian lager in the other (Cockfosters). Despite his inebriated state, Andrea accepted his offer of a drink, and the rest, as they say, is history. They got on so well that they met again the following night, this time alone. From then on, Mark and Andrea became inseparable. They'd spend weekends together whenever they could, and when Mark got his big break in corporate banking in the City of London, they moved into a two-bedroom cottage midway along a Victorian terrace in central London.

They were the golden couple, him proving a success on and off the rugby pitch, and her, the sweet, pretty Welsh lass, happy to laugh at Mark's jokes, whilst matching him pint for pint. They soon bought a Boxer puppy from a local litter and became a family of three. The puppy they chose had two distinctive features: a symmetrical white mark around his neck, which gave the appearance of a permanent neck scarf; and three white paws against one brown paw, which gave the impression of three white ankle socks. The tiny puppy skipped in and out of their legs and was instantly christened Skipper. I'd stayed in the cottage a couple of times with Mark and Andrea, but this would be the first time I'd meet Skipper.

The added attraction this time was that I wouldn't be visiting alone. I'd started to date an Italian girl I'd met while working in Spain. Her name was Chiara Rossi. Chiara was originally from Rome, twenty-six years old, multilingual, and beautiful. Her parents moved to Spain when she was young, and besides being gorgeous, she spoke English with a beautiful sing-song Italian accent, resulting in it sounding like she added an extra "A" on many of her words – so I was always "Frank*a*." She was much more worldly than me, and mature enough to treat our long-distance relationship as a bit of fun, while I was head over heels in love. Despite her being very open about her position, I was constantly trying to impress her in the forlorn hope that she'd eventually fall in love with me, so I saw this as my big chance to win her over. When I invited her to explore London with me, she was over the moon and jumped at the chance. I felt truly blessed. After all, what could go wrong?

Mark and Andrea were flying out to Barbados on Saturday, so we'd planned to arrive on Friday afternoon to allow Skipper time to get used to us. I caught the train from Manchester to Euston, and then another to Victoria, to meet Chiara as she was arriving on the Gatwick Express. Her train arrived mid-afternoon, and it didn't take me long to spot her amongst the many commuters. Wearing shiny black boots, skin-tight black leather trousers, a red turtleneck sweater with an unbuttoned black fur coat showing her voluptuous figure, she was an absolute vision. Her long lustrous jet-black hair and Sophia Loren eyes were the topping on the cake. She was so far out of my league, it was ridiculous. Of course, I had also dressed for the occasion, and in my pointy black and white chequered shoes (I'd seen Elvis Costello wear a similar pair), skinny jeans (think punk, but ten years too late), yellow Fred Perry polo shirt, and a faded Levi jacket, all topped off with my receding hairline, I was also in a league of my own, but for all the wrong reasons. As soon as she saw me, the look in her eyes signalled her disappointment. The vision before her was no longer the suntanned holiday rep who had charmed and entertained her over the summer months. I think that I would have had zero success with the opposite sex if I hadn't worn a holiday rep's uniform every summer, and even more so a ski rep's uniform in the winter. It was no coincidence that I never got so much as a sideways glance from girls in the UK. I guess it's something else to add to my list of things to thank the travel industry for. Anyway, once she'd done her best to disguise her disappointment, I took the handle of her huge suitcase, relieved to find that it was one of those with wheels attached. To her credit, she gripped my other hand tightly and talked excitedly about the sights we planned to see in London over the next two weeks as we made the short walk to the house. Mark and Andrea greeted us at the door.

"Wow, you're punching well above your weight here, Frank!" beamed Mark, while Chiara gazed up into his eyes with a look I could only dream of.

Luckily, Andrea broke the spell.

"Oh my God, Chiara. You're even more beautiful than Frank told us."

What is it about people who meet each other and are immediately in synch with their hugging and kissing? Here was Chiara, meeting Mark and Andrea for the first time, and it was a joy to behold their multiple cheek-kissing. No hesitation or clashing of heads, just a smooth series of gliding movements that they seemed so comfortable with. I've worked in the travel industry for over thirty years, an industry where flamboyant kiss greetings are commonplace, yet I've never really mastered the art. Hugs and kisses over, it was time to be officially introduced to Skipper, and shown his sleeping quarters; an oversized dog basket in a partitioned area at the rear of the kitchen adjacent to the back door. This led out onto a small patio at the rear of the property, where he went for his early morning wee.

Andrea and Mark then began telling a disinterested-looking Skipper that "Mummy and Daddy" were going away for a few days, and that "Uncle Frank and Auntie Chiara" would look after him in the meantime, and of course, they'd be thinking of him every day and would bring him back a doggy present from their trip. Andrea handed me a detailed list of when and where to walk him, what to feed him, and some other bits and bobs that I absent-mindedly nodded along to.

"Look Skipper, Frank and Chiara have a list of everything they need to do to make sure you'll be okay. Come and put your paw out and shake their hands," fawned Andrea.

When Chiara moved forward with her right hand outstretched to hold Skipper's paw, she extended her left hand to stroke his head. A dog after my own heart, Skipper wildly misinterpreted this innocent gesture as the green flag to take the relationship to the next level. With his tail wagging ten to the dozen, he launched his front paws above Chiara's left hip and immediately started dry-humping her leg. Naturally, I stepped forward to protect her honour and push him away.

"C'mon there, Skipper. Leave Auntie Chiara alone. We promise we'll find you a nice girlfriend this week. C'mon, off you get, boy."

However, what I expected to be a gentle push turned into a real battle of wills as Skipper dug his rear legs in and refused to back up. As I put more weight into it, he started growling, his tail no longer wagging, and the hackles on his back rising. *Bloody Nora!* Skipper was much stronger than I had expected, and with his upper lip curled to bare his teeth, and his beady hazel eyes boring into mine, we spent the next thirty seconds in a highly unedifying push and shove routine. Then suddenly, out of nowhere, he gave up, causing me to lose my footing. Falling forward, I reached out to grab onto something, which, to put it as sensitively as possible, well… let's just say, it was erect and purple, and leave it at that. Skipper let out a short yelp, and I squealed like a young child as we fell together into his basket. It wasn't the most elegant way of protecting a girl's honour, and it was made worse by the embarrassed silence of the three stunned onlookers. I quickly returned to my feet and meekly suggested that now the introductions were out of the way, we should retire to the lounge. As we did, I could feel Skipper's stare deep into the back of my head, and I knew that there'd be no love lost between us from here on in.

Once in the lounge, Andrea broke the ice, "Sorry about that. He can get a little frisky. He'll be fine once he gets to know you."

Over a couple of gin and tonics, I rallied with a quickfire canine routine.

"I was surprised Skipper didn't like me; my last two dogs, Timex and Rolex, loved me."

"Timex and Rolex?" asked Mark.

"Yes. Well, they were watchdogs."

Cue the muted chuckles, and off we went for our night out.

On Mark's recommendation, we dined at Santini's, an Italian restaurant nearby. Despite the time of year, we sat outside in a pretty tree-lined patio area with huge gas patio heaters and blankets to keep us warm. Chiara sat close to me and didn't fawn over Mark too much, so all was well with the world. As they had to leave for the airport early the next morning, we didn't go crazy on the drinks, which made for a lovely relaxed start to our extended city break.

Later that night, as I snuggled up to Chiara in bed, she looked at me with her dreamy hazel eyes and I waited for an equally dreamy compliment to go with it. However, the compliment didn't come my way.

"Zat Skipper is a lovely aneemal, Franka. I canta wait to walka with heem," she whispered.

"Really? I thought he'd be a better-looking dog than that, but I guess it's each to their own," I responded, in the most childish way imaginable.

Thank goodness she wasn't English and the inference of what I was saying had been lost, because my insecurity had reached an all-time high. Being jealous of Mark was bad enough, but not the family pet. I immediately made a mental note to revise the list of what I needed to get tomorrow.

1. Dog biscuits.
2. Milk.
3. A bloody grip!

We were told to follow Andrea's instructions carefully, which included two dog walks a day in Hyde Park; one in the morning and one main walk later in the afternoon. The routine gave us plenty of time to explore London, especially in the evening, so it was set to be an idyllic week. We had to remember to crush two doggy tablets into whatever Skipper was eating, and that was about it.

My relationship with Skipper was set from the very first morning. When I went to make breakfast and open the back door, I was greeted with a growl and an icy stare. Conversely, as soon as Chiara came onto the scene, it was all tail-wagging and happy yelping (not unlike how I reacted to her).

Chiara took control and organised everything, including our list of things to do and see. She'd even researched the latest films she wanted us to watch at the local cinema. We duly went to see *Big*, which was a new release starring Tom Hanks, about a boy who becomes an adult overnight, and *The Big Blue*, a French film about two friends competing in the freediving championships in the Mediterranean. I wasn't particularly bothered about seeing either film, yet I loved them both. Maybe it was down to the natural high of being with such a beautiful girl or the thrill of the bright lights of London, but either way, I was having a ball.

I found parts of *The Big Blue* to be surprisingly moving. It's a film where nothing really happens, but I got drawn in, and before I knew it, I had a lump in my throat. It wasn't a good look for the hard-as-nails sex god I was pretending to be. Becoming emotional at the most insignificant point of a film or TV show is a burden I've had to live with all of my life. Like most people, I've shed the odd tear at films such as *Ghost* and *Titanic*, but sobbing at films such as *Father of the Bride* and random episodes of *Cheers* are particularly low points. And no matter how many versions of *King Kong* I've seen, as soon as those planes start shooting at him at the top of the Empire State Building, off we go again. *King Kong* also has a superb last line of dialogue when, in the final scene, Carl Denham, the PR impresario and chief protagonist, ends the film with, *"Oh no, it wasn't the airplanes…it was beauty killed the beast."*

Anyway, back to 1988 and my own beauty, Chiara, and our own beast, Skipper.

We were now approaching the end of the first week, and our roles were becoming more defined. I'd be the one to feed Skipper, whilst Chiara would be the one to fuss over him. It had all fallen into place nicely. The week had flown by, and I awoke early on Sunday without a care in the world, to make my way to the kitchen. With Skipper still asleep, I went about boiling the kettle and making egg on toast for Chiara's breakfast in bed. By tiptoeing around, I managed not to wake Skipper, and by the time I returned with the breakfast, Chiara was sitting up in bed.

"I'll just nip back, let Skipper out for a wee, and then come straight back," I said.

"Okaya, Franka. Thanka you, my darleeng. Don't be longa; I needa your toucha."

It was absolute heaven.

Back in the kitchen, I gave Skipper a gentle shake, but there was no response. I gave him a more vigorous shake. Still no response. I raised my voice, "C'mon Skip, rise and shine." Still no response. Another shake, and then a more frantic shake, but still no response. As a parent, when you lose sight of your young child in a busy shop, the panic is instant and overwhelming, and the wave of relief when you see them again is immeasurable. Well, on this occasion, there was no wave of relief. Skipper's lifeless body lay on its right side, so I placed my palms on his chest and belly, and felt for a heartbeat without really knowing where to feel. I crouched down, opened his jaws, and put my ear to his mouth. Nothing. I opened his left eye between my forefinger and thumb, and as soon as I let go, it closed again. I sat on the floor in a state of shock, which was quickly interrupted by Chiara.

"Franka, wattya doing on the florra?"

"I'm so sorry, Chiara, but I...I...I don't think Skipper is breathing. I'm not sure, but I think he might be de...dead."

"AAAGHHH! DEDDA? DEDDA? WATTA APPENNA, FRANKA? CHECKA FOR DE PULLSA!"

Having no idea how to check for a pulse on a dog, I went about putting my finger to his neck, behind his ear, his groin, everywhere I could think of. Nothing. I spent the next few minutes consoling a sobbing Chiara and then sat silently at the kitchen table. Here I was, 8 a.m. on a sunny autumnal morning in the heart of London, sitting at the kitchen table next to a heartbroken Italian girl, and staring in disbelief at the prone body of my cousin's dead dog.

Before reading the rest of this story, please try not to judge me on the decisions made and actions taken. It was the 1980s, there was no internet, and we had no mobile phones. Although, in hindsight, I am sure that we could have approached things differently. Anyway, here goes.

"What shoulda we do, Franka?" Chiara wailed.

"Honestly, Chiara, I have absolutely no idea," I responded frankly.

"But we canta leave heem lying there, Franka!" she added, ashen-faced.

Chiara went back to the bedroom, brought through a blanket, and covered Skipper's body.

Before the internet existed, most people had a trusted friend to turn to for advice in times like this - mine was Graham. Graham was around five years older than me, married, sensible, and knew a little bit about most things. I'd met him whilst working briefly at a rubber-manufacturing factory in Manchester where he'd taken me under his wing, and we'd been friends ever since. Luckily, being a Sunday morning, he was at home and answered the phone immediately. Once I'd told him the story, he was on it in a flash.

"You're kidding? A healthy dog just dropped dead?" he summarised.

"Yep."

"Had he eaten anything unusual beforehand?"

"No. Only what we gave him."

"Was there a sign of anything wrong with him yesterday?"

"No."

"Did he have a medical condition?"

"No, but he was taking some tablets each day."

"Tablets?"

"Yep."

"Have you got the packet?"

"Probably."

"Go and fetch it, and read the instructions."

Doing as I was told, I duly read them out.

"I can't understand most of it, but it says something about 'aortic stenosis' in big letters," I told him.

"That's it then."

"That's what?"

"He's had heart failure. It's fairly common in Boxers, but it's strange if he's been taking his tablets," he mused.

For the second time that morning, I felt a sharp pang of dread as I noticed yesterday's tablets still in their packet on the kitchen table. I'd planned to give him a double dose today. *Shit, it was all my fault. I'd killed Skipper!*

"Listen, Graham, I didn't give him his tablets yesterday. Could that have been the cause?"

"No chance, mate. After just one day and he drops dead? Not a chance."

"Thank goodness for that, but what should I do?"

"Call a bloody vet, you knob!"

"What, on a Sunday? Will there be one open?"

"Probably not. Is there a garden there?"

"Yes. There's a small patio and a garden area at the back."

"Perfect. Bury him there. It will save you a few bob," he concluded (you don't get that level of insight from Google).

"Are you kidding me, Graham? Can you imagine me

explaining that when my cousin gets home? *'Welcome home guys. How was the holiday?' 'It was great. We had a lovely time. Really relaxing. We loved it! Hey, where's Skipper?' 'Oh him, he's dead, but don't worry, you can find him under the patio. Anyway, we must dash, keep in touch, bye!'"*

Graham rose above the sarcasm. "Well, how are you going to find a vet on a Sunday? He'll be stiff as a board soon, and you won't be able to take him anywhere - rigor mortis, mate. Anyway, I'm late for the footie and I need to pick some of the lads up enroute; we're playing the Horse & Farrier in Rochdale. It'll be a mudbath and a bloodbath, so gotta go. Good luck, Frank. See you when you get back."

It was clear that we needed to get professional help, so out came the Yellow Pages to search for pet cemeteries. After half an hour with no luck, and with despair setting in, one of them finally answered. They told us they had space, would treat the dead body with respect, and outlined the costs for burial plots and cremations. We decided to pay for a burial plot and were delighted when they said we could bring him over that afternoon. Relieved, the only problem now was that they were located in East Grinstead, which was too far by taxi, so it meant going by train from Victoria.

"Franka?" asked Chiara.

"Yes, darling," I replied.

"How will we carry Skeepa?"

"Hmm, I'm sorry darling, but I think we'll have to use your suitcase. It's the only one big enough."

"No, Franka. We can't put Skeepa in my case; I could never use it againa!"

"Look darling, I'll buy you a new one. Yours has wheels, so it makes sense, otherwise it would be too heavy to carry," I reasoned.

With that, we solemnly wrapped Skipper in two blankets,

removed his collar, and lifted him into the suitcase as a sobbing Chiara said a prayer. As we walked to the station, I couldn't shake the feeling that we were doing something wrong, maybe even illegal, but I had no idea what it was or what else to do.

Once on the train, I relaxed, and Chiara calmed down a little. The benefit of it being Sunday was that there were fewer people on board to take much notice of us. We managed to find some table seats and placed the case across the two seats opposite us. Everything was going to plan until we reached Croydon, where the train started to get busier. However, all seemed fine until I saw a couple making their way along the carriage in our direction.

My ears pricked up as I heard the woman say, "Please don't make a scene, Brian."

This wasn't a good sign.

Nowadays, I'd applaud Brian for taking a stand against people who put their luggage on train seats, but at that moment, he was the enemy, and he was the first to engage.

"Hi there. Are these seats taken?" he asked cheerfully.

"No, they're not," I responded in kind.

"Is this your case?" he continued.

"Yes, it is, thanks."

"Do you want me to put it on the overhead rack for you?" he asked, still smiling.

"No thanks. We've tried that, but it's too big and heavy," I replied, equally friendly.

"Oh, I'm sure that it's no problem. Let me try it for you," he persevered.

"We have some fragile items in there, so we'd prefer it if you didn't," I said more sternly.

"Don't worry, I'll be careful," Brian continued.

I was now praying that the locks would hold as he moved

towards the case, but he'd barely touched it when all hell broke loose.

"What the Fuck? Something is moving in there!" Brian shouted.

"Calm down, mate. You must be mistaken," I shouted back.

"I tell you, something moved in there. What the hell is in there?"

Chiara and I now looked at each other in complete panic, while Brian's wife tugged at his sleeve.

"I asked you not to make a scene, Brian," she whispered loudly.

"I tell you, Doris, that bloody case moved of its own accord. Something is moving in there!"

By now, we'd caught the attention of nearby passengers, and I could also see the ticket inspector making his way down the carriage towards us. I was in meltdown but continued to bluff.

"Look, we are moving house and we have lots of breakables in there, so please just leave it where it is."

Before I could fully finish the sentence, the case suddenly lurched sideways on the seat. Chiara looked as though she was about to faint, and there was an audible gasp from the people around us as Brian leaned forward and began talking to the case.

"Hello? Hello? Are you okay in there? Don't worry, help is on the way."

The ticket inspector was now on the scene, and Brian was bursting to update him.

"Thank God you're here Inspector. We have reason to believe that there is something alive inside this man's case, and he refuses to tell us what it is."

Thankfully, the inspector remained calm and professional.

"I'm sorry, sir, but if the case belongs to this man, then it is his business, not yours."

But Brian now had his audience, and there was no way he was going away quietly.

"But…but…but it could be…a child!"

The atmosphere was now charged, and I heard a faint, "Open the case, you sick bastard," amid the background chatter.

Chiara had now had enough, and with tears starting to flow again, she wailed, "It's notta childa…it'sa Skeepa."

"A bloody kipper? I'm sorry, lady, but I wasn't born yesterday. Whatever is in that case is much bigger than a fish," Brian responded.

"Look, she didn't say kipper, she said Skipper. It's the dog's name. And it's not a child, it's a dog - a dead dog!" I admitted.

The ticket inspector had heard enough.

"Sir, you do realise that we don't charge extra for dogs? There is no reason for you to take this course of action."

"You don'ta understanda. It's our friendsa dogga, we just wanna bury it under the grounda in Grinstedda," shouted Chiara, not particularly helping matters.

I tried to defuse the situation.

"Look, everybody, calm down. It's my cousin's dog and we're taking it to be buried. There's no big deal here."

"Calm down? No big deal? Burying a dog alive is NO BIG DEAL? Why did you tell us that bullshit about moving house? You kind of people make me sick," shouted Brian, still playing to the crowd.

"I'm sorry about that, but I panicked. You don't understand, the dog is DEAD."

With dozens of eyes now on us, the inspector stepped in once more.

"Sir, I believe the best thing for all concerned would be for you to open the case and show us the contents."

I am so ashamed to admit this now, but my mind was so frazzled that as I reached across to open the case, I was praying that Skipper was actually dead. The tension was palpable as the clips sprang open and I lifted the lid. The answer to the question on everyone's lips was now revealed. There he was, his innocent little face stretching out from under the blankets. With eyes and mouth wide open, he let out the longest yawn I'd ever seen. Skipper was well and truly alive, and seemingly none the worse for wear. Lazarus! Except for a single sound, you could have heard a pin drop. That one sound was the thud of Chiara's head as it hit the table.

The ticket inspector now took control.

"I'm sorry sir, but unless you have a collar and lead for this dog, you can't bring it on the train and you'll need to alight at the next stop. I've also contacted the railway police who will meet us there, as there is a suspicion that you are mistreating an animal that might not belong to you."

In what seemed like no time at all, the train came to a stop, and, as if in a trance, the four of us - the ticket inspector, me, Chiara, and a wobbly Skipper, made our way from the train. The police were indeed waiting for us on the platform, and after the ticket inspector briefed them, we were taken to the local police station to be interrogated, while Skipper was fed, watered and treated like royalty.

After more than two hours of questioning, they finally accepted our story; partly because the cemetery corroborated what we said, and partly because Skipper wagged his tail and jumped onto Chiara's lap at every opportunity. So, after leaving my contact details, we were finally allowed to leave.

To be fair to the police, they kindly gave us a dog collar

and lead so that we could reboard a train back to London later that evening. Chiara slept most of the way home, exhausted by the events of the day, but from that moment on, it was never quite the same between us. It wasn't helped by the fact that Chiara wanted to tell Mark and Andrea the whole story, while I didn't want to go through it all again. We eventually compromised and agreed to give a half-truth, saying that Skipper had stopped breathing in his basket and we feared he might be dead, but that he had miraculously come to life again a few minutes later. It was just enough to alert them to the fact that he might have some kind of medical condition they might need to follow up on. We did still have some lovely moments, but the spark had gone, and it felt like we were going through the motions. A bizarre side-effect was that, as well as still adoring Chiara, Skipper was also now well-behaved and obedient around me. No more snarls and growls, he'd happily come to me to be stroked, and didn't seem to have any animosity towards me at all.

However, there was a new focus for Skipper's anger - the suitcase. In fact, we had to lock it in a cupboard for the remainder of the stay to stop it from being attacked. In the end, we bought a new one and ditched the original, but the new one didn't prove too popular with him either. To be honest, it was a bit of a relief when we reached the end of the fortnight and the sun-kissed couple burst through the door, brimming with excitement from their trip. They couldn't wait to give Skipper his presents: a huge squeaky rubber dog bone in the Bajan colours of blue and yellow, and a hand-woven blanket for his basket. I thought Mark might have sensed that something was amiss when he opened up a conversation later that evening.

"I have to say, Frank, I've noticed a definite change in mood since we left."

"Oh yeah? What's that then?" I replied.

"How the hell have you got Skipper to like you so much? We were worried that you wouldn't get along after we saw the way the introduction went. We kept imagining that you'd have trouble controlling him, but we needn't have worried at all. In fact, we're really impressed. To be able to turn Skipper around, the way you have, in such a short space of time, is impressive. You might just have a special gift with animals, Frank."

I smiled and changed the subject.

We had a lovely final night together, listening to all the holiday stories, and their excitement was infectious, but I could tell that Chiara was counting down the hours until she could return home. As we said our goodbyes the following morning, the inevitable happened; Skipper barked furiously at Chiara's case and launched himself onto it as she wheeled it down the hallway.

"Wow, that's so sweet. He doesn't want you to leave, Chiara. Look, he's pawing at your suitcase. He probably wants to get in it so you can take him with you!" Andrea exclaimed.

Mark and Andrea were in fits of laughter and seemed a little bemused when Chiara and I responded with thin-lipped smiles.

Predictably, I never saw Chiara again, but Skipper went on to live a full and healthy life. I last visited Mark and Andrea a couple of years ago at their home on the south coast. They now have two dachshunds for company, or as I call them, "hand luggage."

Chapter 7

Winter Wonderland

In the summer of 2018, I attended a significant birthday party for my old friend, Richard Turdlow, in the West Midlands. Richard and I met through our mutual love of skiing. Following my less-than-auspicious debut on the white stuff, I'd grown to love the sport, and over a period of ten years Richard and I worked together for various winter sports companies in ski resorts across the Alps. However, the reason we are still close after so long has less to do with skiing and more to do with the fact that even approaching sixty, Richard remains as daft as a brush, and it's impossible to dislike the guy.

We first met in the ski resort of Kitzbühel, in Austria, in the mid-to-late eighties. It was early December, and we were desperately waiting for some snow to fall, ahead of our first winter arrivals. To integrate us into the local community, the tourist board had organised a football match between the local ski workers and those working for overseas holiday companies. As we gathered in the changing rooms to sort out our playing positions, nobody wanted to be the goalkeeper. It was then that an older-looking, muscley, dark-haired lad with a broad West Midlands accent and a Desperate Dan face took control.

"Hey, you. You're a gangly fucker. Why don't you go in goal?"

Incredibly (and embarrassingly), he was looking at me.

"Thanks for that. By the way, I'm Frank. Pleased to meet you, too!" I responded.

He strode over and offered his hand.

"Rich Turdlow, but you can call me Turd."

"What? Are you serious? Turd?"

"Yeah, short for Turdlow. It's a nickname, mate. Are you a bit thick, or what? Because if you are a bit thick, you'll be perfect to play in goal and dive around on that icy pitch."

All eyes were on me, and being the (gangly) wimp I am, I nodded and mumbled a meek, "Okay then, I'll give it a go."

I needn't have worried, as the match was pretty uneventful. I had very little to do, and we returned to the changing rooms as comfortable 2-0 winners, with my new friend, Turd, bagging both goals.

Now, this might sound odd today, but back then, tattoos weren't a thing.

If you had tattoos in the 80s, you were either in the army, a football hooligan, the wrong side of the law, a fairground worker, or just plain scary. So, as Turd came out of the shower to get changed, I couldn't help noticing some primitive inking on his arms.

"You did well today, mate. I told you you'd be a good goalie. Always trust 'The Turd,'" he beamed.

"Thanks. I was just admiring your tats."

"Cheers. Which do you like best?"

I hadn't expected that, so I had to look properly now. The one that caught my eye was on his forearm and looked like a homemade tattoo of a red cabbage with an arrow through it. It had the word "TURD" above it and "TRACEY" below. Intriguingly, it also had the words "THIS IS A ROSE" underneath the names. I asked him what it all meant.

"Ah, that's because I got nicked for stealing a car to go joyriding when I was sixteen, and when the copper asked if I had any distinguishing features, I showed him my arm. Unbelievably, the cheeky bastard wrote, *tattoo of red cabbage on right arm!* The muppet refused to change it, no matter how many times I told him it was a rose. The bastard wouldn't listen. Anyway, not to worry, I had "THIS IS A ROSE" added so no one would make the same mistake again."

He was far too menacing to laugh in his face, so I continued, "Ah, interesting. And who's Tracey? Your girlfriend?"

"Yeah, my fiancée. She's back in Shifnal. We'll get married next year so I'm only doing this for one winter season. I learned to ski in the army, so I might as well make use of it."

It turned out that Richard was a thoroughly decent lad who had a train of thought and logic all of his own. He was a simple guy, but in the nicest and most noble way. Unlike me, he didn't have part-time morals and wasn't short of female attention.

His party trick was to ask a girl her first and last name, and when they'd tell him, he'd say, "I can't believe that. I have your full name tattooed on my arse."

Invariably, they'd come back with, "No way!"

"Yep, your full name," he'd insist.

With that, he'd look them in the eye and say, "If I prove that I've got your full name tattooed on my backside, you buy me lunch on the slopes tomorrow. And if I haven't, then I'll buy you lunch."

They'd happily agree, and he'd pull down his trousers to

show the words "*YOUR FULL NAME*" tattooed on his backside.

But despite his flirty nature, he remained faithful to his fiancée, Tracey. To prove the point, later on that winter, a minor UK celebrity, of the Page Three variety, came out to Kitzbühel and was quite taken with Rich (I refused to call him Turd) to the point where she turned to me on her last night to say, "What the hell is the matter with your friend? I came onto him, but he told me he can't be unfaithful to his girlfriend because she's waiting for him in somewhere called bloody Shifnal!"

Fast-forward to the start of the following winter season, and I was standing in the arrivals hall of Munich airport, waiting to welcome the first arrivals of the winter, when who should saunter through? None other than Richard Turdlow!

"Rich? What the hell are you doing here? I thought you'd be a happily married man in Shifnal by now."

"So did I, Frank, but when I got back from Kitzbühel last year, I found out that Tracey had been cheating on me with my best mate, Keith. I was devastated, but I'm over it now. He's welcome to the bitch. I wouldn't mind, but he's a right ugly fucker - a spotty-faced, lanky twat - looks a bit like you."

"Cheers Rich, but seriously, I'm sorry to hear that. It must have buggered up your tattoo too," I commented.

"Don't worry about that, Frank. I got it sorted."

"Laser treatment?" I asked.

"No way, that's far too much of a faff. I worked out a much cheaper option."

With a beaming grin, he rolled up his sleeve to reveal the red cabbage tattoo with his name above and the name "TRACEY" below. Except now, it was no longer just the name "TRACEY;" it had now been extended to read

"TRACEY… IS A SLAG." I did a double-take to make sure that the addition was a real tattoo and not some kind of joke, but sure enough, it was real, and he seemed over the moon with the new wording.

Anyway, here we were, sitting in a Wolverhampton wine bar some twenty-five years later, celebrating his fiftieth birthday. With his shock of silver hair and still-toned physique, I was pleased to see him looking so well, as we reminisced about the good old days working in the mountains. We chatted long into the night, as the party continued around us. We were having a great time until Rich mentioned the one season we were to work together in Colorado; the first time I had skied outside of Europe.

"Hey Frank, remember that season we almost worked together in the States?"

And just at that moment, the birthday boy got dragged onto the dance floor by a group of his sister's friends, and I was left alone to think about a chapter of my career I rarely revisited, a chapter so surreal that my brain usually went into freeze mode to stop me dwelling on it. Yet, somehow Richard had awakened the dragon, and I was about to revisit one of the most bizarre winters imaginable. As I drifted off into my own world, somewhere on the dance floor, I could hear a familiar deep West Midlands accent moving through the gears.

"Honestly, luv, if I prove that I have your full name tattooed on my arse…"

* * *

In the winter of 1991, a well-established UK travel company offered me the opportunity to work in North America for the first time, namely in the glitzy ski resort of Vail, Colorado. I had worked for them in Austria in the preceding summer and had been on the brink of leaving for pastures new, but the lure of one more ski season in the mountains of Colorado was too appealing to turn down. Better still, my mate, Rich, was returning for his second season in Colorado, working for a competitor in the neighbouring resort of Breckenridge, so it was all set to be a superb ski season for us both.

My winter accommodation was to be in East Vail, where the company had booked me a room within the large ranch-like home of Vail resident and business owner, Don Torissi. I was told that Don owned a local clothes shop where his wife Lydia also worked, and they had the room spare as their son had recently moved out.

Me and Rich had flown out on the same flight in the last week of November. Rich was a godsend on the flight over. Besides telling me all about the deep snow, immaculately groomed ski runs and friendly atmosphere of skiing in the States, he also briefed me on the USA protocol of actually gaining access into the country. Specifically, how I should say that I was a tourist doing some travelling, and not there in a work capacity. The reason was that the supply of "alien" work permits (green cards) was strictly limited. He told me what to say at customs checkpoints, and how I shouldn't carry any business-related literature with me, in case I was searched. Once we landed at Denver Airport I felt some trepidation as I filled out my visa form and queued at passport control. Rich and I had joined different queues, and I glanced over as he sailed through and chatted to some locals as he made his way to collect his bags. As I got closer to the officer at the control booth, I became more and more nervous as I inwardly rehearsed my pitch.

"Next!" came the shout from the booth, so up I went.

As I handed my passport over, the questions began.

"Howdy, sir. What is the nature of your visit? Business or leisure?"

"Leisure. I'm here on holiday," I replied.

"For how long?"

"Four months. I'm doing some travelling while I'm here."

"Do you have proof of funds to support your stay?" he quizzed.

"Yes. I have my credit card and bank statements if you'd like to see them."

"Okay, sonny. Where are you visiting first?" he continued.

"I'm staying on the outskirts of Vail with some friends to do some skiing for a few weeks before going west to California. My contact details are here on the visa form," I stated confidently.

Another couple of minutes passed while keyboard keys were tapped and my ID scrutinised. Eventually, I got the green light along with an enthusiastic stamping of my passport and visa card. I then collected my luggage and sailed through the subsequent customs control without a hitch. Walking through to the arrivals hall I was relieved at how smoothy it had gone. I knew Rich had come through some time before me, but I was still a bit surprised that he'd taken an earlier shuttle bus over to Breckenridge rather than wait and check that I'd made it through safely. Not to worry, I caught the next available shuttle, and two hours later, I was knocking on the door of 1 Eagle Drive in East Vail, a huge wooden structure blending in perfectly with the surrounding snow-laden forest. Don, my landlord for the season, was immediately at the door to meet me.

"Welcome to our humble abode, partner," he beamed.

He was a large, deeply tanned man, and clearly no stranger to the gym. He exuded health, and talked in a deep baritone midwestern drawl. Standing just behind him was

Lydia, similarly tanned, and smiling widely. Wearing a figure-hugging white ski suit, and with her hair tied back in a ponytail, they looked like something out of the pages of a health magazine. I was then shown to my huge ensuite basement room, that their son, Donny, had vacated that summer to hang out with his girlfriend in Minturn, a small town around ten miles away. Don was quick to tell me he was less than impressed by Donny's career choices, describing the 24-year-old as a "dumb-ass pothead drifter." Donny worked in a ski and boot hire shop "for a few measly bucks a week," and Don wasn't at all happy. This was obviously not a family to mince words, and we got on like a house on fire from day one. He explained that he only rented Donny's room out so Donny didn't think he'd always have a free place to stay if he ever got lazy and gave up work. As the tour of my new home continued, I could see that I'd fallen on my feet, as the place was massive, and despite its rustic surroundings, was fully kitted out with the latest high-quality furnishings and gadgets. Add to that the two high-powered pickup trucks in the drive, and it was obvious that Don and Lydia were doing well for themselves. Don's business was a swanky store on the main street - ILD Traditional Colorado Clothing - and Lydia explained that ILD stood for "I Love Denim" as the shop focused mainly on selling quality denim apparel.

Later that afternoon, they took me into town for a look around and to get something to eat. I was blown away by Vail, a hugely impressive ski resort. The town was built in the style of a stately, upmarket Tyrolean village. I loved it instantly. Don and Lydia told me all about the endless skiing trails, and how the front of the mountain was dedicated to more traditional ski runs, whilst the rear of the mountain was left pretty wild with huge back-bowls of snow, and acre after acre of skiing terrain. It sounded tremendous. They arranged to take me skiing on the Sunday of my first week, and had invited Donny and his girlfriend, Jo, to join us. This was to be followed by dinner back at the ranch as part of my formal family welcome.

It's said that, irrespective of natural talent, if you practice a sport or pastime for a minimum of 10,000 hours you will reach expert level. I believe that this is true of skiing, where progression is all about miles under the ski. By the time I rocked up in Colorado, I'd averaged around seventy days skiing per winter for six winters, so despite my lack of natural talent, I could realistically be classed as an expert skier, and I couldn't wait to go skiing with the family. Sunday came around quickly enough, and Don, Lydia and I met up with Donny and Jo at the bottom of the main Highline Express lift. I felt overdressed in my brand-new company Ski outfit, as although Lydia was dressed in her figure-hugging white ski suit, Don had donned a pair of old faded ski pants and an old parka, whilst Donny and Jo both wore jeans and ill-fitting lumberjack jackets. Neither of them seemed to care. They looked like they'd stepped straight out of a Scooby-Doo cartoon where Donny could easily have played the part of Shaggy. They were so laid back. I almost burst out laughing when I saw Donny's ski boots. They were like something from the 1970s, and two out of the four buckles on each boot were broken. I shook my head and felt a little sorry for him.

The journey up the lift consisted of Don baiting Donny, telling him he needed to "get real" and settle down into a proper job rather than working in a lousy ski hire shop. I warmed to Donny as he didn't rise to any of it, his main response being, "Yeah, you are right, man. I need to get my shit together." The other topic of conversation was me explaining what an expert skier I was, and how skiing had been invented by the Brits. Basically, I was being a complete prat.

Once at the top, we had a choice of three runs marked "black diamond," meaning they had been rated as difficult.

Unlike in Europe, where ski runs are usually numbered, the runs in Vail had names, such as Rogers Run, Blue Ox, and Highline. Proper names gave them so much more personality and could be highly amusing, as I found out later that season in Aspen, where one of the ski areas was called Sam's Knob. To hear chairlift conversations enthusing about the prospect of *riding on Sam's Knob,* or enthusing that *Sam's Knob is awesome!* warmed my heart. Anyway, each one of the three runs facing us was steep and bumpy, and Don went first on Highline. Despite bump runs not really being my forte, I knew that I'd be the strongest skier in the group and got ready to follow Don down the mountain. I then spent the next ten seconds staring open-mouthed as Don set off at breakneck speed, bouncing from bump to bump in an almost straight line, but maintaining total control. Donny then followed, no more than a metre behind him, and in absolute unison. I turned to look at Jo and Lydia, but it was too late, as they both set off at a similar pace and skill level.

"Un-bloody-believable. You are bloody kidding me!" I shouted to no one in particular as soon as they were out of earshot.

I stared in disbelief as, on the third or fourth mogul, Lydia threw an Olympics-standard 360-degree turn in mid-air and continued at full speed down the slope. It looked effortless. I now realised what an idiot I'd been. I'd not once asked about their skiing experience, just blathered on about myself, presuming that a shop owner and his wife in their late forties couldn't possibly be top skiers, and as for their "pot-head" son and girlfriend - no chance. In no time at all, I reverted to the insecure Frank I'd spent years trying to escape from. My head flooded with self-doubt. Momentarily, I became that nervous charlatan, taking my first ski lesson with Choco again.

"C'mon, Frank. Get your bloody act together. You've talked the talk, now walk the walk, for crying out loud. You can do this. You're a great skier. Now go and bloody prove it," I shouted to myself.

Off I went, skiing as fast as I could, crashing into the moguls, one after the other, knees pumping like pistons as I tried to catch up. Within a couple of minutes, I was at the very limit of my capability. My muscles were starting to burn, and yet I was still losing ground. I was so focused on my technique that I'd reached the last fifty metres without looking too far ahead. But as I glanced up, I could see that the four of them were gathered at the bottom of the run, ready to take the next lift back up to go again. By now, my knees were throbbing, and I was gasping for air with every movement. I made one big sweeping turn and stopped to catch my breath. They looked up and waved to me, so I waved back as enthusiastically as I could, knowing that they'd now be watching me ski down to them. I'd need to get my excuses in early. I took a deep breath, and off I went, trying to stay neat and tidy while going at pace over some pretty steep bumps. Legs racked with pain and increasingly ragged, I continued to bounce from one bump to the next. I managed it as well as I could and came to a sharp stop right in front of them. As I bent double, barely able to breathe, Don smiled.

"Okay, that's the warm-up run out of the way. Let's get back up there and do some real skiing."

"Hold on a second, Don," I rasped. "I twisted my knee on one of the first turns and had to take it easy from then on. It's an old injury, but I'll probably need to go easy for the rest of the afternoon. I'm gutted because I'd love to carry on skiing with you guys," I lied.

"Well, that was pretty impressive skiing for someone with a twisted knee, Frank. I take my hat off to you; you're a strong intermediate skier. Much better than most Brits I see," he responded.

And there it was, the perfect response to my earlier hubris. I had been damned by faint praise. I was a *strong bloody, fucking, intermediate skier*! Six winters working in the Alps, skiing almost daily, and that's as far as I'd got. The most hurtful part was that compared to them, it was true, probably even generous. Like life in general, it's all about levels, and when it came to skiing, theirs was a very different level to mine. However, there was one sport where I was a few levels ahead of them, and that was the ancient art of bullshit. And, as they had kindly chosen to believe the knee-injury story, it was duly embellished to involve a leg-saving helicopter dash to the hospital.

Donny and Jo volunteered to stay with me for the rest of the afternoon and we pottered around the mountain at a much easier pace, punctuated by plenty of drink stops. It was much more my scene. I got to see another side of Donny that afternoon. Beneath the laid-back facade, he was a real character, wisecracking and easy-going, yet sensible and serious when he needed to be. I couldn't help thinking that he'd make a great ski rep. Later that evening, following a sumptuous home-cooked dinner, I relaxed with the family around their open fire and asked a question that had been on my mind since I was first shown around the place.

"Don, I'm intrigued. When you first showed me around - the painting you have on your bedroom wall - the one with the words 'ILD thanks America' underneath, what's that all about? It looks like a giant dildo!"

"Well, it looks like a giant dildo because that's exactly what it is, Frank. Anyway, why has it got you so intrigued?"

"Well, I know that ILD stands for 'I Love Denim,' but why the giant dildo?"

"Get ready for this, Frank," Lydia squealed with delight. "You've just asked Don about his favourite subject - himself!"

Donny and Jo looked at each other before Donny turned to me, rolled his eyes, and said, "You've gone and started something now, Frank."

Don just smiled to himself and lit a cigar.

Exhaling high into the air in dramatic fashion, he continued, "Ignore the heathens around us, Frank. Before I answer that question, I need to tell you a little story about my Ma and Pa. My folks settled in New York in the 1930s. My dad was from Sicily and my mum from Naples. They came here to start a new life, and life was tough. My Pa was a humble man and went to work in a shoe shop, and over time, convinced the owner to specialise in imported Italian leather shoes, which turned out to be a great move. He worked every hour he could to look after me, my sister, and his own Ma and Pa, and eventually became shop manager. Much later, he bought the shop."

Cigar smoke now billowing, Don was on a roll, with his deep baritone voice perfect for storytelling.

"Well, the thing is, Frank, my Pa continued to work right up to the day he died at the ripe old age of ninety-two, and I'll always remember him for three things. The first was that he had the biggest legs in New York. You don't spend sixty years bending down at people's feet without growing the biggest calves in town, that's for sure. The second is that he gave us the most love possible in the least possible time. As kids, we'd only ever see him first thing in the morning, and on Sundays when he'd cook lunch and tell us story after story about the old days in Italy. Never once did he ever mention his job in the shoe shop. In truth, although I loved my Ma, it was Pa I always felt desperate to spend more time with, and I would hate Sunday evenings more than any other, as I knew I'd lose him for another week. I feel cheated about that to this very day."

With that, he blew out another circle of smoke and fell silent.

"So, what's the third thing, Don?" I ventured, now completely transfixed.

"The third thing is the most important one, Frank. The third thing is that he taught me my biggest life lesson. He taught me that having big legs isn't the only thing you should have at the end of your life. In later years, he got cancer and all his money went towards paying for his medical treatment. By the time he died, he had nothing left, and the shop had to be sold to pay the bills. You know what, Frank? That was the moment I knew that my life would take a very different path, and that's how the ILD brand was born."

I was engrossed. I had no idea where this was going, but he was clearly enjoying the moment and the others seemed just as eager for him to continue.

"Shortly after his passing, I got talking to my friend, Marty, in a bar in downtown New York. We were having some fun as he'd recently got a job selling "exotic adult gifts," specialising in sexy lingerie, vibrators, and the like. He told me how much demand there was - so much that they could hardly keep up with it all. They had no shop or store costs, as nobody wanted to be seen in that kind of establishment. They simply advertised in adult magazines and offered a discreet mail-order service. I was intrigued, and it got me a-thinkin'. I went home that night and came up with an idea that made me three million dollars over the next twelve months."

I quickly glanced over at Lydia in case it was a joke, but she looked back and nodded. Don continued.

"The next day, I bought every adult magazine I could lay my hands on. They must have thought I was the biggest pervert in New York! I worked out the average price for the best brand of dildos, and ordered fifty of them in various sizes at a trade price of around $12 each, retailing at $21.99. That's a pretty good markup. I then put a half-page advert in every single adult magazine in the country advertising them under my company name, ILD, and priced them at $16.99 to undercut the competition. The orders came rolling in, so many, that the postman was turning up at my door every day with my own cart full of mail. In the first two weeks, I'd taken 10,000 orders from all over our beautiful country. Not bad. But I decided to cut the price even more to $15.99 and kept the ads in for another three months. By the end of that time, I'd taken over 200,000 orders, money up front. I tell you, Frank, we are one sexy nation. Anyway, I called it quits at that. I'd made my money; I just needed to wait a few months before I knew for sure how much."

With that, Don passed around the whisky, and we all had a refill. I'd had a few drinks by now, but could still do basic maths, and I knew that the story didn't add up.

"I don't get it, Don," I said.

"What don't you get, Frank?"

"Well, you were making around $4 per vibrator - and that's without your advertising, storage, and postage costs - so I'm not sure how there was any profit?"

I was starting to feel a bit sorry for Don and assumed he'd either had too much to drink, or maybe he was winding me up. He looked at me, shook his head, and smiled.

"C'mon, Frank. Are you serious? I had no real postage to talk about, and fifty vibrators don't need much storage, just a single wardrobe."

"I don't understand, Don. I thought you said you took over 200,000 orders?"

"I did, but I only had fifty vibrators, so once I'd sent those, I had no more to send."

Silence.

"Sorry, I still don't get it. I thought you said you made three million dollars?" I said, now less sure of my logic.

"More than that, but, well, I couldn't be sure of that straight away, Frank. I had to be patient and wait until I'd refunded everybody's money."

This made so little sense that I briefly wondered whether Don was a distant relative of Kevin Hand.

"My head's hurting now, Don. This makes no sense to me. Refunds? You need to help me out."

Don turned to Lydia. "Honey, bring a refund cheque to show Frank. The English guy is struggling with basic math."

Lydia went to their bedroom while Donny looked across and said, "You're going to love the next bit, Frank. It's his party piece."

Lydia re-entered the room, walked across, and handed me a cheque marked simply "Refund," made payable "To whom it concerns," for a sum of $15.99. On the payee line, in bold red letters, it said "I Love Dildos Ltd," and in the background was a silhouette of a huge purple dildo. "Thank You for being a loyal customer of 'I Love Dildos Ltd'" was also written across the bottom of the cheque, in the same bold red ink.

"I sent a cheque just like that to refund every customer, and guess what?"

"What?" I responded, as the penny slowly started to drop.

"Out of 200,000 refunds, less than 100 people cashed the

refund cheque. That left me with just over $3m sitting in my bank account after paying my advertising and postage costs. Look, Frank, there's something you need to know about the USA. We are a bunch of hypocritical motherfuckers. We are some of the most sexually depraved fuckers on the planet, but we're also some of the most religious and self-righteous, so what goes on behind closed doors stays behind closed doors and, as sure as eggs are eggs, there aren't many people willing to let their local bank manager know they engage in, let's say, 'dubious extra-curricular activity.' Certainly not for the sake of fifteen bucks! Well, I say not many, in my experience, less than 100 out of 200,000."

With that, he roared with laughter and raised his glass high in a toast to the huge vaulted ceiling above.

"Do you know how many complaints I received? None… Nil…Zilch. Not one single word of complaint from one single dildo lover. Anyway, what was there to complain about?"

I stared at him as the penny finally dropped.

A few seconds later, I muttered in admiration, "What a superb scam, Don. That's bloody brilliant."

"Hey, careful there, Buddy. This was no scam, and no rules were broken. I simply hadn't enough stock to fulfil the orders, and I made the legally required refunds to the letter of the law. It's not my fault that the cheques weren't cashed. If the authorities came knocking, I'd followed the law and could prove that I had wilful intent to fulfil the orders by the fact that I'd dispatched fifty dildos in good faith. After all, being such a poor businessman, I hadn't expected the level of demand, and my piss-poor operation just couldn't cope. In all honesty, Frank, as soon as Marty told me that customers were too embarrassed to come into a shop to buy them, I knew I was onto something, and the rest was simply a matter of logistics. To be on the safe side, I left the money in the bank for a full twelve months before I spent any of it, and by that time, it had earned me almost another quarter of a million bucks in interest. I could have carried on for longer, but why do that when in the space of twelve months, I could walk away with over $3m, no questions asked? Unlike my old man, I knew when to quit, God rest his soul. I used the money to relocate here to Colorado, kept the brand name, ILD, for old times' sake, and it's been a perfect fit for my clothing shop."

After a minute or two of silence, he brought the story to an end with some sound advice.

"Don't ever forget, Frank, imagination is more valuable than education. Knowing something is fine, but imagining how you can use that something to make yourself some real money is much more valuable."

Over the next few months, Don proved to be a font of inspirational quotes, and like Choco before him, he became something of a mentor to me. As luck would have it, I was able to repay that mentorship pretty quickly.

That same week, news filtered through from head office that Rich hadn't actually made it through the customs checkpoint at Denver airport after all. They'd found some business cards he'd forgotten to hide, and from there, they'd tracked down his entry and exit into Denver the previous year. In short, he was found to be attempting to work by illegal means, and was deemed an illegal alien. It transpired that he was strip-searched and kept in a small, poorly ventilated cell alongside a dozen Mexicans for four days while they arranged his return flight back to the UK. I bet he never told any of the Mexicans that he had their name tattooed on his arse!

So, there was now a vacancy in Breckenridge for a ski rep, and I immediately threw Donny's name into the ring.

Great skier, local knowledge, honest, outgoing, personable, and best of all, fully legal. Happily, Donny interviewed well, was offered the job, and went on to become an absolute star. He was popular with customers, hoteliers, service providers, and even his dad. This move cemented my relationship with Don and Lydia, and they never tired of telling me they'd be ever grateful for helping to get Donny back on the right track.

Working in Vail was far less taxing than working in a European ski resort. I had fewer arrivals, and only two flights a week: Gatwick and Manchester. I'd generally only need a minibus to meet my guests at Denver airport and accompany them back to Vail. My customers were mostly well-heeled, well-travelled and polite, while the hotels were professional and gave exceptional service. I was so happy that I'd decided to work this one final ski season as it was semi-retirement compared to the constant exhaustion of looking after the British hordes descending on the Austrian Alps. But, of course, there were exceptions. It was now mid-February, the snow conditions were great, I was doing plenty of skiing, the après-ski programme was selling well, and my newly added excursion of a weekly day trip to Aspen was sold out.

I was in good spirits as I waited for my latest arrivals on a flight from Manchester - a group of six lads from Liverpool. It was an unusual booking in that they'd booked two triple rooms in one of the best hotels, but hadn't pre-booked lift passes or ski equipment, so I presumed that they'd bring lots of their own ski gear with them.

As they came shuffling across to where I was holding my welcome clipboard, I had an instant feeling that I'd need to be on my guard, although there was no obvious reason to feel that way, as they looked harmless enough. So, I put it down to my natural instinct and previous experience, where I'd found groups of Scots and Scousers to have similar traits as holidaymakers. They'd tend be one extreme or another; either a rep's dream, the funniest and most amiable group of people you could ever meet, or aggressive and unreasonable, with very little in between. As they approached, the first chap held out his hand in a warm greeting.

"Hi mate. We're the Willis group, staying in Vail at the Sonnenalp Hotel for seven nights. I'm Vinnie. Pleased to meet you."

With that, each of the lads shook my hand in turn.

"Barry, hi."

"Stevie, hi."

"Terry, hi."

"Duke, hi."

"Greg, pleased to meet you, Frank." (after squinting at my name badge).

With the formalities out of the way, they explained that they didn't have any ski gear with them as they weren't sure how much skiing they'd do. They wanted to play it by ear. As we walked to the minibus, they were chatty and in good spirits, so I had no reason for concern. One thing struck me as odd though, they all wore ill-fitting ski jackets, each one at least one size bigger than they needed. I laughed to myself that the reason they didn't want to ski was probably because of their poor eyesight.

They were superb company on the two-hour minibus ride to Vail and had me laughing all the way. Vinnie did most of the talking and was clearly the leader of the pack. They'd been friends since school, and as it was both "Lanky Greg's" and Barry's birthdays that week, they'd decided to do something different and try skiing. The journey flew by, and I told them all about the different excursions they could go on. They immediately booked the "Freedom Skidoos" half-day snowmobile tour early in the week to celebrate the birthdays.

The excursion included a champagne lunch, so it would be a birthday to remember, I told them, as I wrote out their tickets.

Fast forward a couple of nights, and I'd met up with some of the other local workers in the Shakedown Bar. It had live music, was always jam-packed, and with half-price drinks for resort workers, it was my kind of place. I was at the bar with my pals, Ian and Ali, who worked in the ski and boot rental shop, when I spotted the scouse lads sitting at a table at the back of the room. I gave them a wave and made my way over.

"Alright lads? How was the Skidoo trip?" I shouted above the din.

"Brilliant, Frank. We bloody loved it!" Greg shouted back.

The other lads raised their glasses as if to agree and we had a quick chat before I returned back to Ian and Ali. Towards the end of the night, with the dance floor still packed, I saw the scouse lads pushing and shoving a couple of guys near the coat stand and feared the worst, but it seemed to stop quickly enough, and by the time I'd come off the dance floor they were nowhere to be seen. The following morning, I made my breakfast visit to the Sonnenalp Hotel feeling slightly the worse for wear, and the first people to come and say hello were Mr and Mrs Stubbs, a lovely couple from the West Midlands.

"Good morning, Frank. The snow looks champion today," said Mr Stubbs cheerily.

"Morning, you're up nice and early. You'll be able to catch the first lift up the mountain at this rate," I said.

"Well, we have to do some shopping first, Frank. Our ski jackets went missing from the bar we were in last night. We hope that someone took them by mistake, but we heard that a few more went missing as well, so we're not sure we'll see them again. Never mind," he continued.

"Oh no. Let's hope it was just a harmless mistake. I hope you didn't have any valuables in the pockets," I sympathised.

"Around $300 in cash, but another chap had a lot more taken, so I guess we were lucky. You just don't expect that kind of thing out here."

With that, they turned and walked across to the lift. As the lift doors opened, Vinnie walked out, larger than life, and with no sign of a hangover. As he made his way to the breakfast area, I shouted across to him.

"Morning Vinnie. Just a quick one. I'll need payment for the snowmobiling trip so I can settle up with the Skidoo guys. Can you remind the others so we can sort it out later tonight when I'm back for my evening visit?"

"Yeah, no worries, mate," he called back, with a thumbs up.

Looking at Vinnie, I couldn't help but have a suspicion about the ski jackets, but with my hangover at full-throb, I was probably overthinking it.

After that, I headed over to meet Ali, Ian, and some of the others to ski away the cobwebs. We had a great afternoon on the slopes; no lift queues, great snow, and we skied off the hangovers. Feeling tired but relaxed after such a good day, I arrived back at the Sonnenalp for my evening visit in good spirits, and after around ten minutes sitting at the rep's desk, saw Vinnie enter the lobby and head for the lift.

"Hi Vinnie. How's it going?" I called over.

"Yeah, fine, mate."

"Did you catch up with the others about paying for the snowmobiling?"

With that, he turned back from the lift and came across to

settle the bill. But, as he got closer, he gave me a hard look that I hadn't seen from him before.

"Look mate, enough's enough. Stop goin' on about the fucking money. We ain't payin' yer, so fuck off, right?"

I was completely taken aback by his ferocity and heard myself splutter, "But…but…but you've been on the excursion and it needs paying for, Vinnie."

"That's your fucking problem, mate. You've been warned. Now fuck off out of my face before you get hurt, tosser."

He then put his head inches from my face, and in case I hadn't got the message, he kindly spelt it out in layman's terms.

"Now. Fuck. Off."

Shaken and shocked, and not one to ignore a customer request, I promptly did as I was told. I put my papers into my backpack, and, not to put too fine a point on it, I fucked off. I was really rattled. I hadn't been subjected to such unexpected and unwarranted aggression like that since, well, pretty much ever. I was humiliated, and was sure that the scene had been overheard by other guests, including Mr and Mrs Stubbs, who were sitting nearby.

On a practical level, I already knew that the money had gone, and I'd have to pay Freedom Skidoos from my own pocket. At around $1,000, I was angry at myself for breaking the golden rule of only confirming a booking after it had been paid for. It was a schoolboy error that would have had Choco shaking his head in despair. I also knew that it was no good reporting it to the head office, as they'd say the same thing. I thought about refusing them transport to the airport on their departure day, but I was too scared to really contemplate it. There were still another four days before they left, and I dreaded seeing them again.

That night, back at Don and Lydia's place, I cracked open a beer and sat on the terrace in contemplation.

"What's bothering you, big fella?" said Don, as he joined me for a drink.

"Oh, just had a bit of hassle from some of my guests today."

"Oh yeah? What kind of hassle?"

I replayed my earlier humiliation and expected either some ribbing for being an idiot, or some sympathy, but I got neither - just a few more bland questions.

"So, these boys are from Liverpool? Staying at the Sonnenalp Hotel, you say?"

"Yes, but they aren't exactly 'boys.' They're probably in their late twenties, early thirties."

"Shit, Frank, I'm in my late forties and I'm still a boy."

"In all honesty, Don, I feel embarrassed more than anything else, but I guess that's life."

"Sure is, Frank. Don't worry about it. Shit happens."

Over the next few days, my fear and embarrassment gradually turned to anger, mostly with myself for letting my guard down, and I was now convinced that Vinnie and his team had more than a hand in the missing coat shenanigans. As it happened, I didn't see any more of them until the evening before their departure, when I was again sitting at the desk in the hotel reception. The lift doors opened and one of the gang, Stevie, made his way over to me. I hated how nervous this made me, and braced myself for more abuse, determined to stay calm and professional no matter what. I stayed seated, looked up, and smiled.

"Hi Stevie, everything alright? Did you have a good day?"

"Yeah, mate. I wanted to come and pay you the money for

our Skidoo trip the other day, and apologise for not paying earlier."

I couldn't believe what I was hearing and waited for the punchline. The best I could do was to tentatively continue the chat.

"Okay…" I continued, waiting for some kind of explanation.

"I'll pay for all six of us, if that's alright. I think it was $1140, but I've no change so here's $1200. Keep the change, mate. Cheers."

With that, he handed me the bundle of notes and walked back towards the lift.

Just before he got there, he turned and said, "Oh, by the way, what time will the minibus collect us tomorrow?"

"Six-thirty A M. It's an early pick-up," I shouted back.

"No worries. Cheers," he responded, almost meekly.

I couldn't believe what had happened. I didn't know whether to laugh or cry. They must have felt some remorse, or maybe it was just Vinnie being an arse, and they'd been good guys all along. I was absolutely delighted and felt bad about blaming them for stealing the coats. Over the past two days, I'd mentally decided to boycott anything to do with Liverpool for the rest of my life, but suddenly, I found myself craving Beatles music, and could happily laugh along with Cilla, Tarby, and Doddy again.

Anyway, it was with a spring in my step that I boarded the minibus early the following morning to collect my scouse friends from the hotel and take them back to the airport. There they were, the little beauties. Only Vinnie was missing - probably still getting ready after a heavy last night. As they boarded the bus, the lanky one, Greg, turned to me.

"Don't bother waiting for Vinnie. He'll see us at the airport, mate."

"Are you sure? We can wait if he's still getting ready."

"No. He's already left. He's making his own way."

Strange, but at least it saved me the embarrassment of sitting in a minibus with him for the next two hours. It was a win-win situation, as far as I was concerned.

Two hours later we arrived at Denver International, and as I was saying my goodbyes, I noticed something of a commotion and a crowd gathering close to the nearest check-in desk. Before I clocked what was happening, the five scousers sprinted towards the throng and started to pull bystanders away. I caught up moments later, only to see airport security surrounding a bubble-wrapped object lying on the floor. It was the same bubble wrap used to wrap suitcases, only this time it wasn't a suitcase inside the wrapping, it was a naked man! And not any man - a scouse man. A scouse man called Vinnie. A scouse man called Vinnie, with a UK passport stuck in his mouth. Greg was the first to shout at the airport security guards.

"Leave him alone. He's with us," he wailed.

Stevie joined in, "Just unwrap him and let's get the fuck out of here!"

Utterly confused, I turned to Greg.

"I don't know what's going on, but is there anything I can do to help?"

Greg looked at me with wild, almost frightened eyes.

"Why don't you just fuck off? Haven't you done enough damage already, you FUCKING MANIAC?"

It took some time for all the hullabaloo to calm down, and for Vinnie to be released and clothed. I watched it all from a distance, and tried to make sense of what had happened. As I had new arrivals to welcome, I couldn't stay long enough to see the lads finally check in, but I was confident that they wouldn't be looking to come back anytime soon. I don't remember much about the ride back to Vail with the new arrivals later that evening, as I was still in shock. Two of my new arrivals were a lovely couple from Oswestry who had also booked the Sonnenalp Hotel, and as I checked them in, the receptionist collared me.

"Hi, Frank. The Willis party that departed this morning left lots of ski jackets in their rooms. I have them here."

I knew instantly who at least two of the jackets belonged to, and it wasn't the Willis party. What did surprise me was that all the money, credit cards, and driving licences reported missing were all accounted for and untouched in the jacket pockets. The day really couldn't get any stranger.

Back home that night, mentally and physically exhausted, I sat in the lounge waiting for Don and Lydia to get back from a night out in nearby Beaver Creek. Once they arrived, as usual, Lydia was the first to hit the sack, leaving me to tell Don the incredible story of the day. Don listened intently as I took him through the events of the past twenty-four hours, from the scouse lads coughing up the Skidoo money and the debacle at the airport, to finding the stolen coats in their hotel rooms.

"Sounds like someone gave those boys a little reminder that they need to show some manners around these parts," Don mused, as he blew smoke from one of his favourite Cuban cigars.

We carried on listening to music and drinking the last of the Jack Daniels in silence before Don eventually turned to me.

"I reckon I'd better turn in for the evening, Frank. Lydia will be wondering where the hell I've got to, and you can't keep a good woman waiting."

However, after a few steps, he stopped and slowly turned to face me.

"Oh, by the way, Frank. Remember when I said I owed you one for finding Donny the job?" he drawled.

"I sure do," I replied.

"Well, now we're even. Goodnight, Frank."

* * *

I kept in touch with Don and Lydia for a few years after that winter, mainly through postcards and the odd letter, but eventually we lost touch. The last I'd heard, Don had sold his business and bought a huge house in a gated community in Florida, somewhere between Fort Lauderdale and Miami. And, that's where the story might have ended, but around eight years later, I unexpectedly bumped into Donny at Berlin's Tegel airport of all places, where I learned that he was now Vice President of sales for a US real estate company. I didn't get the opportunity to quiz him on how he'd reached this lofty height, as the story he was about to tell me shocked me to the core.

Here goes…

It was late October, some three years earlier, when Don and Lydia drove to Miami to attend a business dinner with some potential business partners. As usual, they had plenty to drink, but Don insisted on driving their pickup truck the fifteen miles back home in the early hours of the morning. It was poor visibility and hammering with rain, but they got home in one piece. Unfortunately, the remote gate entry mechanism didn't work as they approached their property, so Lydia got out to open the gates manually, and went on to open the house whilst Don waited. Once the gates were open, and keen to get out of the torrid conditions, Don parked up in the garage as fast as he could. In true Don-style, he then decided to have a nightcap before going upstairs to join Lydia. One nightcap led to two, and two led to three until he fell asleep on the settee. He was sleeping like a baby until the sound of police sirens and loud knocking at his front door woke him at around 8.30 a.m. Fully dressed, bleary-eyed, and foggy-brained, Don opened the door to two police officers.

"Excuse me, sir, could you please accompany us to help identify a body found on your premises?" asked the first.

"Excuse me? A body?" Don responded fuzzily.

"Yes, sir. Please come with us," the second officer added.

With the rain still pouring, they led Don down to the area in front of his still-open property gates where a sodden body bag was about to be loaded into an ambulance. As he neared, he noticed a drenched red handbag abandoned to one side. With his brain now struggling to compute, the paramedic helped him into the back of the ambulance where the black body bag had been laid. As the bag was slowly unzipped, a woman's head fell to one side, congealed blood hiding a huge gash to the side of her scalp.

"Do you recognise this person, sir?" asked one of the officers.

The fog inside Don's head had now been replaced by nothingness. His mouth opened and closed like a goldfish, with no thinking, no realisation, just a few mumbled words.

"Oh, God…Lydia."

The police investigation later showed that Lydia had slipped to the floor as she opened the gates. In a hurry, blinded by the rain and deafened by the wind, Don had accelerated over Lydia's body, killing her instantly. The blood tests showed that Don's alcohol level was still three times over the limit, ten hours after the incident, and he was sentenced to twenty years in the state penitentiary on a charge of manslaughter. He was due for parole in another eight years.

"Well, I guess that's something. At least he'll be able to

walk free again," I muttered stupidly, completely at a loss for anything appropriate to say.

"It don't matter one bit," Donny fired back. "He don't wanna come out. Can't forgive himself for killing the love of his life. He's even pleaded to be put on death row. He don't eat, don't exercise, don't accept visitors; just sits there. He's lost the fucking will to live. He's lost a wife, and I've lost a mom *and* a dad."

Sitting in the soulless airport, I couldn't get to grips with what I'd heard. I, too, felt a hollow, aching sense of loss. I'd always thought of Don as my hero, and Don and Lydia together as the most dynamic, well-suited, larger-than-life, and fun-loving couple I'd ever met.

On my flight back to the UK, and for months after, I couldn't stop thinking about it, about how fragile life is, and how grief can end a life as easily as death itself.

RIP Lydia Torissi.

Chapter 8

No more Garys

A recent online news article screamed "No Garys left by 2050!" According to the UK register of baby names, so few babies had been christened Gary in recent times that the name was becoming extinct in the UK. Apparently, Alan and Kenneth were going the same way, and although it didn't say so, it is hard to believe there are many baby Keiths out there right now. So why did this headline catch my eye? Well, in 1999, I was very close to accelerating this statistic.

Working in the travel industry has many notable upsides. Forging a decent career despite having no readily definable skill set being one of them. Another is that you regularly meet successful people with even less going for them than yourself. Often, you will have worked with them at some point in your career, and enjoy catching up at the countless business and social events. They'll usually be keen to impress you with their seniority, and will delight in telling you about their various share options, stock investments, and other such palaver. The irony is that your abiding memory of them will always be that campsite barbecue in the South of France some thirty years earlier. The one that saw them staggering around the campsite at three in the morning, after a skinful of French brandy, sobbing, and telling everybody that they loved them.

So, let me introduce you to Gary Boyle. Gary and I worked together in the South of France in the late 1980s on a campsite called Mar Estang. He's since gone on to greater things, and by 2012 he was Vice President of sales at a major UK tour operator. It was in that year that we found ourselves sitting at the same table at the Travel Weekly Awards dinner on a crisp November evening at a newly opened venue in the heart of the Battersea Power Station development. Both of our companies were up for nomination in the endless awards categories. The winners were chosen by an independent panel of travel experts, and so carried more credibility than those where the event sponsors win all the awards. Attending this type of event fulfils two purposes. The first, particularly for the middle manager, is that by classing the evening knees-up as a networking opportunity, it sets a precedent for them to attend similar social shindigs in the future. It's a time-honoured process that goes something like this:

1. Overhear the odd snippet of innocuous business information from someone over dinner. Something as simple as, *online sales are up 15% year on year,* will do nicely.
2. Back at the office, at the next senior meeting the middle manager attends, they turn this harmless snippet into "breaking news." They shake their head and soberly share the intelligence, making it sound much more relevant than it actually is.
3. In the style of a courtroom barrister, they pace the room, stating that the rival is performing ahead of the market and add random meaningless phrases

such as "speed to market" and "multi-variant testing" as they vow to outperform the competitor.
4. The senior people in the room nod sagely at the insight, thank them for their diligence, and happily sign off any future attendance at such events.

Travel is no different to any other business, being seen to be credible is just as important as actually being credible. Luckily for me, I was at the point of my career where I was free to focus on the other purpose of the evening, which was to reminisce with old industry colleagues over a few glasses of wine. And that's where Gary and I reminded ourselves how close I'd come to removing him from the travel industry altogether.

The biggest event in the travel calendar is the ABTA Travel Convention; a very earnest affair. The Association of British Travel Agents holds the annual event in a different country every year. With over 1,000 members of the UK travel industry in attendance, it presents and debates the major travel issues of the day, predicts the trends and challenges for the following year, and has changed little in terms of format over the past thirty years. The event is sponsored to the hilt as well as being funded by the local Tourist Board of whichever country is hosting it. In 1999, the host city was Cairns, situated in Northern Queensland on the East coast of Australia. A location which, because of travel costs, ruled out most middle management from attending and ensured that the senior echelons were well represented. At this time, I was working for a major UK tour operator and was a late addition to the event guest list as one of the senior team had pulled out. To this day, I can't fathom why I was chosen, as my role within the business was pretty insignificant, but I had built up some decent alliances at senior level, and was seen as a good all-rounder. So, off I went to the "lucky country." It was a cold and wet November morning when I boarded the flight at London Heathrow, and as I entered the cabin, I was met with an unexpected greeting from somewhere further down the plane.

"Oi, O'Hare, you streak of piss!"

I'd have recognised the voice anywhere. It was unmistakably a well-oiled Gary Boyle, the newly appointed Head of Sales at a fast-growing holiday car hire agency based in Surrey. I hadn't seen Gary since his days as a campsite rep for Intasun Holidays in the South of France, where his dark curly perm (it was the 80s), athletic frame, and loud, confident persona meant he was always a favourite with the female holidaymakers. His strong cockney accent only added to his popularity. Unlike me, he didn't have to rely on chat-up lines, as his looks and his natural swagger did the job for him. Whereas I relied on a variety of quips ranging from the silly, *Hi, my name is Mr. Right. I believe you've been looking for me?* to the imbecilic, *My talking watch says you aren't wearing any underwear (pauses, puts watch to ear) Oh, sorry, it's an hour fast.* Unsurprisingly, I was pretty lonely that summer.

"Oi, O'Hare, over here," came the voice again as I continued down the aisle.

Sure enough, it was Gary. Or, I should say, an older, chubby, grey-haired version of Gary. In fact, if not for the voice and unfounded confidence, I'd hardly have recognised him. The intervening twenty-five years hadn't been kind, and he was failing the test of time. Being Gary, he persuaded whoever was next to him to move so we could sit together, and I spent the next few hours listening to story after story of his exploits - hugely entertaining and great value throughout. He confided that he was on his second marriage and with a much younger wife, so he was on a strict fitness regime trying to cut down from his bloated sixteen stone to his "fighting weight" of thirteen and a half stone by cutting out "the shit" from his diet. I'm not sure that the surrounding people appreciated some of the raw language, but, as Gary kindly reminded me somewhere above the Indian Ocean when I tried to quieten him down, "You always were a soft-arse, O'Hare."

As luck would have it, we were both staying at the same hotel, a five-minute walk from the conference, which tends to follow a similar pattern each year; a jam-packed attendance for the opening day presentations, and a full house again for the final session on day three. In between, there would be a smattering of attendees as most delegates turned their focus to drinking until the early hours, enjoying multiple sightseeing trips, and taking part in various charitable events.

Gary and I had signed up for the charity bungee jump taking place on the second afternoon; the proceeds going to one of the many good causes supported by the travel industry. As someone who is scared of heights, I was glad that I was going with somebody who nonchalantly described it as a "piece of piss."

On the day of the jump, we took advantage of the lunchtime hotel buffet. Now, it might only be me, but I can never fully enjoy a buffet because I have a weird phobia that whatever I put on my plate will be scrutinised by everyone else as I walk back to my seat. So, rather than choosing the amount and type of food I really want, I compromise to please my audience (I told you it was weird). This nonsense normally results in a plate of unhealthy food hidden beneath a smattering of vegetables and salad leaves. However, on this occasion my routine was further complicated by a long queue and too much choice. This meant there would be little time for a second visit should I mess up the first. But, as I worked my way along the buffet, it became apparent that I'd gone too big too soon. My plate was piled with chicken, pork, and beef which meant that there was little space left with half of the buffet still to go. I suddenly regretted choosing so much meat, especially as we were close to the ocean, so I capitulated at the fish section, and swiftly swapped two large pieces of pork from my plate with two pieces of tuna, leaving the pork amongst the remaining pieces of tuna and hoping nobody would notice. Once back at the table, I spotted Gary working his way down the queue and hovering at the tuna section. Surely not… But he did; he selected my two discarded pieces of pork from the fish section and added them to his plate. Once he'd made his way back to our table, I glanced at his plate of salad leaves, tomatoes, and the pork.

I casually asked, "What have you gone for, matey?"

"I went for the tuna. It's part of the diet. Got to keep to the regime."

I then watched him wince as he chewed the tomatoes, but happily wolf down the "tuna."

Once he'd finished, he turned to me.

"C'mon, Frank. We'd better get ready for the jump."

"Yeah, no problem. By the way, how was the tuna?"

"Best fuckin' fish I've ever had. Much better than the shit we get back home."

The jump was to take place at the AJ Rocket Bungee Centre, two hours north of Cairns, and our minibus struggled with some of the rough rainforest terrain as we approached our destination. Eventually the trees opened up to reveal a vast clearing, dominated by a huge wooden platform overlooking a deep-turquoise lake around 50 metres below. The wooden construction beneath the platform had hundreds of interwoven steps, winding around like those you see in a holiday waterpark, only much higher and much more terrifying. Shielding my eyes from the glare, and sticky with humidity, I peered up at the platform towering high above and felt my stomach churn. The only reason that I didn't climb straight back into the minibus was that none of the other participants seemed at all phased. Instead, they chatted excitedly about what lay ahead, while I stood stock still, overcome by my feeling of dread.

"Is that it?" bellowed Gary. "It's a bit Junior Showtime. What is this? Amateur Hour?" he said, winking at the girls next to us.

We shuffled into a log cabin at the foot of the huge construction, where we signed the disclaimer forms and were weighed on what looked like a set of cattle scales. Our weights were then written in felt pen on the back of our right hands; 88 kg on mine and a swiftly hidden "hand-in-the pocket" number on Gary's (104 kg).

From there, we were each given a bottle of water and told to take our time walking up the wooden steps as it could take twenty minutes or more to reach the top in such humidity. I followed Gary up, one slow step at a time, stopping to rest at every mini-platform, wiping our brows and drinking the water, until we eventually reached the top platform. Despite being much bigger than it looked from below - at least five metres wide and ten metres long, with high balcony rails all around, I was still petrified. However, I tried to stay calm as we were approached by three of the most beautiful girls imaginable, each kitted out in minuscule denim shorts, navy-blue AJ Rockett T-shirts tied in a knot around the midriff, and topped off with the compulsory flip-flops.

"Hey, guys. Welcome to the hottest experience in Australia," they chimed in unison. "Here's your complimentary shot."

They handed us a tray with two shot glasses filled to the

brim with tequila. Their name badges told us they were called Ronah, Mia, and Kylie. Mia was the first to compliment Gary.

"Strong looking pair o'legs ya got there, blue," she beamed.

"Yours aren't so bad either," Gary fired back, as he ogled her tanned legs.

"Let's check your weight, fellas," said Mia, pen and clipboard at the ready.

I showed her the back of my hand with a by-now very faint "88 kg" due to the excessive sweating and brow wiping. Next came Gary's turn, only his number was now totally illegible with the digit "4" just about visible.

Quick as a flash, Gary tucked in his stomach and with a cheery smile said, "ninety-four kilos, and every one paid for in full."

With that, we took our place behind an elderly couple and waited to have the safety procedures explained. I turned to Gary.

"How come you said ninety-four kilos?"

"Are you kidding? Did you see the way she was looking at me? I'd have no chance if she thought I was a fat fucker," he shot back.

Maybe there was logic in there somewhere, but all I could do was laugh.

It was Gary's turn to jump first, and before adjusting the elastic, Ben, one of the male members of the Rockett team, asked him, "Tips, shoulders, or hips, mate?"

As we were both bemused, he explained he could adjust the elastic tension so that Gary's fingers would just about touch the water (tips), dunk his head (shoulders), or he could be submerged in the water all the way to his waist (hips).

Gary surprised me by saying, "Tips."

Knowing that he'd never know what I chose as he would have already jumped, I took my chance. "Soft-arse," I said.

Gary took the bait. "What?" he snapped.

"Tips? I thought you'd be 'Hips' for sure. I thought I was the soft-arse?" I goaded.

"Bollocks! You'll only do 'Tips,' you northern wimp."

"Actually, I'm going to go for 'shoulders' or even 'hips,'" I lied.

"Okay, you lying bastard, I'll do the same. Make that 'shoulders,' Ben."

"Right you are, blue!" confirmed Ben.

With the necessary adjustments made, Gary took a couple of paces back, ran forward, and launched himself into an impressive swallow dive, hurtling through the air like a majestic, accelerating arrow, downwards towards the deep water below.

THHHWAAACCCKKKAAAASPLASH!

Outside of cartoons, I don't think I've ever heard such a noise, and seen a splash like the one Gary made on entry into the water. We all held our breath for what seemed like minutes, but was probably only a few seconds, before he catapulted back up to the surface, a spluttering mass of blubber, with shorts halfway down his legs, underwear up near his chest, and his bare arse cheeks glistening in the sunlight.

Up on the platform, the girls were wide-eyed with their hands over their mouths, as Ben reeled round to me and shrieked, "It says here ninety-four bloody kilos!"

Later that evening, I visited Gary in Cairns Hospital

where there was a frosty silence before he murmured, "How was I to know the fucking weight affected the elastic that much?"

I agreed with him and told him he at least had the glory of being the final jump of the day as the rest of the afternoon had been cancelled because of the "unforeseen incident."

He was to stay in hospital for another week as they treated his broken collarbone, dislocated shoulder, and cracked ribs. Now that I knew he was okay, I chided him for stopping me from doing my "hips" dive, and told him he'd have to pay me for all the sponsorship money I'd now have to reimburse. Towards the end of the chat, he threw in something I had anticipated.

"Frank?"

"Yes, Gary."

"I know you were trying to get me to say 'hips.' You know that if I'd have taken the bait, it would have probably killed me?"

"I do know that, but I also know that you lied about your weight to impress a girl who couldn't give a monkey's about either of us. So maybe we've both learned a lesson."

We both laughed nervously, but the thought that it could so easily have been curtains for him wasn't lost on me.

As I reached the door, Gary shouted across, "A couple of last questions before you go, Frank?"

"Fire away, mate," I replied.

"Would you really have gone for 'shoulders,' too?"

I couldn't lie. "No. Sorry, mate. Probably 'tips.'"

"I thought so, you soft arse," he laughed, shaking his head.

"What was the other question?" I asked.

"Are you sure that Mia girl didn't fancy me? Even a little bit?"

"Of course she did Gary, she's only human" I replied, giving him the answer he was looking for.

On the flight back home, I smiled as I thought about that last exchange, and instinctively raised my glass as I pictured Gary sitting up in his hospital bed, eating the food from his tray and saying to the nurse...

"This tuna tastes like shite!"

Chapter 9

Gut Feeling

Increasingly, the online travel industry is driven by systems, data, and analytics. Whatever the metric, you can be sure that there is an algorithm tracking its performance, and the best businesses consistently choose the most logical course of action based on what the data tells them. In the age of the algorithm, there's rarely a place for good old gut feeling, but having an innate business intuition to help make the right decision at the right time is still a powerful tool to possess.

Back in the early 1990s, Julie Jones arrived at the Flytours head office to be interviewed for the position of Senior Marketing Executive. As she entered the building that bleak and wet Lancashire morning, she was in full calamity mode. She was waiting in the busy reception foyer when I came down to meet her.

"Hello. Do we have a Julie Jones here?" I asked.

"Guilty as charged," piped up Julie, who seemed embarrassed as soon as she said it, and offered an enthusiastic handshake.

"You've got cold hands there, Julie. It must be chilly outside," I commented.

"Ah, yes. But you know what they say? Cold hands, warm heart," she responded, before again shaking her head.

Once in the interview room, it only got worse.

"Have you come far today, Julie?" I opened.

"Not too far. I can do it in my boyfriend's car in twenty minutes…I mean, the journey…nothing sexual. I mean, driving in his car; he wasn't in it with me. Oh shit! I'm sorry. I'm so nervous. I want this job so much."

She then burst into tears and explained that she'd been up all night looking after a sick relative and didn't feel that she was able to continue the interview. She then asked to cancel her application for the role. It hadn't gone well, and Julie was clearly under some stress, but we invited her back for a second attempt. She got the job, and five years later, she became a company director. Julie is now a leading figure in the travel industry, a strong CEO, and a sought-after non-executive board member. I take no credit for her career other than to demonstrate that everybody has bad days, and making long-standing judgements about somebody based on a bad day isn't smart.

The travel industry has been awash with charismatic leaders from the early days of Thomson and Intasun Holidays, and I've worked with, and reported to, plenty over the years. Never more so than in the early days of the dot-com bubble when the traditional travel industry business model struggled to come to terms with a new phenomenon, the "online" travel agent. It was the chance for a new breed of entrepreneur to enter the sector, and it seemed that anybody who was anybody wanted a piece of the action.

It was the early 2000s, and I was enjoying my first real taste of senior management as a director at one of the pioneers of online travel. Our ambitious company was hoovering up businesses across Europe, as our growth plan depended largely on mergers and acquisitions. Any online travel-related business was fair game if our dynamic founders, Lars and Lina, felt it could enhance the value of the brand. Lars and Lina were the poster children of the time. Lars was debonair, super-intelligent, and tech savvy (i.e., slightly nerdy), and Lina was vibrant, vivacious, batty, and a force of nature who was impossible to dislike. They had charm and the likeability factor by the bucket-load, and unlike other business leaders I'd worked with, they were never loud, brash or aggressive. In fact, Lars had a style that was as polite as it was subtle, almost a business version of Hugh Grant's character in *Four Weddings*. He was the classic scattergun leader, often giving multiple people the same task in the knowledge that at least one of them would deliver it for him. He'd ask in such a polite way that you felt as though you were doing him a personal favour - as did the multiple other people he'd asked to complete the same piece of work. At some point, you'd bump into someone working on the very same task as you and then agree between yourselves who would take full ownership, accepting that you'd both been "Larsed."

Importantly, Lars and Lina hadn't grown up within the traditional travel industry, which focused largely on selling packaged holidays through holiday brochures and travel agents. Unhindered by high fixed costs and legacy thinking, the seemingly limitless internet set them free, and they were having a ball. Since launching the business in the late nineties, Lars and Lina had caught the imagination of investors and the public alike. They focused on the late booking market and negotiated the best possible rates so that city-centre hotels filled their otherwise unsold rooms, and the public received deep discounts. The company was soon the name on everybody's lips, and quickly expanded to become a major travel and lifestyle brand. It was start-up heaven, as we'd often have an idea in the morning and put it live on the website in the afternoon. It was an environment that bred creativity, and we seemed to be trying something new every day.

At a strategic level, our focus was firmly set on business acquisitions, and the next target was a fast-growing online business focused on the Mediterranean beach holiday market, Dimitris Holidays. I was designated to lead a team to carry out due diligence on the potential acquisition, and from our first fact-finding visit to their office, it was clear that the leadership style of this business was far removed from that of Lars and Lina. This was a no-frills, no beanbags, and no PR outfit. They were programmed for profit, with minimal meetings, and little time for creativity, trial or error. The goal was simply to negotiate the best deals possible for their customers, in a variety of mediterranean destinations. We were impressed.

Calling the shots was the no-nonsense CEO and co-founder Dimitris Tsintoglou, whose passionate and direct approach was mirrored by his mostly Greek senior team. If Lars was Hugh Grant, then the rotund, greying chain-smoker, Dimitris, was more Jack Nicholson in *The Shining*, with a bit of *Cuckoo's Nest* "crazy" thrown in for good measure. His staff were fiercely loyal and respected him, but he had the air of someone not to be crossed. A great example of Dimitris's unorthodox style came during our introductory meeting at their UK headquarters. A small team of us sat at a meeting table in Dimitris's office and pored over revenue printouts whilst he sat at his desk and answered our questions.

An hour into the session, Dimitris glanced at his PC and suddenly exploded.

"MALAKA!"

It took us all by surprise.

He shouted across to his PA, "Tell Christos to get in here, NOW," and within seconds Christos Galliatsatos, his head of hotel contracting, tentatively entered the office.

"You fucking Malaka! You told me you would get the best rates in the industry at the Agrivos Hotel."

"I did, Dimitris. Nobody has lower daily rates in this hotel than us."

"You lying bastard. The hotel owner has just sent through a copy of our contract, and the contracts of our competitors. We have the cheapest rate by only one euro a night. One fucking euro! That's not cheaper; that's taking the piss. It's disrespectful to me, you, and the whole company. I want a written apology brought into my office in the next hour, and if you don't get a proper discount for every one of our hotels in Corfu by the end of the week, don't ever look me in the eye again."

I was stunned. The whole thing seemed like some kind of performance art, and I half-expected them to turn to us and bow at the end of the crazy charade. We sat there aghast as Christos apologised profusely, accepted what he was told, and duly came back with his handwritten apology.

"That was a bit over the top, wasn't it, Dimitris?" I ventured.

"Trust me, Frank, I know how to get the most out of every one of my team. If you are here again on Friday, you'll see how it works at my staff meeting."

Sure enough, on Friday, he called the office together for his weekly roundup. Dimitris stood with a black binder in his hand and began to talk.

"In this folder are all of our hotel contracts for next summer in Greece. I'm proud to say that this week Christos Galliatsatos and his team have negotiated the best rates in the market for the whole of Greece, with up to 15% discounts at our best-selling hotels in Corfu, including our best-seller, the Hotel Agrivos. To celebrate this magnificent achievement, I am taking everyone out next Thursday night for drinks and some Greek dancing. Thank you, Christos."

As the applause echoed around us, Dimitris turned to me with a satisfied smile.

"Remember, Frank, the reason you are buying my company is that I know what I'm doing, and my team know what they are doing. We get results."

Shortly afterwards, I bumped into Christos in the staff canteen.

"Hey, Christos. Congratulations on a good job."

"Thanks, Frank. Many sleepless nights and many negotiations, but there was no way I was going to let Dimitris down."

"Yes, I felt a bit sorry for you in Dimitris's office. He seemed to give you a hard time."

"No, Frank, that was just what I needed. I should thank Dimitris for that."

At another meeting with Dimitris later that day, the conversation touched on leadership styles and the way he'd dealt with Christos.

"Well, Frank, one thing I've learned is to never treat everybody the same way. In fact, there's nothing so unequal as the equal treatment of unequals."

"What?"

"It doesn't matter, Frank. What does matter is that I know exactly how to get the most from Christos, no matter how unorthodox it looks. I wouldn't dream of speaking to other staff members that way, but it works for him. I've taken the time to understand what makes each of them tick, and treat them all accordingly. Never fall into the trap of basing your opinion of somebody on your first impression; it's a schoolboy error and often wrong. People are complex, and the way you manage them needs to take that into account."

Unorthodox or not, his style seemed to work. The team respected him and his way of working. Yet it was a style which would prove to be in marked contrast to that of my soon-to-be new boss. Things were moving fast, and the predator was about to turn prey as our own business attracted interest from a major travel and technology company from across the Atlantic. Eager to get a foothold in Europe, we were an obvious target, and as they had deep pockets, the deal to buy the company was quickly finalised.

By this time, I'd grasped the fundamentals of what it takes to grow an online travel business, and taken on increased responsibility. Almost overnight, Lina left the business and Lars became a peripheral figure, as a US executive team was parachuted in to work with our pugnacious CEO, Doug Driver. Doug had worked alongside Lars for five years and had been his perfect foil. With a deep Scottish brogue and thick-set appearance, he had the manner of someone equally at home bargaining in the boardroom or brawling in the bar. He took no nonsense, welcomed face-to-face confrontation, and always sat with his legs at twenty past eight. It made perfect sense that he now took over the reins, despite the stark contrast in style. I reported directly to Doug at this point, but that was about to change as part of the US-led restructure.

My new boss was to be Freddie Firestone, a feisty online travel expert recently relocated to London from the New York office as part of the deal. The best way to describe Freddie physically was as a younger, taller, more handsome version of Hollywood actor and film director, Woody Allen. The odd thing about him from a personality perspective was that although he was driven by data and wouldn't make a business decision without multiple scientific proof points, he had the opposite approach when it came to his judgement of people, where he would often make snap decisions. A brash native of Boston, he had supreme confidence in his gut feeling when it came to judging people. And, once he'd made his judgement, it was almost impossible to change it. I got a flavour of his approach less than ten minutes into our first meeting.

"I don't know you, Frank. And other than your job title, I have little information about you or your background, yet I just know that you and I will work well together, buddy. You have the look of someone who's not afraid of hard work, and it's clear just looking at you that you've not had an easy life," he opined.

I wasn't sure whether or not he meant this as a compliment, but I knew it was a bloody cheek! However, I responded as any self-respecting lackey would.

"That's uncanny, Freddie, and very perceptive of you. You are right that it's been far from the easy road for me, but over time, I've realised that unless you are giving everything, you are giving nothing, and I have little time for anybody who doesn't share my bat-shit-crazy work ethic."

Clearly satisfied with the modest response, he continued with some small talk before I gave him an overview of my part of the business, being careful to emphasise the constant merry-go-round of late nights and weekend work I subjected myself to. As the meeting closed, he offered me some heartfelt advice.

"Just be careful of burnout, Frank. I've seen it too often

over the pond. Don't be too hard on yourself, and learn to give yourself a break."

Despite his overt brashness, I knew he was right. We had hit it off, and I was confident we'd work well together.

Freddie was joined on the newly formed board by more industry heavyweights from America. As you'd imagine, all were Stanford or Harvard graduates, five-mile pre-breakfast joggers, and with the dress sense of Top Gear presenters. By now we employed almost 2,000 people across the group, and through plenty of support and good fortune, I was responsible for a team of around 200 across Europe.

It was now time for them to meet Freddie.

The majority of my team were based in the UK, so we gathered everyone together in the ballroom of a luxury London hotel for his introductory presentation. What followed was a mightily impressive charm offensive, which made me realise where Freddie's real skill set lay.

His first slide just had the word "GNAB" written large across the screen.

Freddie did a surprised double-take and said, "I don't know who put that on there, but whoever it was...it's BANG out of order!"

Slowly, the room got the joke and stifled laughs and groans started to spread.

The second slide had the word "ARMAGEDDON" written across it.

This time, he turned to the audience and cracked, "I don't know who wrote that on the slide, but I guess it's not the end of the world."

He continued, giving an entertaining, humble, and sincere presentation that outlined his vision for the business and how we needed the expertise of everyone in the room for us to be successful. By the end, it had been a masterclass in how to get an audience onside.

Next was a flying visit to the Dimitris Holidays office in Thessaloniki, northeastern Greece, where their product and operations team was based. I'd had a soft spot for Greece since my season working in Crete, but Freddie was less than enthused.

"Why do these guys need an office based in Greece? Surely the UK would be easier, and India cheaper?" he complained.

"But Freddie, the team is multilingual, it's not expensive, and they all understand the European travel market," I replied.

He didn't look convinced, but I was confident he'd be happier once he met them.

Having arrived in Greece the night before, we went to the office bright and early to meet the sixty-strong team, and to have a guided tour. Yiannis Limos, Head of Operations, was our host for the day and started with a PowerPoint presentation outlining the roles and performance metrics of the teams we were about to meet. Our next port of call was with Eleni, Assistant Head of Customer Service, but as we approached her desk, it became clear that she was in the middle of a difficult customer call.

"Ah, this is great," beamed Yiannis as we waited. "You can now witness the professional way we deal with our customers, and see why we have such a low customer complaint ratio."

However, despite her polite and professional manner, Eleni was becoming more and more frustrated as she tried to placate the customer, who wanted a full refund for an illness they'd contracted during their recent holiday.

"But please, Mrs Moss, we have confirmation that the

hotel has carried out independent tests on all the food served on the premises. We have validated their cleaning and hygiene records, and they are compliant with all health and safety regulations. Also, there haven't been any other recorded illnesses at the property."

Despite this, we could sense Mrs Moss getting more and more irate as she insisted on a full refund. She threatened to go to the British press, and that it would be "all over the newspapers." It couldn't have helped Eleni that we were listening, and she was struggling to cope with the increasingly difficult customer. Mrs Moss finally demanded to speak to Eleni's superior, and Eleni looked apologetically at Yiannis, who turned to me.

"Excuse me, Frank, while I take this call," smiled Yiannis as he took the receiver from Eleni and began his own charm offensive.

"Hello, Mrs Moss. Yes, this is Yiannis Limos, the Dimitris Holidays Head of Operations... Yes, I do know all the details of your case... Yes, I am taking it seriously... Okay, Mrs Moss, can you please be quiet for a moment and listen to me as I'd like you to do two things for me? Good. Thank you, Mrs Moss. First, I want you to go fuck yourself. Yes, that's right...fuck yourself. Okay, have you got that? Good. Now, once you've done that, I'd like you to do one more thing for me, okay? Good. So, once you've finished, I want you to go back and...FUCK YOURSELF AGAIN!"

With a flourish, he smashed the receiver back down into its cradle, turned his back, and walked away. It was at that moment that I realised two things:

1. The team had a few rough edges.
2. This wouldn't end well for Yiannis.

Although he didn't react immediately, as soon as we were out of earshot, Freddie turned to me.

"What the fuck is going on here, Frank? That was fucking insane."

"I'm as shocked as you. It's certainly a different culture." I responded.

"Different culture! Are you kidding me? What happened to the culture of building relationships, and the customer always being right?" he countered.

"I agree. That was unacceptable at any level. Let's talk to Yiannis and find out what this is all about. There has to be an explanation."

He wasn't convinced. He was even less impressed when we were informed that Yiannis had gone home due to personal reasons, so we couldn't follow it up with him there and then.

Shortly afterwards, we were introduced to Kostas Batarakis, the swarthy head of the hotel negotiating team. As we approached, his team of six sat around their bank of desks, eating cake and drinking wine.

Kostas was the first to greet us. "Hello, Mr Freddie and Mr Frank. We are very pleased that you have come to visit us here in Greece. We don't get many visitors from the head office. Please, have some cake and a sip of wine."

"Hey, Kostas. What's the celebration?" asked Freddie.

"Oh, it's my name day. Here in Greece, we celebrate our names like you do birthdays - although we celebrate those too." Kostas replied cheerily.

"Okay, well, I won't have any wine, but I'll have a slice of cake," Freddie replied.

Over the next thirty minutes, our conversation with Kostas was punctuated by calls, visits, gifts, and handshakes from well-wishers congratulating him for being called Kostas.

I could tell that Freddie wasn't feeling it, and once we moved on, he took me to one side again.

"Is this shit for real, Frank? What the fuck is a 'name day'? You get to sit on your ass drinking wine and eating cake all day just because you have a fucking name?"

"It's a Greek custom, Freddie - don't take it to heart. Anyway, lots of the calls were from hoteliers wishing him well, and it is all about the relationships, just like you said."

He remained incredulous, giving me a quizzical look as he continued, "Can you imagine me trying that at my next New York board meeting, Frank? C'mon man, just imagine the scene... 'Hey folks, I won't be chairing the Group Board Meeting today.' *'Oh, why not, Freddie?'* 'Because I'm sat on my fucking ass, stuffing cake down my throat.' *'And why are you doing that?'* 'Because I'm called Freddie, you fucking morons!'"

To put it mildly, he was a bit miffed. From my point of view, I found it odd and contradictory. The authenticity, honesty and passion of the Greek team was refreshing, but the telephone outburst made no sense at all.

The final incident during our visit to the office summed the day up perfectly. Crammed into a crowded, hot and stuffy lift on our way out, Freddie casually turned to Lakis Lukadis, the head of the translations department.

"Hey, Lakis. What do you have planned tonight?" he asked.

The response was beyond bizarre, but perfectly in keeping with the rest of the day.

"To be honest, Mr. Freddie, I just want to get home before I shit myself."

We stood in silence as the doors opened to the ground floor and we spilled back out into the outside world.

On the flight home, Freddie let rip.

"There's no control over these guys, Frank. They're doing whatever they want, and I'm going to let Dimitris know he needs to make some big changes, starting with the staff. As soon as I walked into their office, I knew that something was wrong - my gut feeling never lets me down."

"I'd be a bit careful there, Freddie. Let's not be too hasty; this was only a flying visit, so it could just be a blip. Their customer satisfaction results are first-class, which makes it even stranger. Don't forget that the best-selling product on our German website for Valentine's Day was an inflatable pole dancing kit; I'm sure your gut feeling would have given that a thumbs down, too."

"Bullshit, Frank. You saw the same as me. The Greeks are a shit show."

At the next board meeting, back in London, Freddie let his feelings be known to the senior team. Dismissing any positives, he gave a damning verdict on the Greek operation, stating that the Dimitris Holidays business was too aggressive, unstructured, and needed to be "professionalised." His recommendation was to introduce a raft of new processes, a new management structure, and to review the quality of the current staff, which included the immediate dismissal of Yiannis Limos. Surprisingly, Dimitris sat there without saying a word until Freddie had finished his summary. Freddie acknowledged Dimitris at the very end.

"I'm sorry, Dimitris. I've not had much time to discuss this with you, and I know you run a profitable business, but my gut tells me you need to make some big changes to your team."

Dimitris responded, "Look, Freddie, I can see that you are passionate about this, so let me go away and come back to you with some recommendations. How does that sound? Let's reconvene when we get back from the tourism convention in a couple of weeks' time."

The calm and control of Dimitris's response was something I hadn't expected, but it defused any escalation at the meeting and brought the subject to a close. Conveniently, the tourism convention was taking place in Thessaloniki and Dimitris and Freddie were due to attend it together. Dimitris was to make the ground arrangements so that Freddie could meet various tourism ministers and make senior level contacts across the European travel community. However, things took a late turn when Dimitris had to pull out due to a family bereavement, and I stepped in to take his place. There was further confusion when, at the very last moment, it transpired that there was a problem with our hotel booking, and Dimitris arranged for someone to meet us upon arrival to take us to our new accommodation.

As we made our way through the arrivals hall, we were greeted by a smiling Yiannis Limos. As soon as Freddie saw Yiannis, he turned to me, dripping with irony.

"Oh look, Frank, it's Mr Customer Service. Let's hope he isn't here to tell us to go fuck ourselves."

Yiannis was more upbeat.

"Welcome back to Greece, guys. Come with me to the car and we'll get on our way."

It seemed strange to be getting in the back of Yiannis's car rather than a taxi, but things were about to get even stranger.

"My family is so honoured to host you both. We live to the northwest of Thessaloniki in a village called Aridaia, and I will drive you to and from the conference each day, and be your personal chauffeur."

"I'm sorry, I don't understand, Yiannis. Aren't you taking us to our hotel?" Freddie asked.

"No. There was a mix-up with your room bookings, so Dimitris asked me to host you. I thought you knew. Don't worry, you will have your own bedrooms and a bathroom. We will look after you like you are family."

"With all due respect, Yiannis, we really need to be in a hotel within walking distance of the event, so can you please sort that out?" Freddie responded more firmly.

"I'm sorry, Freddie, but everywhere is full because of the conference. Don't worry, everything will be okay. My family is looking forward to meeting the big boss of the company."

"I don't give a fu…"

Luckily, I intervened before Freddie said something he might regret.

"That will be lovely, Yiannis. We appreciate the fact that you and your family are going out of your way for us," I interjected.

"It's no problem, Frank. It is an honour for us."

The remainder of the journey was pretty tense with Freddie making several unsuccessful calls to Dimitris's cell phone to make it very clear that he was a "dead man" when we got back to the UK.

An hour or so later, we hurtled down a dusty farm track and pulled up outside a huge wooden ranch surrounded by lots of green fields, with vines and fruit plants stretching for what seemed like miles. There was a large wooden veranda at the front of the house, and as we pulled up, the family spilled out onto it. Yiannis made the introductions.

"Guys, please meet my mother and father, Christos and Fotini."

As we shook hands, another older couple appeared.

"And these are my grandparents, Yiannis and Soula, along with my younger sister Katarina." He gestured to a girl of around fourteen years of age. "Katarina speaks good English and is studying hard at school to one day get into an English university."

"Three generations living under one roof? Isn't that a bit unusual?" I asked.

"Not in this part of Greece. Sometimes it's four generations. We are one big family and we all look after each other," he replied.

"I'd love to do the same, but my mother has dementia, so she has to be looked after in a care home," I said.

Yiannis looked bemused. "A care home?"

"Yes, so she can get specialist care. Surely you have the same here?"

"Not really, Frank. We don't have care homes. Each family looks after their own."

We quickly freshened up and joined the family gathering, out on the veranda to eat dinner. I don't think I've ever seen so much food - steak, meatballs, pork, sausage, salads, grilled cheese, huge hot peppers, stuffed vine leaves, and warm bread - the table was straining under the weight. Even Freddie seemed impressed.

"This is a great spread, Yiannis. It looks fantastic," he gushed.

"I hope it will taste the same way, Freddie. Everything is made using our local produce, either from our fields, or from our cousins. Even the wines are our own."

With that, we got stuck in, and as the food tasted even better than it looked, it made for a lovely evening. Freddie had been fairly relaxed during the feast, but suddenly became more animated as he looked down from the veranda.

"Jeez, Yiannis, there's a huge pack of dogs in the front yard. Are they yours?"

"They don't belong to anyone, Freddie. In this part of Greece, most dogs and cats are wild. They come here to eat any leftovers and drink water from the water trough outside. Some stay overnight, and some move on to other farms. If you feed them your scraps, they'll stay and protect your land, scaring off intruders. If you don't, they'll go elsewhere. We normally have two or three that stay on our land long-term, and the others drift."

"So, they're running a protection racket! Feed them, and they'll protect you; don't, and you're on your own. That's brilliant!" exclaimed Freddie.

"Pretty much, yes. It's the law of the wild; the brightest and strongest survive, and the weak ones die at the side of the road. It's just the way it is."

"What about the cats?" Freddie continued.

"Same as anywhere. They keep the mice away and try to beat the dogs to the food. Look, I'll show you."

With that, he went to the fridge, took out two large chicken carcasses and some bread, put them on a tray, and threw them off the veranda. Sure enough, like a bolt of lightning, the cats got there first, took a mouthful, and shot away before the dogs reached the scene. Once there, the dogs noisily ravished every scrap of meat, skin, bone, bread, grass, and dirt in the vicinity. The whole process was over in less than a minute with nothing remotely edible surviving. From there, they sauntered over to drink from the water trough, which seemed to have a variety of frogs and other amphibians in it. Then, on cue, a couple of the dogs settled down for the night, leaving the rest to go elsewhere. Freddie was impressed.

"These guys have quite a racket going on here. By the way, Yiannis, we're going for a run tomorrow morning before breakfast. Are there any good routes around here?"

"Well, if you go straight out of the farm, follow the track to the left, head across the next field, and then come back, it will be a run of around four kilometres. Is that far enough?"

"Perfect. Do you want to join us? We'll start at around 7 a.m." Freddie offered.

"No thanks, Freddie. I'll be busy around that time, but please remember that you'll be running past a couple of farms, and the stray dogs will chase you. They won't bite, but they can be a nuisance."

"Don't worry about that, Yiannis, it takes more than a few stray dogs to worry a Bostonian! In any case, we'll be careful not to wake you."

Yiannis smiled. "Okay, kalinikta,guys."

Just before we went to our rooms, Freddie turned to me and whispered, "Just as I was starting to warm to the guy, he can't be assed to get up early for a run. The exercise would have done the lazy fuck some good. Never mind, he won't be around much longer. I'll just have to whup your English ass instead."

At six-thirty the next morning, we quietly made our way outside onto the veranda, where Freddie started his warm-up routine.

"Kalimera, guys!" boomed a voice from the adjacent field.

Our eyes shot across to see a waving Yiannis, his sister, their mum and dad, and their grandparents, all either on their knees, or climbing amongst the trees, as huge wicker baskets lay all around them.

"Good luck with your run today, my friends. We will have breakfast ready for when you return," shouted Yiannis, as the rest of his family waved and shouted an enthusiastic, "Kalimera!" across to us.

"What the hell are you guys doing out there?" Freddie shouted.

"We are harvesting our asparagus and peaches. It's a great crop this year. We'll tell you more over breakfast, when you return. By the way, I've left bread and biscuits in a small bag on the veranda for you to feed the stray dogs on your run."

"Many thanks, Yiannis," I shouted, and picked up the bag while Freddie muttered something about not being scared of a few mangy dogs, and that feeding them would show weakness.

Seconds later, we were off, with Freddie making the pace a few yards ahead of me. Running has never been my forte, and I knew that I'd struggle to even complete the 4 km, let alone stay close to Freddie, especially in the surprisingly humid early-morning conditions. To be fair to Freddie, he was clearly running within himself to make sure I wasn't too embarrassed, and the first half kilometre or so was pretty enjoyable as we jogged down the dusty lanes. Further along, Freddie started to pick up the pace, turning the corner to the first farmhouse around five metres ahead of me. Suddenly, a huge white dog burst through the undergrowth from one side of the track. Two smaller brown dogs followed. It was like a planned ambush as they barked and nipped around Freddie's legs.

"There's a good dog. Off you go, boy," he shouted at the lead dog, to no avail.

Around twenty metres past the farm, they were still there, snapping away, inches from Freddie's feet, barging into him whilst occasionally turning to bark at me. Freddie was now getting irked.

"For crying out loud, go-a-fucking way, you furry piece of shit," he yelled, as he kicked out into fresh air every other step.

Meanwhile, pretty much unbothered, I jogged along and watched it all unfold with a mixture of admiration and amusement as the dogs intimidated Freddie while hardly touching him. I could sense that his machismo was about to break at any second.

"Throw them the biscuits, Frank!" he yelled a moment later.

"Are you sure, Freddie? I thought you said it would be a sign of weakness?"

"Just give them the fucking biscuits, smart-ass!"

I opened the bag and threw a couple of pieces of bread and some biscuits to the floor. Within seconds, the dogs noisily devoured the food and trotted back to where they came from without so much as a backward glance. Around twenty hot and sweaty minutes later, I staggered home, a minute or so after an annoyingly fresh-looking Freddie. Once showered and changed, we sat down with Yiannis and his family for a breakfast of homemade cheeses, yoghurt, ham, seeded bread, and fruit.

"Sorry, I couldn't join you this morning, but my grandparents need more help than they used to picking our fruit and vegetables. We normally start at six in the morning until I leave for work, and we continue working the fields in the evening when I get back from work and my sister gets home from her studies. Except for lunch, my parents and grandparents work all day and into the evening."

Freddie was incredulous.

"Are you serious? All that work for a few vegetables, grapes, and bottles of wine?" he challenged.

"But the work and the food keep my family healthy. We don't use pesticides, and we sell some of it at the local market. We are very happy with this lifestyle as we are pretty much self-sufficient. I'd say at least half of our small town grows their own food, and half as many make their own wines and Tsipouro, which you probably know better as 'Grappa'," he said.

"Fair enough Yiannis, but rather you than me." Freddie replied, before we made our way to the car.

Following a busy first day at the trade show, we were invited to a traditional bouzouki night, just outside Thessaloniki. It seemed like half of Greece was there, including most of Yiannis's family. The night was a huge success with the wine flowing and Freddie showing a great aptitude for Greek dancing. Towards the end of the evening, a portly middle-aged man took to the stage, as the music faded into the background, and was handed the microphone. I presumed he was the venue owner, and as he addressed the room, there was complete, almost reverential silence. He spoke for around ten minutes and he finished with a huge "Yamas" as the crowd erupted into spontaneous applause and cheering.

"Wow, he seems popular," said Freddie to the guy standing next to him.

"Yes, he is. He is George Paschalidis, the Minister of Finance for Northern Greece."

Freddie was incredulous. "What? The whole room cheering and applauding…for a politician?"

"Yes. Why not? The reason we have good roads with lighting from all our villages to the city is because of that man. He campaigned for years to improve our roads and build schools. He has worked hard for all of us and we appreciate him - even those who didn't vote for him."

"Well, what the hell did he say?" Freddie asked.

"He said that he was here with his family, and that he felt he had to say how proud he was to see families of three or even four generations together tonight, dancing and singing. He said that it's that sense of family and togetherness that he will never stop fighting for, and it's what makes him so proud to be Greek."

"And you believe that shit?" Freddie said.

"Yes, I do. We all do. Look around and you'll see people aged from nine to ninety-nine all together enjoying themselves. It's one o'clock in the morning, but there is no trouble, no drunken fighting, just happiness and togetherness. We Greeks are as cynical as anyone else, but we recognise a good man when we see one."

Freddie shook his head, looked at me, and slurred, "Hey, Frank, let's get the hell out of here. I need some shut-eye."

On the way home, we shared a cab with Yiannis's young sister, who turned round from the front seat to talk to us.

"This is the first time I've seen Yiannis enjoy himself for almost a year. Thank you. He is finally getting himself back together again. He rarely goes out for fun since his cousin Kostas died last year. It was devastating for our family. They were the same age, they grew up together, and were like brothers."

I suddenly felt 100% sober. "Oh, my goodness! What happened?"

"It was last February. They'd been out drinking in the village, and while Yiannis left his motorcycle there and walked home, Kostas decided to ride home on his. It was dark, and the roads were wet. He lost control and sadly didn't recover from his injuries. Yiannis hasn't forgiven himself for not making sure Kostas didn't ride his motorcycle home that night."

I thought for a moment and then turned to Freddie.

"Freddie, do you remember it was the name day of Kostas when we were in the office in Thessaloniki in May?"

"Yes. How could I forget that nightmare of a day?"

"Well, that would have been the first name day for

Yiannis's cousin, Kostas, since the accident. He must have been devastated. It might go some way to explain his behaviour."

Katarina followed up, "Yiannis should never have gone into the office on Kostas's name day - he was, as you say, an emotional wreck. But he was so proud to meet you, Freddie, and didn't want to let you down. He told us all about what happened, and knows what he said to the customer was so wrong. He was very hard on himself."

I couldn't get it out of my head for the rest of the journey and whispered to Freddie, "We might have to give Yiannis a break, Freddie. What he said was totally unacceptable, but maybe he deserves a second chance."

Freddie just looked at me and shook his head.

The next two days flew by in a whirlwind of early morning runs, business meetings, and late nights. On our last day, we decided on a final morning run before catching a cab to the airport for our midday flight back to the UK. Up bright and early; we were met with the sight of Yiannis's extended family, out on the terrace, bearing gifts for us. They included olives, olive oil, feta cheese, good luck charms, Tsipouro, and wine. You name it; they wanted us to take it with us. While Freddie treated it like an inconvenience, I did my best to show gratitude in proportion to the hospitality and kindness we'd received. In truth, I got a bit emotional when Yiannis's grandmother took my hand and told me she would pray for our health and happiness. As the family dispersed and we began our final run, I attempted to pierce Freddie's hard exterior.

"What lovely people, Freddie. I was actually quite touched by their kindness."

"C'mon Frank, it's just an act. I'm not buying it. Haven't

you heard of the saying, *Beware of Greeks bearing gifts*? You need to toughen up, man!"

Suddenly, something snapped inside and I became determined not to let this ungrateful bastard beat me on our final run. With an energy I'd not known before, I sprinted away, past the first farm, and past the chasing dogs like my life depended on it. Whether it was 4 km or 40 km, I would not make this easy for him. But, competitive as ever, Freddie started to make up the ground, and by the time we were at the halfway stage, he was a few strides ahead as I gasped for breath and felt a dry burning in my chest. The good news was that I could hear Freddie's own laboured breathing and heavier-than-usual footsteps, as he also seemed to struggle with the pace. Now past the halfway point, and running adjacent to the main road, we'd reached the one stile on the route. Normally we'd clamber over it carefully, but this time, instead of slowing up, I could see Freddie accelerating as he approached it. *Surely not… Surely, he wasn't going to try and jump it? For goodness' sake, it was almost waist high on me. He couldn't, could he? Surely not?*

"AGGHHH! MY FUCKING BACK HAS GONE! You English bastard, you've fucked my back!"

I could hear the voice, but couldn't see the body, as the daft bugger had caught his lead foot on the front of the stile, and not to put too fine a point on it, had gone arse over tit into the bushes.

"For God's sake, Freddie, why did you try to jump it? It's like Becher's fucking Brook!"

"What?"

"Never mind. Can you stand up?"

"Stand? I can't move an inch. My back has locked. I'm fucked, and we have less than two hours before we leave for the airport!"

"Keep calm, Freddie. Let me call Yiannis at the office."

Calm as ever, Yiannis did his thing.

"Okay, you have to go and see Dr Nikos in the village. He is the expert when it comes to muscle injuries. He also has an X-ray machine. He'll have you fixed before you get on the flight. The trouble is, he doesn't speak English, so please go with my sister; she isn't at school today, and can translate for you. I'll call the doctor and tell him you have to be seen urgently as you are a friend of the family. I'll also tell Katarina to come to where you are."

A few minutes later, Katarina arrived on her scooter. We somehow managed to get Freddie on the back, and they set off for the doctors while I jogged behind. We arrived at what appeared to be a deserted shop near the village centre, and on entering, discovered it was packed with elderly men and women with no spare seat to sit an impatient Freddie on.

"For God's sake, what the hell is this place? It's like a scene from *Cocoon*," he exclaimed.

Almost immediately, a door opened at the far end of the room and a stooped, grey-haired old man wearing a white lab coat entered the waiting room. It was Doctor Nikos.

Katarina immediately sprang into action, and following a hurried conversation with the doctor, she turned to us.

"Doctor Nikos will see you immediately, as you are in such a hurry."

"Just tell him to get on with it," Freddie groaned, as I thanked Katarina profusely and turned to the packed waiting room to give a stage-whispered, "Thank you," to those waiting.

Entering a side room, we helped Freddie onto a small bed which was next to a larger bed, with a huge X-ray machine hovering above it. Dr Nikos immediately got to work, twisting and turning Freddie with the strength of a man half his age. As he worked, massaging and twisting limbs, back, and hips, Freddie let out an almighty howl of anguish.

He yelled, "For crying out loud, this fucking grandfather clock doesn't know what the hell he's doing, Frank!"

Moments later, the doctor stopped, turned to Katarina, and spoke softly.

Katarina smiled and turned to Freddie.

"You are now fixed, Mr Freddie. Please get under the X-ray machine for some final pictures."

"Are you kidding me? I'm still in absolute agony. Whoa…shit…the pain has gone! I can't believe it; the old fucking witch doctor has cured me."

With that, Freddie tentatively shifted beneath the X-ray machine while Dr Nikos clicked away. We then returned to the doctor's office, where two elderly couples were already sitting, as there was no space in the waiting room. Katerina spoke first.

"Okay, Mr Freddie, Dr Nikos wants to show you the X-ray so you can see what the issue was."

"Okay, no problem. I'm all ears."

Dr Nikos clipped the X-ray onto the large whiteboard mounted on the wall and flicked the light switch so it was fully illuminated for everyone to see. He then pointed to various parts of the X-ray while speaking in Greek to Katarina. Suddenly, Freddie let out a faint gasp beside me.

"Can…you...see...what I can...see, Frank?"

"Er, if you mean, um, you know what…? Yes, I think so."

"I just want you to know that this is the most humiliating moment of my life. I don't get it; I was fully clothed, for Christ's sake."

"I guess that's why they call it an X-ray machine, Freddie."

Unfortunately for Freddie, it wasn't just his spine, hip

bones, and ligaments on show. Taking centre stage were his cock and balls, as clearly as if he'd dropped his trousers and given everyone a close-up. As the doctor continued to point to the illuminated X-ray, Freddie and the old Greek couples sat transfixed as Katarina translated.

"Doctor Nikos says that this part of your leg, to the left of your penis, has a slightly strained ligament. And if you look closely, just beside your left testicle, you can see where you had a trapped nerve. The doctor has fixed that now, so with the painkillers he is prescribing, you will be okay."

She delivered the prognosis with a straight face, before one of the old women got up and pointed to Freddie's cock on the screen and started to talk quickly to her husband, repeatedly saying the name Giorgos. Freddie turned to Katarina and asked what she was saying, but Katarina said she couldn't understand.

"But surely, they're speaking Greek?" ventured Freddie.

"Well, yes, but it really doesn't matter, Mr. Freddie."

"But what did she say?" insisted Freddie.

Katerina lowered her head before answering, "She says your X-ray picture is cute, and that it reminds her of her grandchild Giorgos."

For a brief moment, I thought Freddie was going to cry. Instead, he turned and slowly made his way outside while I asked Katarina how much we owed.

"Dr Nikos says he has not charged you as he has done it as a favour to our family, and in respect to you as our visitors, Mr Frank."

"Wow, that's very kind, Katarina. Please tell him that we really appreciate his kind help. Thank you."

"Don't worry. Mr Freddie was in a lot of pain, and we are very happy that he is now fixed and okay to fly back to the UK."

Thankfully, we made it to the airport with time to spare, but Freddie was uncharacteristically quiet on the flight, so I tried to cheer him up.

"Hey Freddie, at least someone thought you were cute."

"Cute! Fucking cute! We all know what she meant, Frank, so don't go there."

"Well, what would you rather have? Excruciating back pain, or to be cured the way you were?"

Freddie answered immediately, "The back pain."

"Seriously though, did you get what you wanted from the trip?" I asked.

"Well, on the plus side, we made some good business contacts and got a couple of big deals over the line. On the minus side, I've been attacked by wild dogs, nearly broke my back, and shown my cock to half a fucking village."

He then fell silent before continuing, "I've also learnt something about myself in the last few days, Frank."

"Oh yeah? What's that?"

He fell silent again for a few more seconds, then, with a shake of his head, he muttered, "That I'm a fucking asshole who jumps to conclusions about people and their countries. We've been treated with so much kindness, generosity, and respect, and all I could do was bitch and complain. I'm a fucking jerk, Frank, and you know it. You're just too much of a reserved English bastard to say anything. And there is one other thing…"

"What's that, Freddie?"

"If I ever talk about my great gut feeling again, just punch me."

He didn't say much for the rest of the flight. Instead, he looked out of the window, shaking his head, and muttering the occasional, "I'm a fucking asshole."

Back in London, Dimitris arrived at Freddie's office for the debrief meeting.

"Kalimera, Freddie! How did the trip go? Did you achieve everything you wanted?"

Freddie didn't reply, but instead, got up from behind his desk and walked slowly over to Dimitris.

"What's going on, Freddie?" asked Dimitris, bemused.

Freddie put his arms around Dimitris and hugged him tightly. He then closed this briefest of meetings with just four whispered words.

"Se efcharisto file mou."

It sounds fanciful, but from that day on, Freddie was a changed man; equally confident, but calmer, less brash, more tolerant, and much humbler. He didn't stay with the business too much longer, as a year later, he moved back to Boston to start a business of his own. But, considering the short time we worked together, I found him to be one of the smartest, most charismatic, and genuine people I've ever worked with - one of life's good guys.

Moreover, Yiannis kept his job and stayed with the business for many years. The last I heard, he was running a successful chain of beach bars in Halkidiki, northern Greece.

Chapter 10
Lunacy in the Loire

I have a love-hate relationship with Paris, with the hate part mostly centred around transport, prices…and Parisians! One thing I know for sure, though, is that Paris has forgotten more about how to be a majestic capital city than most other capitals will ever know. Like an ageing Marlon Brando, it is bloated, shabby, and past its best, but you sense that if it wanted to spruce itself up and come out of retirement, it could give any city a run for its money. Yet, just like Brando, it has nothing to prove; its historic body of work speaks for itself, it cares little what others think, doesn't conform to popular opinion, and will continue to do whatever it wants to. The Paris Olympic Games were a case in point, from the controversial opening ceremony to the natural, innovative settings for lots of the events, it did things its own way. For me, whether by day or night, this magnificent city of romance still has an air of greatness.

My feelings for Paris were recently reignited as I arrived in the capital for a meeting with Stephanie Dupont, the CEO of a rapidly growing French holiday company. Their business model focused on selling exclusive online holiday packages, and had proved a huge success. So much so that their team had expanded, and they'd taken additional space in a beautiful Georgian building in the north of the city. Although my role was to help them plan the next stage of their European expansion, she was also keen to hear my thoughts on how they could retain their "start-up" mentality with a much larger team of almost 100 employees.

"You know, Frank, we attribute much of our success to our team ethos and values. We look for, and encourage, the softer skills in our employees - humility, empathy, a willingness to share knowledge and information, and to help others along the way. We can't afford to lose that collaborative team spirit," she shared earnestly. "It's the same with the leadership team. We all have egos and argue like hell, but we always look to find the best solution for our business and our customers. However, the team size has almost doubled in the past six months and we feel we are losing some of the magic," she explained. "It's so important to us that we've decided to hold a company offsite next month to not only share our business ambition, but also to instil our values and our unique way of working. We want to get away from the bustle of Paris and spend some time in the countryside, so we've booked a château in the Dordogne for the two-day offsite meeting. As an external pair of eyes, we'd love to share our plan with you and get your thoughts on the best way to organise it."

Did I have any thoughts? You bet. In fact, I had the perfect case study of how NOT to organise such an event. I turned to Stephanie.

"I will be delighted to help you guys, Stephanie. If you have an hour to spare, let's grab lunch, and I'll take you through a real-life example of how a team event can go spectacularly wrong despite the best of intentions. Better still, my example also concerns an offsite at a French château, so if you avoid all the pitfalls that I'll share with you, it will be a great start."

"That sounds like a story worth hearing, Frank. Let's do that. I'll bring our MD, Alexis, along, as he's been working on most of the arrangements."

Two hours later, we settled into our seats at the restaurant, and as the wine flowed, so did my tale of corporate lunacy in the Loire.

Within twelve months of the Thessaloniki X-ray incident, and Freddie Firestone's subsequent departure, I was delighted to be offered a position on the executive committee. However, despite combining American commercial know-how with our sexy brand-led European business, we were still missing our revenue targets, and it became clear that a prudent cost-cutting exercise was the most sensible next step. After plenty of soul-searching, the decision was made to make around 200 roles redundant across Europe. Along with this, the business was primed for a reboot, which included a revised strategy and vision. The strategic direction was broadly agreed between the group board and the executive team, and we all gathered at the quarterly European executive meeting to discuss the roll-out plan. As it was a pivotal time for the business, we were joined by some of the group board members from across the pond. As usual, the meeting was chaired by our CEO, Doug Driver, who by now had adapted the role to suit his more abrasive style. However, on this occasion, he cut a more empathetic tone.

"Okay, guys, it's been a tough year and we've had to make some tough decisions. Morale is low right now, so our job is to re-energise the business, inspire the staff, and build momentum again. We were one of the pioneers of online travel. We still have a great business model and a market-leading brand. So, let's take it to the next level. We owe it to our teams to inspire them with a vision and strategy worthy of both the brand and the outstanding minds we have in this room today." He paused. "So, we're going to start by bringing the senior European and US executive teams together for a three-day workshop, where we'll scrutinise every inch of the strategy until we are all 100% ready to live and breathe the values which underpin this great business. I'm now going to hand over to Hank Mason. For those of you who haven't met him yet, Hank is the Group Strategy Officer, responsible for making sure that everything we do is in line with the overall group strategy."

Speaking in a deep Midwestern drawl, Hank took the reins.

"Many thanks, Doug. It's good to be here to meet so many of you good folks from across Europe. As Doug said, the plan is to reboot the business and get it back on track. So, we're going to take our senior team away for three nights to a French château to double-click on the company strategy, vision, and values, until every one of us becomes a role model for everything this great company stands for. The only way we'll succeed in bringing the strategy to life is if we work together as a team, so the grand finale to the offsite will be our first-ever transatlantic soccer match, USA versus Europe. It will be the perfect way to show how important it is to have fun while working together to achieve results. By the end of the offsite, our exec team will be walking, talking brand evangelists. We'll then roll out similar workshops across the European management teams, and in no time at all, the clarity, direction, and leadership will galvanise the workforce and get us back on track from both a cultural and a commercial perspective."

Naturally, this led to lots of nodding and murmurs of support in the room. Being fairly new to my position, I rarely went against the grain, but on this occasion, something didn't feel right. So, uncharacteristically, I raised my hand.

"Hi, Hank. Many thanks for that summary. It's great that we are all coming together to agree on the strategy and roll-out, but won't it send the wrong message if we fly our senior team to an opulent French château for three nights when we've just made 10% of the workforce redundant? The fact that the event is in a French château in the first place; doesn't that seem even more like *let them eat cake*?"

Before Hank had time to respond, Doug answered for him.

"C'mon, Frank, don't be naïve. The staff are looking for us to lead them to success and expect us to provide a clear vision and direction. We owe it to them to take a few days out together to breathe new life into the business. In any case, we'll make sure that we don't do anything excessive."

I knew it would be foolhardy to continue, especially as I had scant support in the room.

"Fair enough. I guess we can handle any negative feedback if it comes our way," I conceded.

So, in April 2008, seventy of our top business leaders from across the world arrived at Château Lafayette, in the Loire Valley, for two days and three nights of unintentional mayhem. Expectations were high, as the new strategy was to be presented and discussed for the first time. So far, only a select few were aware of the details, and various members of the Group Board were flying in from the States to add gravitas to the event.

The château was breathtaking. The main structure dated

back to the fourteenth century and had been preserved to the highest standard. It was surrounded by acres of the most beautiful gardens and manicured lawns, complete with tennis courts, stables, and helipads. It was stunning.

On the first evening, we gathered in the opulent lounge in readiness for the formal welcome from the château owners, the Lafayette family. As we were served champagne and canapés, I got chatting to David Wordsmith, our new Finance Director. David had recently joined us from American Express and was explaining how different the world of travel was, and how he was hoping to learn a lot from the workshops. A tall, bespectacled, and angular figure, David had an air of awkwardness about him that made me warm to him. In some ways, his shy, gawkish appearance reminded me of myself from some years earlier. He was certainly making the most of the complimentary champagne as we chatted about his upcoming marriage to his childhood sweetheart. I remember thinking that he was the type of guy that every mother-in-law would want in their family; level-headed, decent, and likeably dull.

As David started on his fourth glass of champagne, a distant bell chimed, and three figures descended one of the two sweeping marble staircases, winding down from the sides of the lounge atrium. To the front was a most elegant-looking lady, probably in her mid-fifties. She was dressed in a full-length burgundy velvet dress with a matching brooch in her jet-black hair which was tied tight in a dark bun above her deeply suntanned face. This was clearly Madame Lafayette. One step behind, and on either side, were two much younger figures - a young man, probably in his early thirties, sharply dressed in black tie and suit, and a younger woman in her mid-twenties. From looks alone, it was obvious that these were her children.

You could hear a pin drop as Madame Lafayette addressed the gathering. She explained that the château had been in her family for many generations and that it was her son, Ariel, who largely managed the estate, while her daughter, Florie, helped with the administration and its future planning. Sadly, her husband, Hugo, had tragically died in a sky-diving accident in the Alps some years ago, and their focus was to do everything they could in tribute to his memory. She spoke fluently, and with complete clarity, despite her deep French accent, as she shared the history of the estate and its heavy influence from the French Renaissance movement. In truth, with that accent, she could have said any old tosh and the likes of myself and David would have been captivated.

It was a lovely start to the evening, and was followed by a spectacular dinner in the vast dining room adorned by huge stained-glass windows, a high vaulted stone ceiling, open fireplaces, paintings, historic tapestries, and mediaeval suits of armour. It was truly mesmerising. The seven-course dinner was accompanied by the finest French wines and topped off with local brandy, after which we retired to the cosy late-night bar where a jazz pianist and string quartet serenaded us. Thank goodness we weren't being excessive! At around 1 a.m., I played chaperone to my new buddy, David, as he was getting a little the worse for wear.

"C'mon, David, we'll need a clear head tomorrow. Let's get you to your room, sunshine."

"Aw, thanks a million, Frank. You're a real pal. You could be right; I might just have overdone the wine a tad."

So, with my good deed done, I retired to my room and fell into a deep slumber.

The next morning began with Doug's opening speech. Doug often seemed to treat his presentations as a long-awaited chance to get even with any enemies in the audience. A natural orator, he loved to shoot from the hip and liked nothing more than the challenge of audience participation. You could never be sure if he was mid-hangover or just irked and unnecessarily aggressive. But, despite sometimes having two wrong sides of the bed to get out of each morning, he was invariably good value. On this particular morning, he began his presentation in sparkling form, and did his level best to mask the poor business underperformance with phrases like, *In the current climate, flat is the new growth*, and, *it isn't about how far off target we are, rather, how far we've come.* It was world-class bullshit from a master of the art. However, some of his slides began to malfunction, and despite nobody really caring, Doug was getting narked. When we reached the Q&A section, those of us who knew him best also knew that there could be fireworks. The start was ominous.

"C'mon, we are all senior leaders here today, so don't be shy asking the hard questions. It's in all our interests to deal with the real issues."

For those who knew Doug, this was code for: *I've got the hump today and if you ask anything I don't like, I'll happily end your career here and now.* I was just wondering how Doug would deal with questions from the American contingent when an American hand popped up.

"Hey, Doug. You mentioned that despite the lack of profit, we had strong underlying momentum?" quizzed Brad Crimmings, USA Director of Brand Marketing.

"Correct, Brad," came the unerring reply.

"Can I double-click on that right now and ask you to give some examples of the momentum?"

"Of course, Brad. In Italy, our flight business is literally taking off with double-digit topline growth - pardon the pun."

"I get that, Doug, but earlier, we saw that this was at a negative profit margin," responded Brad cordially.

"Look, Brad, you have to understand the European market and think of the bigger picture. I'm not sure you are quite grasping it."

"But I'm sure you'd agree that margin is key," insisted Brad.

"Well, of course I could agree with you, Brad, but then we'd both be wrong. Next question, please."

You could sense an increased tension in the air as the next victim picked up the baton.

"Hey, Doug. Building on Brad's question, why do you think that the performance of our Spanish business versus the overall Spanish market is so poor?"

"It's a small market for us, Chuck, and not one we need to dwell on," shot Doug as he strode back and forth on stage.

"But you said earlier that it had great potential," continued Chuck, not reading the room.

Doug looked at Chuck without saying a word, the silence broken by Chuck again. "It's okay, Doug, we can take it offline."

"Och, I'm not thinking about your comment, Chuck. I'm just trying to imagine what you'd be like if you had a personality."

The change in atmosphere was now palpable, and over the next ten minutes it was Scotland v America as Doug went into full slugger mode, treading heavy-footed across the stage like a bear with a sore tooth, swatting away every question with a heady mix of scorn and contempt. As a show of senior unity before the big reveal of the new company vision, it left a lot to be desired. By the time Doug stepped down from the stage, we didn't know whether to cheer or start throwing punches. Instead, we applauded politely and headed for the coffee and cakes.

Next up was the big reveal itself; the inaugural presentation of the revamped company vision. We'd flown in Jon Elbheim from our head office in the US for this part. With the grand title of International People Leader, Jon was known as the ultimate motivational speaker, and his booming baritone voice belied his slight, bespectacled frame. Jon climbed onto the stage to wild applause from the American contingent and immediately found his groove.

"Greetings to our fellow leaders from across the Atlantic. Give me a show of hands if you are ready to shed the shackles of the present and embrace the future."

We raised our hands in bedraggled fashion as he continued.

"Thank you, my dear friends and colleagues; now please join with me as we go back... to the future! Hit the lights, Bud."

With that, the curtains slowly closed, and the lights dimmed around us. Eerily, the strains of *Nessun Dorma* began to filter into the room, becoming louder and louder. On the screen, a huge gold-coloured structure came into focus.

"Ladies and gentlemen, I give you... The Parthenon!" screamed the increasingly excited speaker, before lowering his voice to a menacing whisper. In a style reminiscent of Vincent Price, Jon continued, "Dating back to the start of time... 5,000 years before Our lord Jesus Christ... this structure symbolised the power and culture of one of the greatest civilisations known to man. The very foundation of civilisation and strength for thousands - YES, THOUSANDS - of years. It was, and still is...THE ULTIMATE VISION! Today, ladies and gentlemen, we introduce to you a glimpse of our future - our very own company, Parthenon."

With that, a small pyrotechnic exploded apologetically to one side of the screen. It was so over the top it was hard to believe it wasn't a parody, but this was just the beginning; there was more…much more.

"At the very foundation of the Parthenon are our people. YOU are our people. Your teams are OUR PEOPLE. WE ARE YOUR PEOPLE!"

By now, smoke from the fizzled firework had obscured the screen, so whatever was being shown in the background was lost to us. All we could see was Jon becoming increasingly agitated as he left the stage and marched up and down the aisles between our seats. He was telling us that he could feel the energy, feel the love and warmth, and that together we could reach for the stars, but we needed to have a common goal and common vision if we were to reach our full potential. I desperately tried to avoid making eye contact with him, but having made the mistake of sitting at the end of the row, he suddenly stopped his flow and fixed me with a vacant stare. I was bloody petrified.

"What's your name, boy?" (He was clearly younger than me).

"Frank O'Hare, sir."

"Do you have any regrets in life, Frank?"

"Only that I wish I had listened to what my mother told me."

"And what did she tell you, Frank?"

"I don't know; I wasn't listening."

Jon's booming voice immediately drowned out any titters from the crowd.

"A mama always wants her children to follow the right path. Just like Frank's poor mama. She wanted Frank to follow the right path, her path, and she knew the right path because she had a…VISION," he ranted. "Her vision was strong because it had strong foundations, just like the Parthenon. And it had pillars, just like the Parthenon. It had a roof, just like the Parthenon. And OUR mighty Parthenon has four pillars - yes, four mighty columns; the building blocks that support the very roof above our heads. And those columns are: One - Customer Focus. Two – Teamwork. Three - Technical Expertise. And, Four - Revenue Generation."

I presumed that the screen show was bringing the words to life, but by now the smoke was so thick, people were starting to cough and splutter in the front rows.

Still, he wasn't finished.

"And proudly sitting atop our Parthenon is our roof, our roof providing SHELTER, yes, SHELTER against the winds and rains, the tempests and droughts of our industry. Our roof is our reason for being, our reason for LIVING. It is our ultimate goal, and that goal is to be...Europe's most loved online travel agent!"

With that, there was a cracking sound from high above us and golden confetti came streaming down into the room, pretty much covering us from head to foot. It would be churlish not to recognise the sheer brilliance of someone who had kept us spellbound for almost an hour, telling us something most people could have wrapped up in ten minutes. Yet, he still hadn't bloody finished.

"Every email we write, every recruit we employ, every presentation we make, will be guided by the Parthenon. Make no mistake, my friends, we are witnessing history here. No more shall we bemoan a lack of revenue. No more will we bemoan a lack of purpose. And no more shall we doubt the power of unity. We have the Parthenon to guide us."

"Now, all together, Hallelujah and Praise the Lord!" (Disappointingly, he didn't actually say this, but I wish he had; I would have joined in for sure).

"Now, I want you all to follow the light, go next door, shed your clothes, and embrace the change." (Yes, he did say this).

Suddenly, a door behind the stage opened and threw a shaft of light into the room like a hazy path to the promised land. Looking around, I saw rows of expressionless, wide-eyed faces covered in gold confetti, willing themselves to their feet and shuffling groggily towards the light like the lunch queue in a care home. I noticed that some of us were now holding hands for safety and reassurance.

Unknowingly, I'd held onto the arm of Stefano, the MD for our Italian market, who turned to me, glassy-eyed and with a thousand-yard stare.

He mumbled, "Please, Franka, if I don't get out of this alive, please tell my wife I love her."

Tight-lipped and welling up, I nodded to reassure him.

Once through the doorway, we were dazzled by the bright lights of a new room. I blinked in disbelief as I saw Hank Mason and the rest of the executive board members standing in front of us wearing Roman togas and laurel wreaths. They beckoned us forward to get fitted with our own togas and wreaths, before being presented with a red-ribboned parchment scroll. As I reached the front of the line, Hank shook my hand and handed me my scroll.

"What's this all about, Hank?" I pleaded.

"It's your personal declaration to follow the new vision, Frank, and it's written in Latin for authenticity. Look, that's your name, Frank O'Hare, written in Latin. Impressive, eh?"

He seemed so pleased with himself that I almost stopped myself from being a party pooper.

"You know the Parthenon is in Athens, and was built by the ancient Greeks? The Romans built the Pantheon, a different monument. So, shouldn't the scrolls be in Greek?"

Before Hank could answer, Doug appeared like a vision amid the bright light.

"This is typical of you, Frank, looking to find fault. Just go with it, man. Can't you see how excited people are? And don't forget to collect your Parthenon mouse mat and mug before we break for lunch."

Twenty minutes later, there we were, dozens of bemused, confetti-strewn, toga-clad business executives sitting down for lunch, with our parchment scrolls scattered amongst the knives and forks. We soon became the focus of a coachload of Japanese tourists who busied themselves by snapping photos of our wreaths and togas. Amid lots of excited chatter, I'm sure I heard their party leader warn them not to come too close to us, as we looked heavily sedated and potentially dangerous.

In the afternoon, we split into workshops to focus on how we would bring each column of the Parthenon to life across each of our European markets, and although we made some progress, the general feeling was that we'd been presented with a fait accompli, rather than any of us being able to give any meaningful input. In any case, most of us were still in a daze following the histrionics of the morning. More workshops were due to take place the following morning, before the big finale taking place on the final afternoon - the eagerly anticipated USA v Europe "soccer" match.

The game was to take place on the beautifully manicured football pitch as a metaphor for how multinational teams can seamlessly work together to reach a common goal. We'd have a referee from Europe for the first half, and a referee from the United States for the second half. As luck would have it, my name was drawn out of the hat to referee the first half, and I'd be in goal for the European team in the second half, as, true to form, I'd wildly exaggerated my goalkeeping credentials. The teams were competing to win the inaugural "Parthenon Plinth," a huge golden Parthenon-shaped trophy, and our kits of red versus blue were adorned with a crest in the design of the Parthenon. This was to be an annual event which would forever show the unity and bond across the leadership team. Naturally, most of the chat over dinner that evening centred around the following day's big match, and Doug was quick to start the pre-match banter.

"So, O'Hare, I see your name has been pulled out of the hat to referee the first half tomorrow. I certainly hope that you don't start any of that yellow card nonsense for any hard, but fair, tackles."

"Don't worry, Doug. Like any good ref, I'm not averse to the odd brown envelope coming my way."

Then Doug turned his attention to David, who was sitting next to me.

"Despite you being an accountant and probably useless at the game, we've had to put you on the bench. You'll get a run-out, so make sure you don't get in the way tomorrow."

David answered with surprising wit. "Don't worry, Doug. I'll avoid getting in the way, just like Scotland has avoided getting in the way of any trophies for the last fifty years."

The Americans around us erupted in laughter, and Doug joined in, but I'm not sure that he appreciated the riposte quite as much as they did.

The banter continued long into the night with the US team happily accepting the role of underdogs.

The next morning's workshops continued in a similar vein to the previous day, with a half-hearted attempt to live and breathe the vision in a series of set-piece role-plays. Unfortunately, for whatever reason, it didn't gel. Unperturbed, Doug made a rousing speech to close the event and again reiterated that the Parthenon was here to stay, and that by living by its principles, the business would go from strength to strength.

An hour later, there was a mood of anticipation as we gathered by the side of the nearby football pitch. The sky was overcast, but it hadn't stopped a mixture of locals and tourists stopping by to watch. The atmosphere was heightened even more by chants of, "USA. USA," from a group of American tourists.

Bringing the two captains together in the centre circle, I played to the sparse crowd.

"C'mon, guys, let's have a fair game. Play by the rules, and may the best team win. Don't forget that you are playing to win the world-famous Parthenon Plinth. You are each representing a whole continent, so please don't take that lightly. May your God go with you."

Suitably impressed, Doug was the first to respond.

"Fuck off, O'Hare, and blow the bloody whistle."

With the clouds gathering ominously overhead, the rain started to pour. From the kick-off, it was obvious that this would not be the mismatch the Europeans had expected. The US team was much more skilful than anticipated. They were all good on the ball and looked as though they'd played the game at a decent level. This wasn't in the script at all. After ten minutes of good-natured play, it started to get serious. Doug was caught in possession on the halfway line and Scott Minter, from the US team, scampered away with the ball. Our big Spanish centre half came across to snuff out the danger, but Scott was too clever. He tapped it through Juanjo's legs and was off down the wing, putting in a lovely cross for Ed Ness to flick a delightful header into the bottom corner, despite Julie from HR's best effort to pull him back.

Europe 0: USA 1

As the US team began to dominate, the tackles started to fly in, and players began squaring up to each other.

"C'mon guys, it's only a game," yelled Hank, and things seemed to calm down a little.

By now, the rain was teeming down and the more reserved players had wisely started to gather around the edges of the pitch while the more hot-headed slid around, felling each other like skittles. I was trying my best not to show too many cards, but after forty minutes I'd handed out four yellows to the European team and one to the team from the US, receiving a mouthful of abuse each time. I was counting down the minutes to the break when Hank played a lovely through-ball for Scott to run onto again. This time, two of our defenders came from either side to try to take him out, however, they only succeeded in clattering into each other, as he skipped over them, accelerated into the box, and planted a lovely rising shot past our goalkeeper, Reinhart, high into the roof of the net.

Europe 0: USA 2

As I whistled for the goal, I sensed a skirmish behind me.

"You stupid French bastard!"

I turned and saw Juanjo sitting on the floor, clutching his left ankle as he continued his tirade.

"Puta Madre, Pierre. You've broken my ankle. He was my man. You should have left him to me instead of sliding in and taking me down!"

"I'm sorry, Juanjo, but you are too slow. You'd struggle to keep up with a fucking ride-on lawn mower!" retorted Pierre.

Doug now arrived on the scene to add to the fun.

"You pair of useless bastards. Someone, take Juanjo off to the hospital to get his ankle looked at, and let's try to reach half-time without injuring any more of our own players."

Meanwhile, the sodden US supporters on the sideline were going wild with excitement. "USA. USA. USA." Half-time couldn't come quickly enough.

Doug took charge, "Right, O'Hare you go in goal. Reinhart, you big lumbering oaf, get up front and do as much damage as possible to their defence. Wordsmith, you replace Juanjo, and just try to pass the ball to your nearest team mate. I'll bring you back off after fifteen minutes if you're shit. Remember, Brad Mulligan is taking over as ref; he's ex-US military and won't take any nonsense."

I turned to David. "Good luck, mate. Don't forget to take your glasses off."

"I wish I could, Frank, but I'm as blind as a bat without them, and I don't have my contact lenses with me."

This was going from bad to worse. As soon as we kicked off, the US team was on the attack again, and within seconds, the ball was ricocheting around our penalty area. I just managed to throw myself on the ball in time, preventing it from trickling over the line. I've never had a powerful kick, so my clearance barely reached the halfway line where it landed at David's feet. What happened next was sensational. With his back to their goal, he kicked it over his own head, turned, controlled it with his knee, and raced away from the US midfielders. He seemed to glide over the surface before knocking it wide to Doug. Doug then crossed the ball into the box where a soaring Wordsmith met it at full speed to head it powerfully into the goal off the underside of the crossbar. We couldn't quite believe what we'd seen, but David took it in his stride and jogged back to the centre circle as though nothing had happened. I couldn't have scored a headed goal like that to save my life, yet this guy did it wearing bloody glasses! At last, we had some momentum, and although the US team continued to dominate, we made a tactical switch; we brought Reinhart back into defence, let them attack us, and then we'd just hoof it up field for David to run onto. He was so quick, they couldn't catch him, and twenty minutes later, he'd scored two more goals, each time running from the halfway line and rounding the goalkeeper before slotting the ball home.

Europe 3: USA 2

With ten minutes left, it became more difficult as a lumbering Reinhart literally ran through Wendy, from the US strategy team, and got a second yellow card, and was sent off. Wendy was badly winded and taken for a medical check to test for broken ribs. Despite being under non-stop pressure, we'd now managed to get to the final five minutes without conceding again.

With the seconds ticking away, we had possession in their half when we got caught out. David was tackled, and in the blink of an eye, they played the ball through into our half. Pierre slipped, and Scott was suddenly away, sprinting down the left, and through towards the goal once again. I knew he'd want to cut inside onto his right foot, so I charged off the line towards him to cut down his options. Whether I had my angles right and would have saved his effort, I'll never know, because just as he pulled his right foot back to take his shot, a storming, snarling, sweating, muddied bear of a man came sliding across from seemingly nowhere and took Scott down at knee height. The momentum of the clash sent both Doug and Scott sliding towards the edge of the pitch where they eventually came to a muddled, ungainly stop. There was a momentary silence as players, and the crowd, tried to take in what had happened. This was less a tackle and more a full-blown assault. It was the exact thing that an already bad-tempered affair didn't need.

Brad immediately blew the whistle, flashed a yellow card at Doug, and pointed to the spot. My view was that it deserved a straight red card, but I guess that as Doug was the boss, Brad decided to be lenient. With Scott still writhing in agony, Doug was up on his feet.

"C'mon, Brad, I hardly touched him. He's making the most of it."

"Judging by the blood soaking through his sock, I really don't think so, Doug. You know as well as I do that you deserved a straight red card."

Doug came to his senses, stopped arguing, and joined the rest of the players huddled around Scott to make sure he was okay. It became clear that his injury required professional attention, and Scott became the third player sent on his way for medical treatment.

Hank stepped forward as the designated penalty taker, looking to save the day for the US team. Equally, it was now my chance for glory, and to secure the win for Europe. As any goalkeeper knows, and as a certain someone had told me many years earlier, it's important to do your homework, and I'd watched Hank play all the game without once making a side-foot pass or taking a shot with the instep of his right foot. So I was convinced that he'd put his laces through the ball and hit it to my right. Unless he had been fooling us all for ninety minutes, under this sort of pressure, there was no way he'd now attempt to side-foot the ball to my left. To tempt him further, I took a half-step to my left to leave slightly more room to the right for his shot. As Hank went to place the ball on the penalty spot, the scene was set for my match-winning save by diving to my stronger right side. My mind was made up, and I was confident that this was going to be my moment. Yet, as Hank bent down to place the ball on the spot, I saw the unmistakable figure of Doug standing on the edge of the penalty box, looking directly at me with his outstretched right arm at a right angle to his body, pointing to my left. His face was puce red as his eyes bored into mine. Nodding repeatedly, he pointed to my left as theatrically as he could. There was no doubting the message - *Dive to your left, O'Hare.* There was also no doubting that I'd seen his gesture. Having a relatively successful career has had many benefits for me, and one of them should have been to rid me of my natural insecurity. Yet, here I was, feeling intimidated by my desire to please an authority figure once again, and I became unnerved. My mind went into a frenzied conversation with itself. *C'mon, O'Hare. It's a friendly football match, a bit of fun. Grow a backbone, you bloody wimp. Have the courage of your convictions. Show Doug what you're made of and trust your own instincts.*

Meanwhile, Hank took a few paces back from the ball, paused, and took a deep breath while glancing briefly to my right. For sure, this was the side he'd go for. Yet, standing behind him, Doug again vigorously pointed to my left. Crunch time. Hank started his run-up, and I had to react.

Thudddd!

The ball rocketed to my right, and hit the back of the net in a flash, while I feebly fell to my left in a half-hearted attempt to stop the ball from going into a place that I knew it was never going to go.

Europe 3: USA 3

As soon as the ball hit the net, Brad blew the final whistle and so brought to an end one of the most bad-tempered, mean-spirited, and unedifying sporting "team building" exercises you could possibly imagine. Amid the muted US celebrations, David was the first to come across to me.

"You would never have stopped that, even if you'd dived the right way, Frank. Anyway, a draw was a fair result. They didn't deserve to lose."

He was right, but I wasn't really taking in what he was saying, as I was too busy hating myself for being such a bloody wimp.

Doug was second on the scene.

"Well played, Wordsmith. Never doubted you. Superb performance. Nothing you could do about the penalty, O'Hare, although you could have at least dived the right bloody way! In any case, the result wasn't important; it was more about team bonding," he added, without irony.

As team bonding sessions go, it had left some pretty impressive collateral damage in its wake: eight yellow cards, one red card, three medical cases, and festering bad feeling and division among those taking part. Although there was still plenty of banter in the bar that evening, you could feel that it was a little forced. As I was on the early flight the next day, it was the perfect excuse for me to have an earlyish night, so I made my excuses around midnight, and left David to enjoy his newfound fame as the hero of the European team.

The return flight was at 9.30 a.m. from Nantes airport, so we had a meeting time of 5.50 a.m. outside the main entrance, ready for the coach to depart at 6 a.m. sharp. Most of the UK-based team were on the same flight, so I planned to meet David for an early breakfast. As I hadn't gone crazy the night before, I arrived in the breakfast room feeling fresh and ready for the day ahead. However, it appeared that David had bailed on me, as he wasn't answering his phone, so I ate breakfast alone. He'd made me laugh in the bar because, despite being the star of the football match, he seemed intent on showing everyone the pictures of his bride-to-be and telling everyone how lucky he was to be marrying her. I had really warmed to this modest, genuine bloke and hoped that he wasn't too hungover or the worse for wear. After breakfast, I made my way to the meeting point, but David wasn't there either. With the coach due, I started to get concerned and went to the reception to ask them to call him on his room phone. Again, no response. By now, the coach had pulled up at the main entrance, so I ran upstairs to the second floor and banged on his door.

"David, c'mon, mate. The coach is here. Are you okay in there? You need to get your arse into gear, David. C'mon!"

I was sure that I could hear some muffled movement inside, so I tried again.

"C'mon, David. Open up, or just tell me if you're okay. You're going to miss the coach!"

Nothing. No response at all. I had visions of him lying there, choking on his vomit, so I ran downstairs and asked Melodie, the receptionist, to bring the spare key, as it might be an emergency. I must have sounded convincing, because she immediately took the key and ran with me back to David's room. We knocked again and shouted in French and English.

"Okay, David, we have a spare key and we are coming in."

Just as we started to turn the key in the lock, the door opened from the inside. I couldn't believe my eyes. There was David, standing in front of us, stark bollock naked. Obviously still drunk from the night before, and vacantly staring at both of us. To say that we didn't know where to look was an understatement. Although, when Melodie mumbled, "Oh là là," I had a good idea where her eyes were fixed.

"I'm sho shorry, Frank. I am willing to take the conshkwencies. I had one too many lasht night. I'll be okay in the morning."

I was livid. "What? This IS the bloody morning! You've got five minutes to get downstairs, otherwise, the coach is leaving," I ranted.

Suddenly, I noticed that Melodie was talking in French to someone else in the room. Someone was in the bed behind David. I glanced across and could hardly comprehend what I saw. Sat up in bed, sheets pulled up to protect her modesty, smiling and chatting away to Melodie, was none other than Florie Lafayette!

Now, I know that what I'm about to say stretches the bounds of credibility, but here goes. Just as I was trying to take in the scene in front of me, the bathroom door opened and who should emerge into the room, seemingly without a care in the world, Madame Lafayette! She was still wearing her evening clothes, and was casually brushing her hair, as she spoke calmly to Melodie in hushed tones. It was like I'd been thrown into a scene from a Noël Coward farce. Nothing made sense. I glared at David as his bottom lip wobbled.

"It's not what it sheems, Frank. I can explain everything.

Pleash don't tell anyone. Pleash, promise you won't shay a word."

Before I could respond, Melodie had pulled me into the corridor.

"Madame Lafayette says that your friend will make his own way to the airport and you must go without him."

I was now in total shock, and staggered along the corridor, down the stairs, and out to the waiting coach. The coach was a mass of sleeping bodies, dead to the world. I sat there trying to put the jigsaw pieces together. I'd seen David in the bar at midnight the night before. Madame and Florie Lafayette had also attended the drinks party, but I'm sure they had left before I did. And yet, less than six hours later, Florie and David were naked in his room, and God only knows what role Madame Lafayette had played in the proceedings.

Two hours later, we arrived at the airport and passed through security, but still there was no sign of David. In fact, we were boarded and mostly seated by the time he arrived, nervous, but looking every inch the serious business professional. As I looked down the aisle and watched him sink into his seat, I couldn't help wondering how long it would be before he'd be showing pictures of his bride-to-be to the person seated next to him.

When we landed at Gatwick, David made a beeline for me as we waited for our luggage.

"Look, Frank, I'm sorry about what happened earlier. It's a long story and you really don't want to know it."

"You are right, David, I don't. It's none of my business, anyway."

"I know, Frank, but I beg you not to tell anyone and please keep it to yourself. You know I'm getting married soon, and I need you to never utter a word about it, ever."

"Look, David, I don't need to know anything, and you can trust me not to say anything."

Selfishly, I wished the incident had never happened, as although we didn't speak about it again, David was never fully at ease in my company after that. It was a shame, as under normal circumstances, I think we'd have been great pals. He stayed with the company for another eighteen months before being headhunted by a big pharmaceutical corporation based in Amsterdam. The irony was that the head hunter was none other than Doug Driver, who had taken over as CEO of the company a few months earlier. I did wonder whether Doug had made the move based on David's financial acumen or his football ability, as I had visions of Doug plotting the next company offsite and making football the centrepiece again. If so, he clearly didn't need a top goalkeeper, as I didn't get a call.

As often happens with a personality-driven initiative, the enthusiasm for the Parthenon ended with Doug's departure. The new vision had initially been cascaded with some gusto, but following Doug's exit, the concept dwindled from polite enthusiasm to a series of half-hearted references, mostly when senior management was within earshot, until it died a respectful death. I've no idea what happened to the "Parthenon Plinth" either, as we didn't play another soccer match, but I suspect it might make an appearance in the Netherlands at some point.

* * *

Back in Paris, by the time I'd finished telling the story to Stephanie and Alexis, the restaurant tables were starting to empty. They had been engrossed throughout, and other than the odd shake of the head and incredulous gasp, had let me finish without interruption. Stephanie was the first to speak.

"What a story, Frank. So much good intention, but so much bad execution."

"I know. Not only has every practical detail to be thought through in advance, it's pointless taking the team there at all if they are going to be talked at rather than feeling involved and part of the decision making - especially as empathy and knowledge sharing is key to your way of working. It's impossible to do too much planning, so make sure that you allow the time, and involve all the right people. The event starts right now, not when you arrive at the venue."

Despite the farcical events in the Loire, I thought that using the Parthenon as the centrepiece for the vision made it relatable and could have worked well. I'm pretty sure that other businesses will also use the Greek Parthenon analogy at some point. If they do, my advice would be to forgo the Roman togas and keep a close eye on your finance director.

Chapter 11

Peak Distraction

We all experience distractions at work. Sometimes they're self-inflicted and sometimes they are thrust upon us. However, on some occasions, the distraction can lead to an unexpected opportunity.

In the early 1990s, I was working as an area manager in the Canary Islands on Lanzarote. Compared to some destinations I'd worked in, it was heaven. A small volcanic island with strict low-rise building laws meant it was both pretty and not overdeveloped. Better still, there were no night flights, and the longest airport transfer was around forty-five minutes. Add to that a warm year-round climate and a customer base of older couples and families, it made for a very agreeable place to work. That's not to say that it didn't have its challenges; high season overbookings being one of them.

As the popularity of the island grew, so did the pressure to find rooms to accommodate our guests, and in the first two weeks of August, we faced the perfect storm.

One of the largest hotels contacted our office to inform us that they couldn't accommodate fifteen bookings that were due to arrive the following week. No amount of pleading with the hotel manager could make him change his mind. There had been an administrative error at the hotel and he would attempt to find alternatives for our customers, but the island was full, and it was proving impossible. With over fifty customers affected, and such short notice, we had the team working round the clock to find suitable alternatives, and we were making frantic calls to hotel owners all over the island. It was around 7 p.m. local time when I took the latest incoming call.

"Hello, Frank speaking. Can I help you?"

"Hello, Frank? This is Jan Vanderberg. I need a favour from you. Bill Phillips, one of our executive directors, and an important investor in the company, is coming out to Lanzarote with his family next week for ten nights and needs the best three-bedroom apartment or villa you can find. He has a strict list of requirements, and I need you to confirm his options by the end of the day, tomorrow."

Jan was our Group Chief Commercial Officer and had a fearsome reputation for not suffering fools gladly. I'd only met him a couple of times, and each time I had been like jelly.

"Hi, Jan. Unfortunately, it's really bad timing. The island is full and we're overbooked everywhere. We're finding it impossible to find even basic accommodation over the next two weeks. Is it possible that he can rearrange for next month, or maybe try Tenerife or Gran Canaria instead?"

Jan's response was to ignore everything I said and continue where he'd left off.

"It will be Bill, his wife, and his three daughters. They are arriving next Saturday and will need a private transfer from the airport to their accommodation. They'll also need free excursions and a complimentary car rental for use during their stay. I'll ask my secretary to send across the full list of requirements in the morning."

With that, he ended the call.

Short notice VIP requests for complimentary accommodation were both an unwelcome distraction and an occupational hazard. It would often be a family relation, or friend of a board member, and their sense of entitlement was invariably sky-high. Despite being an aspect of the job that I resented; I always did my best to deliver what was asked of me. Yet this time, it really irked me. It was the busiest time of the season. The staff were working round the clock to cope with the workload. And the VIP family was arriving in just six days.

When their list of requirements came through the following day, the options were narrowed further as they were only prepared to stay in, or near, the main resort of Puerto del Carmen. On the plus side, I had been given a budget to work with, although it was nowhere near the going rate for a luxury villa at that time of the year. I worked with our resort agency to call in as many favours as possible, and we spent three sleepless nights calling every property and venue owner on the island trying to find somewhere for the Phillips family to stay. We found a couple of options, but when I visited them, I knew they wouldn't be up to the required standard and so they were rejected. I soon started to dread Jan's increasingly aggressive emails, and on the third evening, I winced as I read his latest message telling me how disappointed he was that we had such an incompetent area manager working for the company. I was physically exhausted and felt mentally tortured by someone who showed no empathy and would not give an inch. It was now 10 p.m. and I was still in the office when the phone rang once more. The caller was Tony Pipe. Tony had emigrated to the island twenty years earlier from

South London with his wife Jen and had established himself as a respected businessman and owner of several nightclubs.

"Hola, Frank. I know you are looking for a villa for a couple of weeks. Well, if you're interested, you can use mine. Jen's dad has just passed away unexpectedly and we need to go back to the UK for a couple of weeks. We'll be flying out tomorrow night. I'm happy to do you a favour for whatever you're prepared to pay, just so long as you promise to keep it in good order, and commit to advertising my nightclubs as part of your reps' welcome meetings for the rest of the season."

I felt a huge wave of relief surge through my body. I'd attended a barbecue at his villa earlier in the year and had been blown away by its size and quality, with stunning views over the town and across the Atlantic. We'd spent the day swimming in his infinity pool, and the evening playing snooker and darts in his games room. He even had a full-size gymnasium overlooking the ocean. It was just the ticket.

"I'm so sorry to hear about Jen's dad, Tony, but we'd love to take you up on the offer. We have a VIP coming over with his family, and it will be perfect for them. We'll make sure that it's cleaned regularly and in perfect shape for when you return," I responded respectfully.

A stroke of ill fortune for Tony had saved the day this time, but despite being relieved, I still resented the way I'd been treated, and wanted the whole thing behind me.

Early the next morning, I drove to the villa to take photos and sent them back to Jan, and of course, the Phillips family happily accepted the offer. On the day of their arrival, I arranged for my friend's limousine company to collect them from the airport, and had champagne, soft drinks and snacks ready for them in the villa. Once they'd settled in, I went to welcome them, sort out their car hire, and book them on the excursions of their choice. Bill Phillips was friendly enough, and I called on them a couple more times during their stay to make sure everything was ok. They weren't overly demanding and seemed to enjoy the excursions, but I was a little miffed that there wasn't a note or call of thanks at the end of their holiday - or maybe I was being too prissy. However, I did receive a pivotal phone call towards the end of that season. Totally out of the blue, I received a call from another board director, this time the Group Commercial Director, Paul Ryan. His introduction was straight to the point.

"Hello, Frank. I don't think we've met before, but I've heard some good things about you and wondered if you'd be interested in a management position back in the UK at the end of the year as part of my team?"

He told me more about the role and that if I was interested, he'd fly out the following week to meet with me and discuss it in more detail. My head was in a spin. Moving back to the UK was something I'd only fleetingly considered, as spending summers in the sun, and winters in the snow, had been my dream existence for almost ten years. However, I realised that by staying overseas indefinitely; I was limiting any future career prospects. I also knew the potential effects of too many late nights, too much partying, and crazy working hours. Going out to eat at 10 p.m. and downing at least a bottle of wine every night was the norm, and a habit I'd had for quite some time. On the flip side, the thought of returning to a management job in the UK intimidated me. *What skills did I have?* Other than using the in-house version of email, I'd barely used a PC, and I was in awe of people who could use spreadsheets. Surely, it wouldn't be long before I was found out.

But slowly I came round to the idea, and with a bit of

Choco-style artificial self-confidence, I decided to take the plunge, so even before Paul came to meet me in person, my mind was pretty much made up. What I hadn't realised was that the past few years working overseas had given me transferable skills that would matter much more in the real world of business than any specific technical ability. The ability to confidently present to an audience, to arbitrate and problem solve, to think on my feet, to give clear direction in pressure situations, and to sell myself to people of all backgrounds, were invaluable skills that would give me an edge for many years to come. When Paul arrived on the island, we hit it off straight away, and he proved to be a charismatic, ebullient, and infectious character; a softer, more business-like version of Choco. He flattered me, telling me how much he needed me on his team, which then begged the question that had been playing on my mind.

"It all sounds great, Paul, and I appreciate the opportunity, but one question; who gave you the feedback about me, and who recommended me in the first place?" I asked.

"Oh, I thought you knew. You actually have a couple of strong advocates back in the UK, namely Jan Vanderberg and Bill Phillips, one of our investors. As soon as I mentioned the role, they both recommended you. In fact, they couldn't speak highly enough of you," he responded.

I don't know which names I'd expected him to say, but it definitely wasn't those. Theirs were names I only associated with stress and resentment, not appreciation or support. Yet, they had given me much more than the instant praise and recognition my fragile ego had been looking for. They had given me the first step on the ladder from the beach, and ultimately to the boardroom. Until then, I had been proud of my overseas journey from holiday representative to area manager, but I knew that this would count for nothing back in the UK. I was about to enter the world of business and office politics, one that the old fake Frank wouldn't have stood a chance in.

Back in the UK, while I was rarely the smartest person in the room, through my approach of engineering situations to showcase my limited skill set, and working hard to improve my knowledge gaps, I started to gain recognition. It was around this time that a colleague made fun of me when they overheard a senior member of staff refer to me as *a safe pair of hands*. They could have their fun, but I was bloody delighted.

My UK career slowly began to flourish and further along the journey, I came face to face with the great-grandfather of the UK travel industry, the mighty Thomas Cook. Having built up a credible catalogue of achievement, much of it in the online arena, I felt I was well positioned to add some commercial value to the iconic brand, so I joined them on a consultancy basis. What I hadn't realised was that I was about to encounter the biggest business distraction I had ever experienced. I would go as far as to say that it was an industry phenomenon.

Like many businesses, the travel industry has a language all of its own. It is littered with acronyms, abbreviations, and travel-specific phrases that you would be hard pushed to understand without a helping hand. Whether talking about empty legs, allotments, guarantees, souls on board, release dates, or RevPAR, it's a minefield for the uninitiated. But, seldom does a word or phrase have so much power that it wreaks havoc throughout the business and its mere mention strikes fear and anxiety into its workforce. Yet, at Thomas Cook, such a thing existed.

For traditional mainstream holiday companies like Thomas Cook, the majority of holidays are booked in the period from January to mid-March, when, following the Christmas break, people turn their attention to booking their summer holidays. For Thomas Cook, this peak booking period was known simply as "Peaks." However, over the years, Peaks had taken on a life form all of its own, and had become a runaway train that was used, misused, and abused in equal measure.

My first experience of the phenomenon came in early January as I tried to arrange a meeting for later that month at the company's head office in Peterborough. Almost immediately, the apologies came back from the invitees - *We won't be able to attend because of Peaks*. At this stage, I wasn't sure about the exact nature of Peaks. *Was it medical, as in "an outbreak of Peaks?" Or maybe it was the name of a senior person I wasn't aware of who had vetoed the meeting, e.g. Mary Peaks?* Having subsequently had Peaks explained to me, I suggested we move the meeting to the following week.

Alex, the Head of Marketing, said, "Sorry, it's still Peaks, Frank. Can we move it to late March, and I can try to fit it in?"

I tried my best to understand the logic at play.

"But how does that affect your marketing team, Alex? Your TV ads, media, and newspaper slots have been booked months in advance, so surely there's not that much impact right now? Granted, the digital marketing team might have some increased workload, but otherwise, shouldn't it be business as usual?"

"Ah, you don't understand, Frank. It's Peaks, and we have

to be ready to support the business through it. It's all hands-on deck," he responded.

Indeed, whoever you spoke to pretty much said the same thing. During this three-month period, everybody agreed that it was "all hands-on deck" across the business, irrespective of whether a particular department was affected by Peaks in the slightest. Over time, it had become the unwritten rule that everyone had to pretend that they were somehow involved with the self-induced charade known as Peaks. Take my meeting with the heads of marketing, product, and hotel contracting as a small example. The product had been contracted and priced, and the brochure and online content had been written months ago, so Peaks had no additional effect on the current workloads of the invitees, and yet the spectre of Peaks still precluded their attendance. In fact, outside of the high street travel agents, call centres, and parts of the finance team, the biggest job should have been to sit and watch the bookings come flooding in.

But of course, I was missing the point; everybody wanted to feel relevant and involved, and nowhere more so than the head office in Peterborough, where leave was often cancelled, and extra staff brought in to cope with the non-existent rise in workload. Gaunt-faced staff would scurry around yelling into their phones. Stressed-out management could be found frantically engaged in arguments that bordered on fistfights. And social activities, or showing signs of having fun, would be immediately curtailed. All this in the name of something that, in reality, had no effect at all on those involved. So much energy and time was wasted on the charade that it had almost entered the realm of high farce. Any visit to the head office during the Peaks period was an education.

I arrived one cold January morning to be greeted by the sight of six staff stationed behind the reception desk rather than the usual three. Thankful for the warmth, as I entered the building, I approached our head receptionist, Joan.

"Morning, Joan. What's going on here today? Is it a staff training day?"

"Morning, Frank. No. We're geared up for Peaks. Taken on three temp staff," she replied breezily.

"Oh, do you do this every year at this time?"

"Sure do. Every single year since I joined ten years ago."

"It must be murder for you guys during this time," I ventured.

"Not really, Frank. It's normally quite quiet for us, but you never know."

Nowhere was safe, not even the staff canteen. One lunchtime, there was a typed notice positioned above some empty hot plates.

SORRY - NO CHICKEN CURRY THIS WEEK (PEAKS)

Nobody was excluded. Having worked late one evening, I was packing my bag in readiness to leave the office, when, out the corner of my eye, I noticed a cleaner knock over her mop bucket, and slump to her knees. Wild-eyed, and shaking her head, she spat the words, "Bloody Peaks!"

If Thomas Cook had thought about it commercially, they could have spawned a whole cottage industry selling Peaks-branded merchandise - mugs, plates, tea towels, and other memorabilia in the staff shop. It was such an obsession that they would have made a fortune. In fact, I had "I survived PEAKS 2013" printed on a white T-shirt and couldn't walk more than a few metres in Peterborough without someone asking me where I'd bought it.

The ultimate irony of Peaks was that you'd be hard-pressed to find a more unproductive period in the whole travel calendar. In the Austrian Alps, there is a natural phenomenon called the Foehn Wind. It is a dry, unforgiving wind that sweeps through the valley every few years, and is said to have an overtly negative effect on the mental wellbeing of the locals. So much so that when it blows, it can be used in mitigation for when crimes are committed, and local school examinations are often cancelled during this period. I swear that if there had been a vote in Peterborough, the locals would have agreed to implement similar laws to cope with their very own Foehn Wind, the travel phenomenon known simply as Peaks.

Maybe I am being unfair and the distraction of Peaks reaped some big-picture benefit for Thomas Cook that I was unaware of. Maybe the "all hands on deck" attitude throughout this period forged stronger teamwork throughout the rest of the year and created a greater sense of company loyalty. For sure, the impact of my fortunate Lanzarote distraction was that it paved the way for my career back in the UK. I guess that it depends on your perspective, but no matter how you look at it, with the right attitude, one person's distraction is another person's opportunity.

Chapter 12

Corporate Survivor

Over the years, I've experienced some hugely dysfunctional boardrooms and senior teams. On the other hand, I've been involved with some that have been a delight to be a part of. Often, the difference between the two is ego. The executive team which can overlook their individual egos for the collective good of the business is usually the one to prosper. Of course, it isn't easy for someone to reach such senior status without developing a certain amount of self-importance, but when it's allowed to thrive among the senior team, you are in trouble.

Over the years, I've been able to adapt to new leadership teams because the profiles within the team rarely change. On the boards I've been involved with, I've witnessed four main profiles, and in terms of ego and self-interest, the last one on the list stands head and shoulders above the others.

> *Subject-Matter Expert:* Often headhunted from a blue-chip organisation or major rival. As a well-qualified business professional, their technical expertise is an asset to the business and gives external credibility.

Company Veteran: Their value is largely based on their longevity within the business. Often coming through the ranks, they understand the ebb and flow of the business, provide context, and ensure that costly historical mistakes aren't repeated.

Plug and Play: With a formal business education and experience across several sectors, this person is at home in any boardroom. With a carefully constructed resumé of blue-chip organisations, they are industry agnostic, gain instant respect, and are a safe bet for the CEO position.

Corporate Survivor: A political animal, their sole focus is to maintain a facade of credibility, and ultimately, their job. Without the expertise of the first three profiles, they have a cunning and survival instinct that others can only dream of. They can talk a good game as long as they aren't pinned down on specifics.

Despite being the least valuable, the Corporate Survivor is by far the most interesting of the profiles. This isn't to say that they're without merit, as anyone who can engineer a pathway to the top cannot be taken lightly. Let's take a closer look at some of their key traits:

- They never play their hand first in the boardroom, and normally articulate a logical reason for having the same viewpoint as the CEO.
- They are highly visible at conferences and social get-togethers, and push their expense account to the limit.

- They often withhold information, using it for their own personal benefit, and are experts in repackaging other people's ideas as their own.
- They have excellent career timing, rarely outstay their welcome, and know exactly when to jump ship.

By definition, the Corporate Survivor is usually outnumbered by credible performers at boardroom level and can be carried to a certain extent, but occasionally they have been known to slip through the net to find themselves in the driving seat, as CEO. This rarely ends well. After a career of sitting on the fence and avoiding being caught in the same room as a decision, they tend to lead by committee, and encourage endless navel-gazing, as they have no idea how to run a business. In turn, this leads to frustration with the lack of direction, inertia, and ultimately a disastrous effect on the bottom line. However, I have been privileged to work alongside some of the best corporate survivors in the industry, and when you see one in full flow, it is a sight to behold. A few years ago, I witnessed a master of the craft at work.

In the mid-2010s, I joined a major online travel agent to help optimise their systems and business processes following a spate of acquisitions, which brought together multiple teams and processes all doing the same thing. Alignment under a single brand would make the business much more efficient and I was enjoying the challenge. As my role touched on most parts of the business, I was given a temporary place on the board, reporting directly to the CEO, Jack Tudor. Jack was a delight to work with. He gave his team the trust and space they needed to manage the business, made sound business decisions, and always kept the bigger picture in mind. He'd strongly support his team, and was ever eager to praise them.

Colin Ferry was a case in point. Colin was the Chief Marketing Officer, having joined from a well-known marketing agency some six months earlier. Jack had been impressed with Colin's glowing CV, his track record of successful marketing campaigns, and his ability to talk knowledgeably about the market in general. In the latter stages of the interview process, Jack asked me to meet with Colin and give him my feedback on this potential new board member.

On the appointed day, Colin arrived ahead of time, and rose to shake my hand as I entered the room. He was a tall, lean man in his mid-forties and looked the archetypal cool marketing executive. He had black-rimmed glasses to match his black roll-neck sweater, a black corduroy jacket, skin-tight jeans rolled up to show sockless ankles, and brown loafers. We quickly built a rapport, and shortly into the conversation, I realised that I'd met him before. I'd been seated next to him at a dinner table on the final night of a travel conference in Phoenix, Arizona, some six months earlier. However, this chat was in stark contrast to our previous encounter. In Phoenix, Colin had spent the whole dinner with his back to me as he chatted with the petite young lady on his right-hand side. I remember thinking it was rude, but didn't care too much, as we had Jurgen Schmitt at the same table. Jurgen was a larger-than-life character who regaled us with stories of his vision for the future of the travel industry. Jurgen had been a keynote speaker at the event where his inspirational speech had been a huge success, and he spent the night entertaining us with his insights and industry-related predictions, including some hilarious stories and analogies. The reason I remembered the night so clearly was that Colin was now repeating each of Jurgen's theories, ideas and analogies, repackaging them as his own. I played along.

"That's an interesting view, Colin, but what if the business is going well? Would you still make the changes you describe?"

"Of course, Frank. If I jump out of a plane without a parachute, I'll be doing well until I reach the ground."

It was Jurgen's line, word for word. I tried another.

"What if the product is so uncompetitive that the marketing spend would be wasted?"

"C'mon Frank, with enough wind, even a turkey can fly!"

Again, word for word, Jurgen Schmitt.

He ended the meeting with another of Jurgen's sayings.

"You know, Frank? If I get the job, I just want to make sure that your brand isn't the first to get in the taxi, but the last to arrive at the party."

He was in cliche heaven, and by the end of our chat, I was in no doubt that I was in the presence of a world-class bullshitter. He might not have remembered me, but his ability to remember and commandeer other people's ideas as his own was commendable.

Jack couldn't wait to hear my feedback as he'd had overwhelmingly positive reports about Colin so far. I didn't spoil the party, as in reality, other than hitting the bullshit bullseye, Colin had done nothing wrong. On the other hand, he had displayed all the early signs of the classic Corporate Survivor.

Once on board, Colin was keen to establish himself in the boardroom. He was bold, brash, and full of promises to reduce marketing spend and improve efficiencies. Around the same time, he'd convinced the board that the company needed a root-and-branch rebrand to retain its cutting-edge reputation, and to future-proof it in an ever-growing and competitive sector. This was classic Corporate Survivor behaviour. Not only did it allow Colin to outsource elements of the rebrand to external agencies, but his future CV credentials would now include the successful rebranding of a major online travel agency. It would be largely cosmetic, consisting of skewing the logo design, some subtle changes to website fonts and colours, followed by a few staff briefings. It was easy pickings for a seasoned Corporate Survivor. After all, how do you really measure whether a rebrand has been successful? How often do you get the chance to grease the palms of an external agency from whom you might well need a favour further down the line? Being a seasoned survivor, Colin knew he had to lobby for the rebrand within his first six months before anyone had any reason to doubt his credibility and push back on any of his requests. Furthermore, such a project guaranteed his tenure for the next twelve months, and gave him breathing space to focus on insulating himself further from any future personal scrutiny.

The Corporate Survivor works best when they parachute in their own team to do the heavy lifting, allowing them to shine and take the credit. This is where Colin had his biggest headache. To land the Chief Marketing Officer (CMO) role, Colin had beaten off lots of external opposition, but crucially, he had also been chosen ahead of two internal applicants, one of whom, Scott Solman, was now Colin's number two in the role of Deputy CMO. A further complication for Colin was that Scott was the son of the CEO's best friend. Smart, ambitious, and commercially driven, Scott had been with the company for just over a year and was highly thought of by the board. Colin had pipped Scott for the role based on experience alone, as it was felt that the opportunity had come slightly too early for Scott. Colin was seen as the ideal role model and mentor for Scott, who was keen to learn everything he could in readiness for the next step up the ladder. Although he hadn't shown it, six months in, Colin had become increasingly frustrated by Scott's endless stream of creativity. Scott's ideas and campaigns were full of flair and innovation, didn't rely on outsourced agencies, and consistently proved to be commercially sound. All this would have been fine if the board hadn't realised that it was Scott setting the pace and the agenda rather than Colin, but they had. For Colin, Scott represented a threat - a red flag - a red flag that needed to be lowered to half-mast. In normal circumstances, Scott would be the dream staff member; willing, diligent and conscientious. However, his thirst for additional responsibility and recognition was wearing thin. Eventually, the chance came for Colin to put Scott at centre stage.

Colin had been invited to speak as part of a panel at a major travel trade event in London. The discussion was to showcase the merits of the online travel agent versus the traditional high street model. The panel was to consist of Colin and two other senior industry figures, one representing traditional offline travel, and the other being a specialist cruise operator who had recently transitioned online. It was a Monday morning when Colin called Scott into his office.

"Hey, Scott. In a couple of weeks' time, I've got a great opportunity for you to raise your profile. I've been invited to speak at the travel trade conference. The only problem is that I will be at the Phocuswright Conference in New York on those dates, so I was hoping that you could fill in for me. The audience will be full of senior execs, including our very own CEO, Jack, so it will be an excellent opportunity for you to get some well-deserved exposure."

"Wow, that's great, Colin. What will I need to talk about?"

"It's all about how different business models operate, and how each grows brand loyalty. It's right up your street. We will be the most innovative and contemporary business on the panel, for sure. I know the moderator and I've asked for the questions in advance, so you'll have plenty of time to rehearse, and we can have a walk-through before I leave for the States."

"That sounds great, Colin. I can't wait to showcase the work we do here and share our success." Scott responded eagerly.

Sure enough, the moderator shared the questions and Scott got to work on his script. A few days later, Colin joined Scott for the final walk-through session.

"Okay, Scott, I've blocked off an hour for us to fine-tune the answers so that you'll be word perfect on the day. There will be five questions posed to the panellists, and then at the end, each of you will have the chance to share your personal thoughts on what the travel industry will look like in another five years' time. I've asked for you to be the last person to answer the first two questions so that you can build on what the other panellists have said, to make a bigger impact. I've also arranged for you to give your view about the future of the travel industry at the very end, so that your words have the most lasting impact on the audience."

"Superb, Colin. Thanks so much. I want to make a big impact with my answer to the first question about building brand loyalty online. I'll talk about how it's expensive to attract a customer to your site. Whether it's through CRM, newsletters, promo codes, or ad campaigns, it all costs money. So, once they are on the site, we have a responsibility to remove all the friction points in the customer's online journey. By inspiring our customers with interactive content, and not giving them a reason to look elsewhere, we can build their trust, increasing our conversion levels and the number of repeat bookings."

"Brilliant, Scott. Well done. I'll record your answers as we go along so we can iron out any issues."

For the next hour, Colin listened, advised, and encouraged until Scott's answers flowed seamlessly. By the end of the session, Scott felt fully prepared and equally grateful.

"I feel bad saying this, Colin, but I've been really surprised and impressed by how you've given up your time and made such an effort to help me prepare for the event. I honestly didn't expect you to care so much."

"Don't worry about it, Scott. We're a team. What each of us does individually reflects on us all. I want you to succeed and know you'll smash it out of the park."

A week later, on the morning of the event, Scott felt confident and well-prepared as he was introduced to Leanne, the moderator, in the packed auditorium. In turn, Leanne introduced Scott to Laura Canon and Phillip Parsons, the other two panellists, while they had their lapel microphones fitted. Scott noted that they all appeared much older and more experienced than him, and congratulated himself on his rapid rise through the ranks. It was now time to go on stage, take his seat, and be introduced to the expectant audience. As Leanne made the introductions, Scott poured himself a glass of water, and looked out into the crowd where he could see his CEO, Jack, sitting alongside Pauline, the Chief Finance Officer, in one of the front rows. Once each panellist had given a high-level overview of their business model, Leanne then kicked off the main debate.

"So, Phillip, as a business that traditionally relies upon a huge travel agency network to take bookings and build loyalty with customers, how is your digital transformation coming along?"

"That's a good question, Leanne. In many ways, our offline experience has taught us so much in terms of best practice, and we've designed our online experience to replicate that. As we all know, it costs a lot of money to attract a customer to your site. Whether it's through CRM, newsletters, promo codes, or ad campaigns, it's a significant expense. So, once our customers have landed on our webpages, we have to do everything we can to give them an experience which replicates the best travel agency experience. That means taking away the friction points in the customer's online journey, and inspiring them with interactive content, not giving them a reason to look elsewhere. This way we can build their trust, increase our conversion levels and the number of repeat bookings."

Scott felt the sweat form on his brow and his mouth slowly opened. Phillip was using Scott's own script! He couldn't believe what was happening. It was his own prepared response, virtually word for word. His mind was such a fog of scrambled thoughts, he hardly heard Leanne's next words.

"That's a great insight into the way you have created an online customer journey to replicate the best offline experience, Phillip. Now, over to you, Scott, to share your thoughts on the way your business builds that online relationship and loyalty from your customers."

Scott cleared his throat and took a sip of water, but he hadn't had enough time to order his thoughts. What came next was a futile struggle to say something meaningful. He couldn't help but say that he agreed wholeheartedly with Phillip and did little more than reinforce Phillip's points with a couple of lukewarm examples of his own. His big opening had been undermined, but he reminded himself that he still had time to recover, and the next question about the adaptation of artificial intelligence was tailor-made for him.

Leanne introduced the question. "One thing we can all be certain of is the need to adapt; whether it's enabling products to be more accessible, or leveraging technological advancements such as AI. How will your business adapt to the ever-changing travel landscape? Laura, you first."

"Sure thing, Leanne. We see AI as a great opportunity to advance our product proposition to another level. Let me give you an example of how it can be used to improve our agents' speed and quality of service."

Laura gave examples of how a complex tour itinerary could be put together for a customer in seconds. Phillip followed this up by exploring how AI could be used to analyse marketing campaigns. The colour had now completely drained from Scott's face. Between them, Laura and Phillip had again used each of his rehearsed examples as their own. Once more, Scott had no time to prepare a revised response, and his mumbled answer to the question brought little to the party. This was becoming a humiliation, as Laura and Phillip's traditional travel business models were sounding more forward-thinking and innovative than anything he was saying.

He acquitted himself better over the next couple of questions, but it had become damage limitation and he could feel a lack of conviction in his voice. His last chance was the finale when he had the opportunity to talk about the future of travel. By this point, he had expected to be the star of the show, and his closing presentation was based on the famous 1963 "I have a Dream" speech by Martin Luther King Jr. To make it work, Scott knew that he'd have to exude a confidence he no longer felt, so he took a deep breath to psych himself up as he waited his turn. Phillip took to his feet first, cleared his throat and stayed silent for a few moments as the anticipation in the room grew. His timing was excellent, and he began.

"I have a dream…"

A few minutes later, Phillip sat back down amidst rapturous applause as an almost teary and apologetic Scott took to his feet. He manfully talked about a travel vision which incorporated machine learning and customer personalization, but his idea of using the Martin Luther King speech as the centrepiece had been usurped by Phillip, so he kept it short and not so sweet. As the speakers left the stage to hand back the lapel mics, Scott turned to Phillip.

"I couldn't believe it, Phillip. You and Laura answered so many of the questions using points and examples I'd prepared, including the *I have a dream* ending. It was a bloody nightmare!"

"I wouldn't worry about it, Scott. Great minds think alike, and all that. I thought you did okay. At least you didn't dry up. Nobody takes too much notice of this kind of thing, anyway."

Despite the kind words, it just didn't add up. Phillip seemed prepared for Scott's challenge, and his response was too rehearsed. Scott's confidence took another knock as he spied Jack and Pauline, giving him a half-hearted wave as they made their way out of the room. He stayed for the buffet lunch, picked forlornly at his food, and made his way back to the office.

Two days later, Colin bowled into the weekly director's meeting fresh from his trip to New York. As the senior team gathered, he turned to Pauline.

"Hey, Pauline. Before I forget, how did Scott get on at the trade conference?"

"Hmm, it was a bit underwhelming, to be honest. I don't

think Jack was impressed. Let's just say that it wasn't Scott's finest hour."

"Oh, my goodness. I'm shocked. Was it anything in particular?" asked Colin.

"Nothing specific, but we felt he was a bit out of his depth."

"I am surprised. I know he was worried about his lack of experience, but I also know that he'd spent hours rehearsing," Colin said earnestly.

Later that day, Colin called Scott into his office and Scott relayed the whole story and asked if there was any way that Laura and Phillip could have seen his script before the event.

"Well, I sent your main points across to the moderator, Leanne, so that she could line up the questions for you, but that was about it. I can only think that it was some kind of unfortunate coincidence."

"C'mon, Colin, quoting Martin Luther King? That's beyond a coincidence; it's enemy activity!"

"I think you are overreacting here, Scott. I used to work with Phillip many years ago, and I also know Laura. I can vouch for their professionalism. There's no way they'd plagiarise someone else's script," Colin responded indignantly. "Anyway, I'll be away for a week now to meet with Canadian Airlines in Montreal, and you'll be in charge while I'm gone, so forget any insecurity and just focus on the business."

And that's where I next crossed paths with Colin Ferry.

The two of us were to fly out to Canada with Stuart Pattinson, our Chief Operation Officer, to pitch for business with Canadian Airlines. I had stepped in for our Technical Director who couldn't make the trip, and Colin was there to talk to them about joint marketing opportunities. As we relaxed in the business lounge at Heathrow, it didn't take

Colin long to tell us how concerned he was about Scott's lack of professionalism, and how he had reservations about his future in the business. He was keen to get the message out there that Scott was a weak link, how he often had to double-check his work, and that the panel presentation was an unavoidable example of Scott's unsuitability at that level. Of course, Colin did his best to come across as caring and concerned, but it was clear that he'd be delighted if we relayed these thoughts back to Jack. What Colin didn't know was that I'd had lunch with Scott following the event and heard all about his own concerns. I also knew the two other panellists and was well aware that they were both close personal friends of Colin's. Scott was too naïve to realise he'd been set up, but he was putty in the hands of this Corporate Survivor, and every day was a step closer to his exit or sideways move. In the real world, youth and raw talent will never be a match for experience, cunning, and guile.

Although I was flying to Canada in a professional capacity, I also had a personal mission to complete. The day before we travelled, Sarah, Colin's Personal Assistant, had asked for a quick chat and ushered me into his office.

"I have a small favour to ask of you Frank," she opened.

"Of course. What is it?"

"I heard that you're travelling out to Canada with Colin to meet with Canadian Airlines," she continued.

"Yes. Why? What do you need?"

"This is going to sound weird, but could you please ask Colin not to bring me anything back?"

"Sorry? How do you mean?"

"It's a bit embarrassing, but he brings me gifts from each of his business trips. In the last six months, he's been to conferences and meetings all over the UK, and overseas, and every time he brings me back a present - expensive chocolates, sweets, fancy wine, and even bloody perfume."

"Are you sure Sarah? It really doesn't sound like much of a problem." I replied.

"This is where it gets embarrassing, Frank. He puts the costs through on his expenses rather than paying himself, so I can see how expensive they are. And he puts the cost through as 'Sarah Munrow - gift.' I feel like I'm costing the company money every time he travels anywhere, and it makes me feel really uncomfortable. His expenses are already sky-high, as he orders the finest food and wine every time he has a business dinner. I've asked him to stop buying me things, but he just laughs and tells me to give them to the other PAs if I don't want them myself. I know it sounds stupid, but I'm at my wit's end, and I get stressed every time he goes anywhere. If you can speak to him and convince him to stop it, you'd be doing me a huge favour," she concluded.

Using expense accounts to impress business associates is established practice, but with the Corporate Survivor, it's often used excessively to garner personal popularity and gain future leverage whenever needed. Colin probably thought nothing of it and lacked the awareness to see the effect it was having on Sarah. I told her I'd speak to him and not to worry.

As we chatted in the airport departure lounge, Colin and Stuart found it highly amusing that I'd booked a seat in economy for the seven-hour flight, especially as members of the "Exec" were allowed to travel business class for any flight over five hours. I was quite happy to fly in economy and save the expense, although they put it down to my "northern peasant roots."

Once we arrived in Montreal, the meetings went well enough. We built a good rapport with the people we needed to impress, and once we had finished our final meeting, I returned a missed call from Jack, back in the UK. Answering it immediately, he explained that a big deal we had been working on with a US tour operator had hit a snag. And, as their CEO was at a conference in Cancún over the next few days, Jack wanted the three of us to fly to Mexico to meet with him and keep the deal on track. It would mean being away for a couple of extra days, which was no problem for me or Colin, although Stuart couldn't make it as he had prior commitments back in the UK.

So, Colin and I amended our travel plans, and the following day boarded a flight to Cancún. Colin was remarkably more relaxed and open on this leg of our journey. His guarded and corporate "Montreal" demeanour had fallen away now that it was just the two of us, and he was great company. It was as though, alone with me in my capacity as temporary board member, he had no reason to impress or have his guard up, and as I was part of his successful interview process, he obviously felt that I was an ally and posed no threat. It all made for a most enjoyable flight as he opened up and shared his background and life outside of work. He told me the story of how he'd met his Polish wife, many years ago in Warsaw, at a marketing conference, and how they'd fallen in love and eventually settled in Tunbridge Wells, a town which he proudly described as "the perfect place to raise kids." He shared numerous photos of his family and his wife, Magdalena, who was pregnant with their third child. It all sounded idyllic, and he even had a go at humility.

"You know, Frank? Even though Magdalena is gorgeous, it really wasn't so hard to impress her. Have you ever been to Poland?"

"Yes, I was in Kraków very briefly a few years ago," I replied.

"Ah, then you'll know that Polish women are some of the

most beautiful in the world, and that Polish guys are some of the ugliest you'll ever come across. There are so many meatheads in Poland, it's not true, so I didn't need to be an oil painting to impress her. And I love Magda today more than ever. It's our wedding anniversary next week, so I went into downtown Montreal early this morning to buy her something special. I went all out and bought her lots of sexy lingerie to show her that even after all these years, she's still super sexy to me."

I was touched by how open he was and how genuine he sounded. It seemed the ideal time to broach Sarah's dilemma.

"Speaking of presents, Colin. I heard you are very generous with your PA, Sarah, and bring her back some nice gifts, too."

"I sure do, Frank. It pays to look after the person who looks after you. It's the way the world works. I love the way she pretends to be embarrassed each time, but I know that she'd never want to work for anyone else."

"I'm not sure she is pretending, Colin. I think that she's concerned that this special treatment could cause issues she can do without. Maybe, if the gifts were simpler, it would be better."

"In that case, the other directors need to get their act together and buy decent gifts for their PAs, because I won't be changing anything. In fact, I'm glad you reminded me, as it had almost slipped my mind."

I decided to leave it for the time being and have another go later in the trip. Instead, I listened to him happily extol the virtues of Poland and the Polish way of life, so much so, he mused, that they could eventually settle down there at some point in the future. He then turned his focus to the in-flight magazine before startling me a few minutes later, suddenly raising his head, and fixing his eyes on mine.

"You know what, Frank? The more I think about it, the more I think you'd love living in Poland. At least think about buying a holiday home in Warsaw, or maybe on the coast in Gdańsk. It's a great place to invest, and you'd fit right in as you look Polish, anyway."

Why on earth he'd decided that I should do that is anybody's guess, as he hadn't asked me a single question about my personal life, career ambitions, or anything else, during the last four hours. However, I believe it was a genuine effort to offer some friendly advice. If so, he'd clearly forgotten his earlier derogatory comment about the menfolk of Poland. What this interchange did, though, was to establish our relationship from his point of view. Despite our age difference, in his eyes, he was the senior partner, and I was his apprentice. It was a role I hadn't played for some time, but one that I had been well versed in over the years, so was happy for him to take the lead. He continued in a similar vein as we came in to land.

"By the way, Frank. Once we get there, let me do the talking. I speak Spanish and find it always works better, and gets things done quicker, if you converse in the local lingo," he opined.

For all he knew, I could have been a fluent Spanish speaker, but he didn't care, and neither did I, to be fair; I was happy to take a back seat.

To put it mildly, the organisation in the arrivals hall at Cancún airport left a lot to be desired. Passport control was mayhem, as the staff at the three desks chatted amongst themselves, and took multiple breaks, despite the long snaking queues. The lack of air conditioning didn't help, but over an hour later, we finally staggered out of the terminal and into the baking hot Cancún sunlight.

Our hotel was around thirty minutes' drive from the

airport and we'd decided to take a taxi from the official taxi rank. However, as we followed the taxi signs, we were surrounded by independent taxi drivers, each offering us the best fares. The most persistent was a slight chap with a pencil moustache, slicked-back hair, and a red shirt cut to his navel. He had the look of a poor man's David Niven. Colin stepped forward and took control.

"Hola, estamos no interesante, solo official taxi para nosotros!" he shouted at the little guy.

As often happens, we then had the scenario of the taxi driver speaking fluent English to a guy replying back to him in schoolboy Spanish.

"But, señor, the taxi rank you want is at least a ten-minute walk away in that direction. There is already a queue of at least thirty minutes, and people have to wait in the hot sun."

The man made a compelling case and pointed to a huge queue in the distance.

"Estamos muy importante business honchos desde London y estamos no pay silly dinero for a taxi," Colin persevered.

"Of course, sir. I can see that you are VIPs and that's why we have strict rules which regulate how much we are allowed to charge. If you tell me the name of your hotel, I will tell you which zone it's in and what the government-regulated cost will be."

"We quedamos en el Hideaway Hotel at Royalton Riviera."

"Ah, this is zone three, and will be a maximum of $40 US, sir," he replied in perfect English.

Colin turned to me and repeated what the man had said, word for word, as though he was translating from Spanish. Adding, "what do you think?" at the end.

"Well, that's around £25 sterling. It's baking hot, and the official taxi queue is huge. I say, let's do it," I replied.

Colin agreed and turned back to the man.

"Okay. We accepto, señor."

A few minutes later, we were sitting in the back of the taxi where a busty lady leaned in through the window on Colin's side with a hand-held payment terminal for Colin to tap his card. I double-checked the payment screen, and sure enough, it was $40, as agreed. The card was declined, so "Niven" appeared like magic at the same window, took the terminal, and explained that Colin would need to key in his PIN number as the terminal was playing up. Once done, Colin then typed in his email address for the receipt to be forwarded to him. With that, "Niven" made a show of telling us we weren't to pay the driver any money, not even a tip, as it wasn't allowed. He then shouted theatrically at the driver, warning him not to ask for any money from us. At last, we were on our way, and as we drove past the huge official taxi queue, we congratulated ourselves on the deal we'd struck.

That evening, we spent dinner preparing for our meeting the following day, and then decided on an early night. Colin was keen to put the dinner on his expenses and was surprised when his Monzo card was declined again. He tried keying in the PIN, but still no luck, so he quickly checked his balance.

"What the fuck? The robbing bastards!" he shouted.

"What's going on, Colin?"

"Look at this, Frank." He showed me his Monzo app, which listed a payment of $400 to "Tax Mexicano." "It must be the taxi we took from the airport."

He quickly checked his email for the receipt he had been promised, but nothing had arrived.

"I don't understand it. We both looked at the payment

screen in the taxi, and it said $40. There must be some mistake," he said.

The whole scenario played out quickly in my mind, and it suddenly became clear. The $40 shown on the display was intentional, but when "Niven" took the terminal and asked for Colin to enter his card PIN number, his thumb had covered the screen after adding an extra zero to change it to $400. His busty lady friend had been busy leaning across to Colin as it was all going on, complimenting him on his Spanish as he keyed in his PIN. The distractions were everywhere, including the charade of shouting at the driver. It was all crystal clear - we'd been had. Colin, the arch manipulator, had had the tables turned on him, and he wasn't happy.

"I'll show those bastards. We'll go to the airport tomorrow, find them, and get our money back. In fact, the hotel must have CCTV of us arriving in the cab. Let's go to reception now. They don't know who they're dealing with."

The hotel reception staff listened intently to Colin's story, but didn't offer the help he was expecting. They sympathised and calmly explained that even if we tracked down the taxi, they could just say that we agreed to pay $400. And as we had no receipt, and no way to prove the agreed fee was $40, there wasn't much we could do. It sounded like it wasn't the first time they'd handled this type of complaint. Colin wasn't amused and reiterated that they didn't know who they were dealing with - as if the knowledge that he was a balding, bespectacled marketing director living with his family in Tunbridge Wells, would be enough to stop a Mexican crime cartel in its tracks. Eventually, he calmed down, and it wasn't until the day of our departure that he raised the subject again.

"You know what, Frank? I can't put a $400 taxi bill through on my expenses. It will make me look a complete idiot. But I've thought of a way round it. Look here…"

With that, he turned his laptop to show me a line item on his online expense claim form that said "emergency underwear Can$550."

"Sorry, Colin, I don't understand. You're claiming 550 Canadian dollars for 'emergency underwear?' What on earth are you talking about?" I replied.

"It's Magda's lingerie. It cost 550 Canadian dollars, which equates to around $400 US. The receipt doesn't say lingerie, and the store was called 'Underworld,' so it's perfectly plausible."

"What's perfectly plausible?"

"That we had to buy extra underwear for our trip to Mexico. We'd only catered for the Montreal trip, so had to buy extra. The only issue is that I need you to go along with it, as $400 is a bit much for one person's underwear."

"Do you know how ridiculous this sounds, Colin? Two board members putting underpants through on expenses?"

But, no matter how I tried to convince him otherwise, he was unwilling to tell the truth, or to just split the taxi cost with me and write it off. His ingrained Corporate Survivor instinct was to devise a plan to mask the facts. He was so set in his Machiavellian ways that the truth seemed almost abhorrent to him. Eventually, I decided to compromise.

"Okay, I'll tell you what I'll do. I'll go along with your 'emergency underwear' nonsense if you agree to stop buying Sarah gifts from each of your trips."

"Okay, Frank, it's a deal. It sounds like my generosity wasn't being appreciated as much as I expected, anyway."

So that's what we did. It's possibly the only time in travel industry history that an expense claim for "emergency underwear" has been made.

Once back in the office, I soon bumped into Sarah again.

Frank O'Hare

"Hi, Frank. How was the trip? Thanks so much for sorting my issue out. Whatever you said seems to have worked."

"No problem, Sarah. Colin was okay with it. You won't have to worry about embarrassing gifts from now on."

"That's a relief, Frank. I owe you one. I know you both had more pressing things to deal with than this, what with all those important meetings, and your unfortunate bout of diarrhoea, you poor love."

I hesitated for a split second before deciding to ignore her last comment and continue on my way. Knowing what story Colin had concocted wouldn't make any difference. In fact, I almost admired his audacity. Although, I was less impressed, some years later, when I bumped into an old colleague at a late-night bar in Madrid. In a fairly inebriated state, he excitedly turned to his friends to say, "Hey guys, this is unbelievable. This is Frank - the guy I was telling you about earlier - the one who shat himself in Mexico!"

Chapter 13

Full Circle

To this day, I am still in touch with the original members of our North Manchester 'O' Club. We meet occasionally, and keep each other grounded. We are all much older, and by and large, a tad wiser. To most of them, I will always be the lanky, spotty chancer who got lucky. There is one exception, though, and that's O'Grady. O'Grady has always believed in synchronicity, the phenomenon of meaningful coincidence, where unforeseen external events result in material benefit to a person. Believers, like O'Grady, insist that preordained synchronicity has already mapped out our lives. Consequently, he is the most laid back amongst us. Serendipity is one aspect of this phenomenon; a set of events that happen by chance, yet have a fortunate and happy impact on the person involved. In the introduction to this book, I talked about serendipity, and how a slip of the tongue by Emre in Istanbul gave me the impetus to put pen to paper. What I didn't share were the uncanny events that unfolded later that evening in Turkey. Events that made me believe that some things in life are indeed just meant to be, be it by chance, or synchronicity.

Following the daytime presentations and breakout sessions at the Istanbul conference, we were invited to the post-conference dinner and drinks party. My flight back to the UK was early the next day, and my plan was well-worn and fail-safe. I'd meet as many of the dignitaries as possible before dinner, one glass of wine with the meal, donate generously to the inevitable good cause, and slip off to bed by 11 p.m.

As I was one of the guest speakers, I had a seat at the VIP table close to the stage, along with the event organisers and other dignitaries. I was one of the first to arrive at the table, so I checked the name cards to see who I would be sitting next to. On my right, was Emre and his wife Defne, and to my left were two name cards marked Aksoy Hotels, a small chain of hotels on Turkey's south coast. As the table filled, the seat immediately to my left was taken by an impossibly beautiful lady, who introduced herself as Aiysha, the owner of the Aksoy Hotel Group. Probably in her mid-forties, her English was as impeccable as her appearance, and she further endeared herself to me by telling me she had found my earlier presentation interesting and enjoyable. I turned to her as the dinner was about to start.

"It looks like your colleague isn't joining us tonight, Aiysha?"

"Oh, don't worry; it's my husband, Mikhail. He'll be here. He's just running a little late."

Before she'd had the chance to say much more, a silver-haired giant of a man took his place next to her, amid lots of head-nodding from around the table. Mikhail was obviously a well-known character. Following a brief conversation between Aiysha and her husband in Turkish, she turned back to me.

"I hope you don't mind, but my husband would like to

swap places and sit next to you. He wants to discuss the wider travel industry with you."

"Of course, absolutely," I responded enthusiastically, although I wasn't overly excited by the prospect of a drawn-out conversation in broken English about the future of travel.

Moments later, Aiysha had swapped seats and Mikhail took her place. As he settled into his seat, he started up the conversation.

"Well, Frank, I see that your presentation skills have improved over the years. More than can be said for your looks, old boy."

I was stunned, and stared at him in silence. The broken nose. The piercing blue eyes. The strong jaw bone... The voice... It couldn't be? No, it really couldn't be? But it bloody was... Choco!

"It's been a long time, Frankie, my dear boy. It's so good to see you again. How has life treated you, old bean? I assume you've spent most of it embarrassing yourself across the ski slopes, and in the prisons of Europe?"

I genuinely didn't know whether to laugh or cry. Instead, I just leant across and hugged him as tightly, and for as long as was socially acceptable.

Being a human being is a strange thing. Here I was, over thirty years later, having been a confident senior executive for many years, yet, at that moment, I was that first-year ski rep all over again; subservient, and inwardly congratulating myself that Choco had remembered me. The dinner flew by as we rudely ignored the rest of the table and loudly relived our season in the Alps, as though it were yesterday. I was intrigued to learn that after meeting Aiysha at a drinks party on a yacht in the South of France (how else!), they'd fallen in love, married within a year, and set up a new life together in Turkey. Choco soon put his star quality into action by growing the hotel chain's international customer base, and helping to establish it as one of Turkey's premium brands. We fell naturally into our teacher/pupil relationship as he told me I was the first person to call him Choco in over thirty years. His real name of Mike had been instantly translated to Mikhail by the Russian owner of the yacht he'd first met Aiysha on, and he'd been Mikhail ever since.

"Why change it, Frankie boy? After all, it translates to 'God-like' in Russian, so it couldn't be more apt."

His self-confidence was clearly undiminished by the passage of time.

The wine soon flowed as effortlessly as the conversation, and my self-imposed limit of one glass was well and truly out of the window. We were two bottles in by the time dessert was served.

"Hey, Frankie. How about me and Aiysha show you some of the local night spots before you go back to your hellhole of an existence, back in the UK?"

Despite feeling a little worse for wear, I couldn't wait to accept.

"You bet, Mikhail. I thought you'd never ask."

Half an hour later, following a Choco-led sightseeing tour along the maze of backstreets, we settled down in a traditional street-side bar where Aiysha and Choco were welcomed like royalty. The rest of the evening was a glorious blur of stories, pastries, wine, raki, and hookah smoking. Aiysha was the perfect foil for Choco; demure and polite, yet with a steely self-assurance needed to keep Choco's hubris under control. She drank tea and patiently watched us get louder and louder as we more than made up for her sobriety. We were nearing the end of a memorable evening when Choco inevitably gave me one final piece of advice.

"Look Frank, it's clear that you've come a long way, and

I'm sincerely delighted for you. I always felt protective of you back in the day, and as we sit here as two middle-aged men, for some reason, I still do. I don't know what it is exactly, but you still have the air of a competition winner who won the chance to spend a day in their dream job, and can't quite believe their luck. Promise me you'll be careful, look after yourself, and remain vigilant. Remember what I told you back in Austria? Always do your homework."

Until this point, Aiysha had politely let us take centre stage, but now it was her turn.

"You're thinking about Anna again, aren't you, Mikhail?" She sighed.

"I suppose I am, but if it can happen to me, it can easily happen to someone as dozy as Frank."

Through my haze, I tried to make sense of what was being said.

"Sorry, who's Anna? Have I missed something, guys?" I asked.

Choco took a deep breath and continued, "Well, remember when we told you about how I met Aiysha at the party on the yacht? Well, we got chatting to a charming Dutch lady at the party. She was driving to Nice the next day to collect her daughter and bring her back to her holiday home in Sainte-Maxime. Unfortunately, the rental companies were fully booked, so she was struggling to find a car. It was only a four-hour round trip, so I had no hesitation in volunteering my Porsche. Remember? The one I had in Austria?"

"Ah, the bright red sex machine!" I nodded.

"That's the one," he laughed.

Aiysha now continued the story.

"Well, the lady was super grateful, and arrived at our villa bright and early the next morning. We arranged to host her and her daughter for dinner later that evening, waved her off at around 10 a.m., and that's the last time we ever saw her, or the car. At first, we were terrified that she'd had an accident. We called all the hospitals and medical centres, but there was no trace of her."

"The next day, I spoke to my friend, Andrei, who owned the yacht. They checked the invitee list from the party, and there was no Anna on it, and nobody else had any recollection of her. It was like she was a ghost," added Choco.

My mind was now working overtime. *A charming con artist called Anna?* Surely it couldn't be "my Anna" from the Costa Brava, all those years ago? It would have been the summer after I met her in Lloret de Mar, so it was perfectly plausible.

I so wanted it to be her.

"Can you remember what she looked like?" I asked tentatively.

"Tall, pretty, blonde, with blue eyes. Typically Dutch, I guess. Anyway, Mikhail has never forgiven himself. Always says he should have done his homework, whatever that means."

Choco finished with, "There you go, Frankie boy. Let that be a lesson to us all. I always thought I was the smartest kid on the block, but if I can get the wool pulled over my eyes, what chance do mere mortals have?"

I was almost giddy with excitement. I didn't want to hear any more. In my mind, it was my Anna, and I didn't want to hear anything else that might prove otherwise. My admiration for her had reached new heights.

I thanked Choco sincerely for his final piece of advice. For me, it was the perfect end to the evening, and, as we got up to leave, I hugged the living daylights out of them both. Once she'd prised herself away from me, Aiysha seemed a little concerned about my welfare.

"We're going in the opposite direction, so do you want me to call you a cab, Frank? It's not far to your hotel, but a cab might be easier in your condition."

"Don't worry about me, Aiysha. The walk will clear my head, and I need the exercise."

"Okay, just walk in that direction and you can't go far wrong," she said, pointing in the opposite direction to where I'd intended to go.

However, after fifteen minutes of stumbling along in the general direction Aiysha had pointed in, I began to feel nauseous and sat down to rest on a dusty wall across from some derelict shops. I felt sick and disorientated and was overcome by tiredness. I began to drift off, and as I did, I could vaguely see Terry from Liverpool standing in front of me, tugging at my shirtsleeve.

"C'mon, Frank. We have to get back to the hotel. If they find out we've been out drinking, we'll get kicked off the training course. They'll be coming down for breakfast soon."

Incredibly, Choco was standing next to him.

"C'mon, Frank. Put these yellow ski boots on. You'll get there much quicker in these."

Chiara had also joined the party.

"Aw, Frankkaa, pleasa come backa to the hotella. I wanna go to beddaa."

As if from nowhere, O'Rourke appeared on the scene and shook his head.

"You really are a thick piece of shit, O'Hare. I told you not to bother with all that holiday rep shit. You could have been out with the lads tonight."

Through my stupor, I just about understood that I was hallucinating, the memories of my past flooding through my mind. This wasn't a good sign, especially as I had no idea where I was. I forced myself to my feet and reached for my phone where the glaring numerals shocked me back into life - it was three-thirty in the bloody morning! Google maps showed that I was still twenty minutes away from the hotel, so I stumbled on, weaving my way down the street, feeling as sick as a dog in a suitcase.

When I finally reached the hotel, I staggered into an ornamental plant display and fell on top of it as it crashed to the floor. By the time I'd disentangled myself and reeled towards the reception, the receptionist had been joined by the night security guard and wasn't about to let me in without an interrogation.

"Good morning, sir. Are you a guest at our hotel?" he asked politely.

"Yesh, of course I am. Now, please can I have my key?" I replied, less politely.

"Certainly, sir. What is your room number?"

"I've no bloody idea. I think it's the seventh floor," I responded unhelpfully.

"We only have six floors, sir."

"Well, it's definitely got a seven in the number," I mumbled.

"Perhaps you can give me the lead name of your booking, sir?"

Before I had time to respond, the hotel manager exploded from the office behind reception and berated the receptionist in Turkish. The only part I semi-understood was when he shouted, "O'Hare VIP," mid-sentence, before apologetically turning to me.

"We are so sorry, Mr O'Hare. Please forgive my colleague. He didn't realise that you are a VIP and a special guest. We are so sorry. Here is your key. Suite number 677."

"Oh, don't worry. No harm done. You can't be too careful," I slurred, as I walked unsteadily towards the lift, barely knowing where I was going or what the heck I was doing.

Once safely in the elevator, I slumped backwards against the inside of the lift and slid down to the floor. I took a deep breath and stared at my reflection in the mirror as the lift ascended. The tired, emotional, and dishevelled old man looking back at me was unrecognisable from the excitable gangly youth who started out on his journey all those years ago.

"Mr Frank O'Hare, VIP," I whispered to myself.

Then burst out laughing.

Afterword

Chuck Palahniuk, the author of *Fight Club*, once said, "Nothing about me is original. I am the combined effort of everyone I've ever known."

Looking back at *Beach to the Boardroom,* I also feel that I'm the product of many of the characters I've met along the way, trying my best to emulate those I've admired the most. Writing this book has also made me realise that superficial badges of achievement, such as job titles and material rewards, mean little when looking back. It's the people and the escapades that bring the easiest smile and the most satisfaction. It's a cliche, but I think that the memory bank really is more important than the piggy bank. One thing I'll always be grateful for is how much trust and patience I've received from people in more senior positions. People took a chance on me, and often backed me, despite my weaknesses. In retrospect, giving people a chance, and supporting them through difficult times and the occasional mishap, is probably the most underrated of managerial traits. Of course, the fact that I was such a blank canvas, naïve and eager to learn,

Afterword

helped me in those early days. After all, if you have no idea where you're going, then any road will take you there. I'm just lucky that I followed the road signposted "Travel."

Frank O'Hare

Acknowledgments

Heartfelt thanks to Martin Skate and Chuck Taylor, whose selfless support, humour, and endless patience have made this book possible.

Printed in Great Britain
by Amazon